THE STRANGE DEATH OF
CONSTABLE GEORGE DIXON

THE STRANGE DEATH OF CONSTABLE GEORGE DIXON

WHY THE POLICE HAVE STOPPED POLICING AND WHAT WE MUST DO ABOUT IT

DAVID MURRAY-GILBERTSON

Copyright © 2023 David Murray-Gilbertson

The moral right of the author has been asserted.

Apart from any fair dealing for the purposes of research or private study, or criticism or review, as permitted under the Copyright, Designs and Patents Act 1988, this publication may only be reproduced, stored or transmitted, in any form or by any means, with the prior permission in writing of the publishers, or in the case of reprographic reproduction in accordance with the terms of licences issued by the Copyright Licensing Agency. Enquiries concerning reproduction outside those terms should be sent to the publishers.

Troubador Publishing Ltd
Unit E2 Airfield Business Park
Harrison Road, Market Harborough
Leicestershire LE16 7UL
Tel: 0116 279 2299
Email: books@troubador.co.uk
Web: www.troubador.co.uk/matador

ISBN 978 1 805141 36 5

British Library Cataloguing in Publication Data.
A catalogue record for this book is available from the British Library.

Printed and bound in Great Britain by 4edge Limited
Typeset in 11pt Minion Pro by Troubador Publishing Ltd, Leicester, UK

Matador is an imprint of Troubador Publishing Ltd

Without the love and support of my wife and family, throughout a long period of research and drafting, this book would never have seen the light of day. For that and so much more I will always be grateful.

Principally however I dedicate my efforts to the memory of Sarah Everard and to that of Peter Woodhams, who were both, in different ways, so cruelly ill-used by a police force which should have safeguarded them but instead did the reverse. Their deaths are a mark of shame on policing that cannot be expunged.

CONTENTS

Foreword		ix
Introduction		xiii
1	**The World We Have Lost**	**1**
	Newham in 1969	1
	Newham in 2009 and 2019	15
2	**'Citizens in Uniform?'**	**38**
	How It Looks today	38
	Almost Police Forces – But Not Quite!	47
	Plastic Police	58
3	**PC PCs? – The Problem of Race and Diversity**	**78**
4	**The Police Workforce**	**128**
	The Shop Floor	128
	Officer Safety and Attitude to the Public	139
	Armed to the Teeth	156
	The Bosses	166

	Photographs	203
5	**Crime, Terrorism and Civil Liberties – A Matter for the Police?**	**208**
	Crime and Criminals	208
	Cautions – 'A Scandal Waiting to Happen'	220
	The War on Terror	223
	Civil Liberties?	235
6	**Sexual Predators – A Betrayal of Trust**	**260**
7	**From the Sublime to the Ridiculous...**	**285**
8	**Where to Now?**	**301**
	The Challenge of Localism	308
	Paying for Policing in a Time of Austerity	316
	Finding the Detectives	322
	Finding the Next Generation of Chief Constables and Commissioners	327
	Redefining the Role of Constable	330

Afterword	340
Acknowledgements	345
Glossary of Terms	346
About the Author	348

FOREWORD

In early 2011, on the first anniversary of the establishment of the ill-starred Cameron-Clegg coalition which was to wreak so much damage on the political and economic well-being of this country, I had a convivial lunch with three former colleagues at a rather expensive West End restaurant, just a short stroll from what was then Scotland Yard. Collectively we had known each other for decades and each of us had followed different paths in our careers. John (I shall call him that) was the only one of us still serving in policing, having recently been appointed as the Chief Constable of a large urban force in the north of England, although he had started on the beat in the east end of London with me many years before. The other two, Peter and Eric (also pseudonyms), were experienced and very senior detectives who had recently retired at the top of their game and were being actively head-hunted by large City firms who wanted to exploit their skills for the benefit of their shareholders and the corporate bottom line. The four of us had been meeting on an 'ad hoc' basis for a number of years, usually over lunch, to savour good company, intelligent conversation, and to indulge in that pastime that senior people in many walks of life enjoy – the deconstructive analysis of our former jobs and organisations.

As senior, albeit mainly retired, police officers with impressive CVs and firm opinions, there was very little about policing over the previous three decades that we did not know. Fuelled by excellent Italian cuisine, we put the world to rights. Time passed, views were exchanged, and gradually a consensus emerged as we surveyed a landscape littered with the wreckage of 21st century policing in the United Kingdom. Eventually, we paid the bill, took our leave from the restaurant, and as we bade goodbye to each other, agreed that the issues we had discussed were too important to be allowed to hang in the ether. We needed to put pen to paper (or finger to keyboard), set out our thoughts and concerns, and get them published for the benefit of a wider readership. Thus was the genesis of the first edition of 'The Strange Death of Constable George Dixon'. Our considered view was that the decline in policing had reached a tipping point, and we hoped that by generating a debate about halting that decline, we might induce colleagues and politicians to take a radically fresh view of what needed to be done. Sadly, then as now, the police in this country had never been held in lower esteem. From Blair Peach to Stephen Lawrence and Jean Charles de Menezes; from the 'War on Terror' to the 'kettling' of peaceful protesters, and on to the rape and murder of an innocent young woman by a predatory animal in police uniform, a path has been beaten towards the edge of a precipice and it is time for thinking people, who are truly concerned about the vital role of policing in a democratic society, to start to challenge what is happening. So much has changed since we lunched together, that a re-evaluation, a decade on from the original publication of our collective views, is overdue. Even ignoring the self-inflicted wounds of Brexit, the political and economic climate since 2011 has become palpably toxic. But I do not intend this as a polemic – indeed I write these words more in sorrow than in anger. Most of my adult life was spent in policing and when I and my contemporaries passed on the baton to the generation that followed, we confidently assumed that the lessons of the past would, in their hands, help to shape the future.

How wrong I was, how wrong we were.

INTRODUCTION

Before we embark upon any analysis of modern policing, there is a need to place the debate in its wider context. No-one ever refers to a 'golden age' of policing – a time when crime was low, the police were unfailingly courteous and efficient, lawbreakers were rapidly apprehended and carted off to prison, and the sun shone every day. No-one ever refers to such a halcyon period because there never was such a time, and probably never will be. However, you would not know this from listening to the current crop of studiously uncritical Chief Constables and Commissioners, for they would have us believe that they have built the New Jerusalem, that under their stellar leadership things have never been better.

Reality TV shows with one eye on the ratings jump on the bandwagon and sing the praises of 'Police Interceptors' or '24 hours in police custody'. The Home Office issues press releases extolling this or that soon-to-be forgotten police initiative, but those discerning souls in the great British public know better. They note the almost total absence of uniform police officers on the streets of our cities, towns and villages and ask why it is that this small country, which has more police officers than the whole of Canada, is policed less effectively and with less consent than it was fifty years ago. Something seems to have gone badly awry.

There is no doubt that there have been numerous brave, resourceful and dedicated men and women who have risked their lives in police uniform over the last two centuries since Robert Peel's top-hatted 'bobbies' ventured forth to confront the Dickensian criminal classes, armed with a truncheon, a cutlass, and a rattle. However, it is equally true that alongside them there have always been corrupt police officers, violent police officers, lazy police officers, stupid police officers and police officers whose only claim to professional skill was the ability to prepare, and submit, an application for overtime. Since the 'Turf Scandal' in 1877 when Detective Inspectors Druscovich, Meiklejohn and Palmer were imprisoned, and a large proportion of the newly formed CID at Scotland Yard were sacked, there have been legion examples of malpractice and downright criminality. The well-reported excesses at the G20 in 2009 and the student demonstrations in 2011 are nothing new, nor is the appalling criminality committed by the rapist and murderer Wayne Couzens and his ilk (of which much more later), but they do not exist in a vacuum – the issues are much more complicated than that.

My tutor at the London School of Economics once described policing as 'the bastard child of social policy and class distinction'. Constables patrolling beats in the palatial squares of Belgravia in the nineteenth century were under strict instructions to, *'offer assistance to members of the gentry when entering or alighting from their carriages'*, and were charged with, *'preventing idle and disorderly persons resorting to, or taking their rest'* in the parks and gardens of Eaton Place and Belgrave Square[1]. Born of a fear of revolution following the Napoleonic Wars, and visceral hatred of all things French (for in France there had been uniformed policing since the days of the *ancien regime),* Peel's 'new police' who appeared on the streets of London in 1829, and in towns, boroughs, and counties elsewhere in the country by 1857, were never envisaged as an engine of social change. Sir Robert Peel had many noble qualities, but he was not a social reformer. As a scion of the ruling classes and elder statesman of the Conservative party, he regarded his overarching duty to be the maintenance of the status quo, which in essence meant preservation of the existing social and class structure. None of this was unusual for the time, indeed any other approach would have been roundly condemned as dangerous radicalism, and thus a model based on deference and rigid adherence to hierarchy was established in those early years.

Surprisingly little, in a philosophical sense, has changed since then for policing was, and is still, largely concerned with the protection of rights and privileges. It has always been about the 'haves' and the 'have-nots'. The landed aristocracy and subservient deference of Victorian times and the early twentieth century have long since disappeared from the social landscape, only to be replaced by a hierarchy based upon the vested interests of a range of other powerbrokers, some old, some very new. A few, such as the enduring interests of the establishment political

---

[1] Metropolitan Police Divisional Orders, Gerald Road Police Station, March 1865 (author's research)

parties and incumbent governments, and the well-being of our major industries and large corporations, have always been with us, but others have forced their way onto the scene in the comparatively recent past and are different in form and function to what existed before. Once upon a time the middle-classes and the professions, indeed all the property-owning elite, as fully paid-up members of the 'haves', could confidently expect deferential service from their local constabulary to protect them from predation by the working classes who lived on the margins of society and periodically needed to be reminded of their place in the grand scheme of things, usually with the flat of the sabre, or a blow from a truncheon. All of this was seen as the natural order and was questioned by no-one. It was not fair, it did not purport to offer social justice, but as the flow of history changed society, decade by decade, throughout the twentieth century the relationship between the police and those on the receiving end of law enforcement subtly changed. A uniquely British model of civilian policing shrugged off many of its faux-military and class-based origins and gradually adapted to the new social landscape. What emerged, particularly in the years immediately following the trauma of the Second World War, was an easy accommodation. It had its roots in the continuing respect for authority figures of all kinds that was the prevailing attitude of the time, a desire for order and stability after the dislocation of the war years, and a recognition that civil society needed effective policing as crime rates soared in the late 1940s and early 1950s. More importantly however this 'easy accommodation' was a function of the fact that from the late 1920s changing attitudes had subtly altered the experience of policing insofar as it affected the majority of the 'have-nots' – those at the bottom of society with little economic commitment to the status quo.

A largely artisan and working-class police force started, slowly at first but with gathering pace, to deliver something new to the majority of the population who had for so long been regarded as the 'lumpen proletariat'. By degrees, there was an acknowledgement that most victims of crime were those at the bottom of the social pyramid. Operational necessity, quite apart from common sense and common decency, demanded that the 'deserving poor' be treated, if not as the social equals of their betters, then certainly as equal to them under the law and therefore deserving of support, protection and assistance from the police. In short, the concept of service was born.

So it was that the comforting, decent and heroic figure of Constable George Dixon appeared on the scene – a fictional representation of the sort of policeman and the sort of policing that people in post-war austerity Britain yearned for. 'The Blue Lamp', directed by Basil Dearden and Michael Balcon, was produced at Ealing Studios and released in early 1950. It was an instant box office hit, winning a BAFTA in 1951 for 'Best British Film' and clearly touched the psyche of the cinema-going public. The screenplay was written by an ex-policeman, Thomas Bennett Clarke, and was an early example of the 'social realism' films that would emerge later in the decade. It starred Jack Warner (then a much loved star), as PC George Dixon, who played the friendly avuncular copper, diligently working his lonely night beat around Paddington Green. He knew all the local people and all their children by name; he knew their small triumphs and he knew their problems; he cared because he lived amongst them. The plotline was based upon a simple moral premise in which the police are the honest guardians of a decent society, battling the disorganised crime of a few unruly youths. As Dixon is shot dead by one such youth when disturbed in the foyer of a cinema during a sordid robbery for a few pounds, the message that comes across, loud and clear, is that good men such as George Dixon are willing to lay down their lives so that their fellow citizens, no matter what their social standing, can live theirs in safety. The film was the progenitor of the television series '*Dixon of Dock Green*' which ran on prime-time TV for twenty-one years between 1955 and 1976, screening over 430 episodes.

The 'Blue Lamp' and the TV series were fiction, although the active involvement of the Metropolitan Police in their making and the documentary style of the original film (with footage of real activity at Scotland Yard, and minute attention to detail in terms of locations, procedures, and even the buttons on uniforms) conferred upon both a degree of authority that has seldom been seen since. Nonetheless, to many people at the time and to many today George was and is the archetypal police officer who should be patrolling our streets.

It is impossible to overstate the impact that Constable George Dixon has had on attitudes to policing since that time. Until the late 1960s, 'The Blue Lamp' was shown to every recruit constable at every Police Training Centre in the UK. Without any embarrassment, Dixon was presented as an exemplar of what a 'good copper' should be, and recruits were encouraged to model themselves upon him. To an entire generation of police officers and police leaders who were trained during those years (and who retired during the 1980s and 1990s) their policing mindset, consciously or unconsciously, was affected by the image, and by the expectations of a public who likewise wanted, indeed expected, a constable like George on every beat and around every corner. Even though it is almost fifty years since he was on our TV screens and over seven decades since 'The Blue Lamp' was released, many in the press and media and a large proportion of the public, still refer to 'the Dixon of Dock Green style of policing', with honest coppers 'pounding their beats like George Dixon'. Newspapers regularly refer, almost wistfully, to the days when 'Dixon of Dock Green' protected our communities.

Today, the George Dixon style is viewed by the police establishment and by the PCs on the shop floor and their leaders, who probably have no idea who he was, as something between an embarrassment and an anachronism. To the present generation of police officers, their Commissioners and Chief Constables, and most importantly to those Home Office officials who shape and develop police policy for their political masters, George Dixon, and all that he stood for in the minds of the public, is ancient history. Frankly, they wish that all the talk of Dixon, and 'walking beats', and 'knowing your patch', would just go away. Modern policing, they argue, is about targets and performance; about meeting the needs of diverse communities *'within a complex socio-economic, inter-generational, and operationally challenging milieu'*[2]. It's about *'citizen focus'* and *'customer satisfaction'*,

---

2 ACPO Strategy document on 'Citizen Focus' (2011) (author's research)

spurred on by '*collaborative strategic partnerships*' and myriad 'pilot initiatives' which miraculously always seem to be a success. Indeed, an erstwhile colleague at Scotland Yard once remarked to me wryly, 'We've got more pilots in the Met than Goering had in the Luftwaffe – but the majority of ours will end up doing more damage to London than his ever could'.

Sadly, the vast majority of Constables and Sergeants in today's modern police service have the same level of animosity towards dear old George Dixon, but for entirely different reasons to their bosses. They do not want to see a return to patrolling beats in all weathers, having face-to-face encounters with the public, the majority of whom they have been trained to regard as the enemy. They would actively resist any suggestion, on 'health and safety' grounds that, heaven forefend, they should patrol alone. Policing, for the generation born between 1985 and 1995, who now form the larger part of the police operational presence across the UK, is about fast cars, body armour, officer safety, and 'hitting the bad guys where it hurts' – anything less is boring. Community and Neighbourhood policing of the Dixonesque sort is beneath them, they say in hushed but nonetheless emphatic tones. It's for 'lazy uniform carriers' and 'plonkers who aren't good at anything else', or for those who want a quiet life as they glide towards retirement – it's not for *real* cops.

Simultaneously the new powerbrokers, the 'haves' who demand attention and dictate the direction of policy, have become so influential that servicing their needs has become a (some would say *the*) core activity of many forces – largely to the detriment of the service given to the public at large.

Health and Safety, Risk Assessment, and the concept of 'Officer Safety' (of which much more later), have been raised as totems before which all must genuflect and to which tribute must be paid. Where once, barely a decade ago, such matters were regarded as important, but peripheral, elements in core policing, they have now assumed a level of significance such that no decision on any operational or policy matter can be made at any level in the organisation without the involvement of H & S professionals. Without any debate, policing has changed from an activity which, almost by definition, required police officers to take risks and rewarded them for doing so, to a wholly 'risk-averse' occupation in which physical cowardice *(I choose my words carefully)* is overlooked on a daily basis.

Nothing however can rival the power and influence of the Diversity/Equality agenda, which since the late 1990s has rolled liked a tsunami over all aspects of public life and public policy, but in terms of policing has created an operational and organisational empire of such complexity that it touches upon everything that is spoken about and done. It was born of existential guilt for decades of poor policing in our urban heartlands, and the provision of an admittedly less than satisfactory service to Britain's growing, and largely urbanised, black and Asian minorities. Offences have been created where none existed before to protect 'communities' which never existed before, but who now indulge in special pleading for their rights. Thus, we now have, and the police service prostrates itself to serve, a transgender community; a gay, lesbian, and bi-sexual community; a Romany and Travellers community, and myriad faith communities. This is in addition to communities based upon race and ethnicity which at least have the advantage and justification of identity and residence in one place or another. Even here, however, the police service and their political masters (certainly since 1997) have adopted a counter-intuitive and downright divisive approach.

Sikhs from the Indian sub-continent who live cheek by jowl with Moslems from Somalia, or Catholics from the Congo, in some of the most challenging urban areas, are not treated as members of the same community as they deserve to be, but as discrete groups. The investment of time, energy and manpower, in offering little more than patronising cosmetic support to these self-defined communities, is immense. Every command unit in every one of the police forces in the United Kingdom has at least one, and sometimes many more, designated officers to act as 'liaison' to such communities. Note well, that 'liaison' should not be confused with policing – that is a matter for others; liaison officers are there to listen and empathise, to 'understand' and 'facilitate' at vast cost to the public purse.

The impact of the diversity agenda on the police service as an organisation has been even more profound. It would not be an exaggeration to say that an almost Orwellian atmosphere prevails in the upper echelons of policing in the UK, which has filtered down to the shop floor. An officer is now more likely to be dismissed without pension from the police service, for some throwaway remark about a female colleague or a member of an ethnic minority group, than if convicted of a criminal offence before a court. Indeed, there are officers serving today in many forces with criminal convictions for serious breaches of the law which would formerly have justified instant dismissal, whereas others have been peremptorily removed from the service for little more than 'thought crimes' having offended against the prevailing diversity/equality mantra. In selecting personnel for promotion and appointment to key specialist posts, almost all forces have indulged in the most outrageous tokenism by selecting wholly ill-qualified officers to bolster their anti-discriminatory credentials, not seeing that by doing so they patronise and devalue the contribution of truly able black, Asian, and female officers elsewhere in the organisation.

Jack Warner died in 1981, together with the fictional Constable (later Sergeant) George Dixon that he had played for over twenty-five years. Appropriately, the pallbearers who carried his coffin to the grave were six real police officers from Paddington Green. There is little doubt that he and they would have been amazed at the extent to which policing was to change in the four decades thereafter. Indeed it is unlikely that they would have recognised most of it as policing, in the accepted sense, at all. More importantly, nor would the two thousand ordinary Londoners who came to pay their respects at the East London Cemetery as George Dixon was laid to rest.

It is a common failing in many, when looking back, to ignore contrary evidence and blithely claim that 'things were done better then'. It would certainly be wrong to argue that the whole structure of modern policing should be condemned; there have been technical and operational advances that have benefited many. However, the fact remains that it is undoubtedly the case that something has gone badly wrong. In terms of what the average man or woman in the street wants from the police service that they pay for, this new breed of twenty-first century policemen and women offer but a pale imitation of what the public expect and rightly deserve. Viewed from a wider perspective it is increasingly clear that the rate of change is accelerating. The alienation of the police service from the public that they are charged with protecting is now such that it would have been acknowledged as a crisis as recently as ten years ago, yet today it is meekly accepted as the norm and barely registers as a matter of concern in the senior echelons of policing, in the media, or amongst our political classes, except when some crisis or another arises. As Mr and Mrs Ordinary-Voter settle down on the sofa to watch yet another episode of 'Strictly Come Dancing' or 'Love Island', they seem neither to know nor care that one of the most important contributory elements of a healthy functioning democracy is changing and almost certainly failing.

Significantly, much of the change is a function of the parlous state of leadership and supervision in the police service with management intervention, such as it is, notable by its absence. The majority of senior officers act as cheerleaders for their junior personnel and are distinctly uncomfortable when faced with the necessity of criticising them. Strong leadership skills and the power to inspire by example have somehow been left out of their tool bag. This may be due to the way in which the current generation of police leaders have been identified and promoted but is more likely to represent a desire to avoid rocking the boat. Sadly, those entrusted with leadership of the 166,000 police officers in the United Kingdom are rarely seen doing very much other than selling one false prospectus after another in the form of 'Charters' and 'Policing Pledges', whilst ignoring the behaviour of their subordinates who continue to actively disengage from the public.

It was not always this way.

CHAPTER 1
THE WORLD WE HAVE LOST

NEWHAM IN 1969

The London borough of Newham is archetypal 'Eastenders' territory. Created on 1st April 1965 from an amalgamation of the old Essex County boroughs of East Ham and West Ham and the docklands region of North Woolwich, it was comprehensively bombed by the Luftwaffe during the Second World War. During the 1950s and 1960s it was the test bed for some of the most innovative, and some of the most depressing, local authority social housing in the country. The ill-starred Ronan Point stood in the south of the borough until it collapsed like a house of cards in May 1968, taking four residents to their deaths. Indeed by the late 1960s slab-built tower-blocks stood on most of the cleared bombsites, surrounded by streets of working-class Edwardian terraced housing which had somehow escaped Hitler's attention. Apart from the Port of London docks, which were in terminal decline as freight moved to containers and the east coast ports, there were precious few employers other than a few warehouses, beyond which the only option for many was a low-paid retail job in one of the newly built shopping centres in East Ham and Stratford.

Life was tough for most people, but with a population of over a quarter of a million there was a genuine sense of community and shared experience. Many of the inhabitants of the borough of Newham were the sons and daughters of 'real' Eastenders who in the 1920s and 1930s had escaped the grinding poverty of Stepney and Whitechapel by moving to what were then regarded as the leafy suburbs of East Ham and Stratford, where clean and cheap housing was available. These good people, immortalised in Noël Coward's 'This Happy Breed', had raised their families under the most difficult conditions before, during, and immediately after the Second World War and by the 1960s their children were embarking upon life on their own.

Each of the principal centres of population in the borough had its own police station. There were no less than five, at West Ham, East Ham, Forest Gate, Plaistow, and North Woolwich. All were open 24 hours a day and each had a full complement of policemen (almost exclusively police*men*, there were still very few police*women* in those days), who would patrol beats alone on foot – rarely in pairs unless ordered to do so under extremely unusual circumstances. They were directed to calls from their local station by use of the new 'personal radios' – a great innovation – or upon their return to the station during their shift. Just two constables at each station on each shift, experienced and street-smart, were selected to crew the fast response Jaguar 'area-car' which dealt with all the 999 calls via its radio link to Scotland Yard. If you were chosen by your sergeant for this duty, it was confirmation that you had 'arrived'. In addition, one or two PCs at each station were authorised to drive the new blue and white unit beat cars, nicknamed 'panda cars' because of their colour scheme, which had been introduced as part of a package of reforms and modernisation championed by Roy Jenkins in 1966 and 1967 when he was Home Secretary. There had been concern at the time that they would replace foot beats, but in fact that seldom happened, as the unit beat cars were merely superimposed upon the existing beats, acting as a support system for the foot patrols. Once all these specialist posts had been filled, every other constable was allocated to a foot beat for his entire shift.

The Metropolitan Police had an operational strength of just over 25,000 in the late 1960s, eighty per cent of what it is today, but unlike today the vast majority were employed on duties in uniform at local police stations. Thus it was that at a fairly average, 'semi-inner' London police station such as West Ham, around twenty constables, three sergeants and an Inspector would parade for duty on each of the three shifts (i.e. at 6am, 2pm and 10pm), 365 days a year. The same sort of coverage was provided at the other stations in the borough, with a few less at North Woolwich due to the fact that the docks had closed and there was precious little activity or crime. So, at any given time, around a hundred police officers were on duty in uniform in Newham, the vast majority on foot patrol on beats. There was also other coverage, not so obvious but nonetheless providing a service to the borough.

Each station had its own complement of CID officers, usually ten or fifteen, under the control of a Detective Inspector who investigated everything from domestic murders (of which there were few), to everyday burglaries and thefts. There was a plain-clothes 'Q' car, crewed by trainee CID officers and driven by a highly trained uniform branch driver, which patrolled the whole borough until the wee small hours of each morning, on the lookout for crime and local criminals. There were traffic patrol cars designated to patrol East Ham and West Ham from their east London base in Stepney – crewed by specialists, who dealt with all the serious road accidents and unfit vehicles. There were traffic patrol motorcyclists, who spent much of their time pursuing the 1960s version of 'boy racers' before summonsing them for speeding. There were no fixed penalty tickets at the time, which was actually a good thing because offenders had to go through the process of losing a day's work in order to spend an hour or two at court before appearing before the magistrate to answer their summons, an exercise in public shaming.

Discipline was paramount, and in many forces, including the Metropolitan Police, was rigid. The police service proudly referred to itself as 'a disciplined body' and from the moment that they entered recruit training school, young constables were left in no doubt that failure to obey a 'lawful order' was the most heinous of offences. The word of their sergeant was law. Their inspector, on the few occasions that they had face-to-face contact with him, was to be regarded as the Almighty's vicar on Earth. Their superintendent, whom they glimpsed from afar and ruled them from the constabulary equivalent of Mount Olympus, was, to all intents and purposes, the Almighty. They were bound by a legal duty to conform to 'Police Regulations' enshrined in statute, which governed their conduct both on and off duty. It was, for example, an offence to 'take an active part in politics', to 'wilfully neglect to discharge any lawful debt', and officers were particularly enjoined to, 'abstain from any activity which is likely to interfere with the impartial discharge of [their] duties or which is likely to give rise to the impression amongst members of the public that it may so interfere'.

From the earliest days of their career, police officers were made to understand that they had to march to the beat of a different drum, compared with the average man in the street. Their conduct, appearance, attitude, and behaviour were the subject of close attention. In those days before any sort of requirement to disclose confidential appraisals to officers, the most damaging information and comments were often set out in explicit terms on confidential personnel files. Some of the content held on such files could bring an officer's career to a grinding halt. It was, for example, not at all unusual for a particularly serious or salacious matter to be committed to paper and then sealed in an envelope boldly marked, 'CONFIDENTIAL – ONLY TO BE OPENED BY SUPT. OR ABOVE' and placed on the officer's file. A career-stopping time bomb waiting to go off.

Management science was only just appearing on the scene as a subject worthy of attention at the Police Staff College and was regarded as 'management nonsense' at shop-floor level. Sergeants and Inspectors enforced discipline in ways that today would generate employment tribunal proceedings at the drop of a hat. In 1969 however such techniques were remarkably effective and ensured that officers did as they were told – greatly to the benefit of the public. Two reminiscences from long-retired veterans of West Ham in the sixties give a flavour of how things were done.

'I was 20 years old, had been a PC for less than six months, and was posted to the early-turn shift so I had to be on parade in uniform by 5.45am. It was December, freezing cold and pouring with rain and I overslept by half an hour. I lived about three miles from the station at the time, so I jumped on my bike and pedalled like mad to get to West Ham. I ran into the locker room, quickly changed into my tunic and helmet and managed to get on parade at one minute past six. I was bathed in sweat, soaked to the skin from the rain, and completely out of breath. I nodded to the Sergeant and said, "Sorry I'm late sarge, problems with my bike". To my surprise he just smiled at me benignly and I thought I was off the hook, then with a nod of greeting to the Inspector, who had just walked into the parade room, he said, "That's alright son, you're not late at all. In fact you're about eight hours early. Come back at 2.00pm – you can do a late turn, and I'll see you again at a quarter to six tomorrow morning". A wasted day, a quick changeover as a punishment, and a lesson I never forgot. I was never late for duty again during my entire service'.[3]

And this from an officer who retired many years later as the Deputy Chief Constable and head of CID in a police force in the Midlands.

'I was on night duty and was posted to Stratford Broadway patrol, which basically gave me a mile and

---

3   Research Interview March 2011

a half of shops, offices and half a dozen pubs to look after. For the first couple of hours I diligently checked doors and windows and dealt with the occasional drunk, but by 3am I was tired out, so I hid myself in the doorway of Woolworths to keep out of the rain. In those days, unlike today, Sergeants used to patrol their sections on foot, checking that their PCs were doing what they were supposed to be doing, and after about two minutes I was spotted by my sergeant as he emerged from a turning on the other side of the road. He made straight for me and said, "All quiet, anything to report?" I replied that everything was "All correct". "Really?" he said, "Come with me", and led me along to the far end of the Broadway where there was a camera shop. Whilst I had been at the other end of my patrol someone had sprayed insulating foam into the alarm box, had forced the front door and had clearly made off with most of the stock. A PC from the neighbouring beat had discovered the break-in and was standing guard outside. The sergeant's only comment to me was, "You're not on this patrol for the sake of your health, you're here to do a job of work. You obviously need a lot of practice", and for the next two weeks he posted me to that same patrol on every shift. The strange thing was that I didn't actually mind, because I got to know most of the people who worked there, and that came in really handy as time went by'.[4]

---

4   Interview with DCC Tom Williamson (Nottinghamshire Police) (2001)

All police stations shared common boundaries with their local magistrates' court and in those long distant days before the Crown Prosecution Service had even been thought of, there were distinct advantages in such an arrangement. As had been the case since the nineteenth century, the law required that the arresting officer in any proceedings was the 'informant' – the named individual who was charged with bringing the offender before the court and, in the first instance, prosecuting the case against him. This was so whether or not the officer was a raw recruit in his first few weeks of service, or a senior CID officer with decades of experience. All officers learned quickly how to present simple, and then more complex, cases before the magistrate. Each morning, courts across the land would be filled with prisoners answering their bail, or held in custody in cells, and every one of them would be accompanied by 'his' arresting officer. The vast majority of cases before the courts, as today, were fairly inconsequential in nature. Drunkenness, petty thefts and burglary, minor assaults, and what now would be grandly referred to as anti-social behaviour, were the meat and drink of the magistracy. A fundamental difference, however, was the speed at which the system operated.

The old adage, 'justice delayed is justice denied', was true then as it is now. With a link between the local police station and the local court, and officers having a personal responsibility for the conduct of 'their' cases, proceedings were seldom delayed unnecessarily. West Ham Court was just 250 yards from West Ham police station; East Ham Court was directly across the road from East Ham police station. Elsewhere in London and the rest of the country, police stations and courts often shared the same building. In practical terms this meant that a drunken reveller could smash a shop window at 2am, be arrested, charged and held in custody at the police station by 5am, be in the court cells by 9.30am, plead guilty and be sentenced by the magistrate before 11am. No expensive adjournments requiring attendance after attendance by police witnesses and others, no court lists filled with abortive hearings, no reams of paper submitted to faceless lawyers at some far distant CPS office, no expenditure of public money on unnecessary overtime payments. Most importantly of all, the hapless owner of the shop with a shattered window, who as the victim in the case should always be the focus of attention in criminal proceedings (but so seldom is these days), could be assured by lunchtime that the lout who had damaged his property had been dealt with. In the majority of cases justice was swift and resolution was often immediate. Nowadays, access to prompt justice is rare. More than half of all magistrates' courts in England and Wales have closed since 2010, forcing defendants, witnesses, police, lawyers and justices of the peace to travel, sometimes more than 50 miles, to access local justice.[5]

Most officers in those days, before there was an explosion in home ownership and an exodus to the suburbs, lived locally. The majority were in married quarters or rented

---

[5] Since 2010, 162 of the 323 magistrates' courts in England and Wales have shut – a loss of 50.2% of the estate. In addition, over the same period, including crown courts, county courts and tribunals, more than 250 further hearing centres have ceased operating. *(House of Commons Justice Select Committee Report 2019 [downloaded December 2022].)*

accommodation, or if they were single, lived in barrack-like section-houses. As a result they got to know the area as residents rather than as an 'army of occupation'. Their children attended local schools; their wives shopped locally; they spent their off-duty leisure time in the borough. To use a somewhat hackneyed term, they 'identified' with the locality and had a vested interest in keeping it free from crime and loutish behaviour. The knock-on effect was that many demonstrated a level of commitment to their beats and patrols that is seldom if ever seen in these early years of the twenty-first century. Not being subject to an all-consuming targets-regime that would emerge from the ether decades later, officers had the time and the inclination to put more into their day-to-day relationships with people who were often neighbours, or at the very least people that they had grown to care about, rather than mistrust.

The following is an example of the efforts that an individual constable in the late 1960s would go to, undirected, to lend assistance to someone on his beat who needed the help of police. It was not altruism, or slavish following of some community policing initiative, it was simply what he believed was expected of him.

'I had just finished my probation, so I suppose I had about two years' service. Trevelyan Road, a quiet street near West Ham Cemetery, was on my beat, and I lived about half a mile away, where Forest Gate borders Wanstead. I was walking through one morning when a chap came out of one of the houses and told me a story about the trouble that he and a neighbour were having with a group of local kids,

who were climbing over the wall from the cemetery at night and nicking stuff from their gardens. I said I'd speak to the parents, and that seemed to do the trick, but about a fortnight later he contacted me to say that they were at it again. I decided that I needed to be a bit more assertive, so when I was next on nights, I got the OK from my sergeant and went to the chap's house. We sat in his garden shed in the dark and sure enough, after about thirty minutes, we heard the sound of feet on the roof and then saw three lads aged about fifteen drop into the garden. They were pretty surprised when I emerged from the shed in full uniform, including helmet, and nicked them, and even more surprised when I called for a police van and had them taken down to the station. They weren't bad kids actually and they ended up with Juvenile Bureau cautions and thick ears from their parents. Everyone was satisfied; the householder in Trevelyan Road, his neighbour, and me. A few years later I was a police training instructor at Hendon, and who should turn up in one of my recruit classes but one of the kids I had nicked. Over a pint at the end of the course he told me that I had probably turned him around at a difficult time in his life. I was really pleased about that.[6]

In essence, this was the style of policing that people wanted then and would probably opt for today if given the choice. It was about visibility, involvement, and prompt

---

6   Research Interview February 2009

intervention to deal with street level problems. Gangs of putative young hooligans were known, split up and sent packing with the ever-present threat of being 'nicked' and handed over to shamed and contrite parents. Operational choices were not dressed up in pseudo-professional jargon such as *'intelligence-led policing'* and *'problem-oriented strategies'*, nor were they constrained by bureaucratic reporting arrangements; they were simple, to the point, and effective.

Recent research has shown that whilst police numbers have increased over time, they have not matched rapidly rising crime rates; that the police in 2020 faced around 40 crimes per officer, four times the number in the 1960s and twenty times the number in the 1920s. In addition, it is argued, the sheer volume of anti-social behaviour presents a significant new challenge. On the basis of crime figures alone, it is true that theoretically each officer in 1969 Newham did indeed have a smaller workload than his successors fifty years later, but statistics can and do lie. An appreciable number of offences, recorded in the 2020 statistics, simply did not exist as recordable crimes in 1969 and therefore did not appear in the totals. The best example is 'Common Assault' which accounted for almost two million of the 'Assaults without Injury' that were recorded in 2018/19. None of these allegations would have gone anywhere near a 1969 crime book, but they still took place – it was just that they were dealt with by officers as 'civil disputes' or 'neighbour arguments' and made the subject of nothing more than a few lines in an officer's pocketbook. So it is with 'anti-social behaviour offences' which did not exist at all before 1997 and their invention by New Labour.

They cover a multitude of sins, from insulting behaviour, through disputes between tenants on social housing estates, and on to criminal damage, graffiti and assaults. Although all were studiously recorded as crimes in 2009, as they are now, and feature in national statistics, none save the most serious assaults or damage would have been recorded as crimes in 1969. But they still took place, they were just called something else. Once again, they were the day-to-day experience of the beat PC, requiring intervention, resolution with a few well-chosen words and perhaps a threat about what might happen if the incident occurred again, followed by a brief pocket book report and a word to the station's intelligence 'collator' so that he could update his record cards on what Mr and Mrs Smith's boy Darren was up to. In the context of activity, comparing raw crime data in 2019, 1969 or even 1929 is largely meaningless; what is important is how officers fill their time. Busy, committed, and active police officers in 1969 were as busy, perhaps busier, than those who followed them in 2019. The same would apply in respect of those who were lazy, disinterested or disengaged in 1969. They could avoid work just as easily as twenty-first century police officers. Indeed the 2023 generation can probably 'dodge the column' more easily because there are more of them and supervision by Sergeants and Inspectors is virtually non-existent.

As if not content with existing levels of crime, the senior echelons of policing have now discovered a wholly new form of criminality, something that has been forced upon the long-suffering population of these islands as a major priority requiring the investment of personnel and resources – it is the ill-defined concept of 'hate crime'.

In England and Wales, hate crimes are defined as any criminal offence which is perceived by the victim or any other person to be motivated by hostility or prejudice based on a personal characteristic such as race, religion, sexual orientation, disability, or transgender identity and are distinct from ordinary crimes in that they specifically involve an element of hostility or prejudice towards a particular group of people. However, hate crime has now assumed a life of its own, and police forces now use the definition (whilst studiously ignoring the fact that an actual criminal offence has to be committed in the first place) to include any and all comments on social media or in public discourse, which anyone disagrees with – a flagrant assault on free speech. Thus challenging the lifestyle of LGBTQ+ people on religious grounds in a public place or online can render the perpetrator liable to arrest and detention, as can misogyny or even 'fat shaming', whatever that might be. We have arrived at a position where the police take action in respect of things that are not actually crimes or breaches of legislation at all, solely on the basis of 'virtue signalling', whilst blithely ignoring real crime every day. In 2021/2022 the police in England and Wales recorded over 160,000 allegations of hate crime, up from less than 20,000 in 2011/2012. That is an awful lot of offended people whose feelings have been hurt, demanding the attention of police.

In many respects the way in which Newham was policed in 1969 was hardly different from the way in which it had been policed in 1929, or even 1909. There had obviously been social, operational, and organisational change aplenty. There had been a technological revolution and the introduction of scientific and communications equipment that could not even have been imagined decades before, but basically policing continued to be about a face-to-face presence on the streets, commitment to a service ethos, and a degree of respect for the expectations of those on the receiving end as an integral part of an unwritten social contract.

It was not perfect, it never had been, but it worked.

NEWHAM IN 2009 AND 2019

Peter Woodhams was just 22 years and 34 days old when he was shot dead outside his home in Canning Town on 21st August 2006. A satellite TV engineer, he lived with his partner Jane and their three-year-old son in Tallis Close, which is cheek by jowl with ExCel, one of London's premier international exhibition and conference centres. Tallis Close and ExCel are in the same Newham electoral ward, separated only by the tracks of the Docklands Light Railway, yet in terms of affluence they might just as well be located on different planets. ExCel is landscaped into an attractive waterfront development comprising top-drawer hotels, sophisticated wine bars, restaurants and penthouses which even in the aftermath of the 2012 economic downturn still command prices of almost a million pounds. Tallis Close is in a depressing, local authority social-housing estate, a mixture of old multi-storey flats, newer low-rise blocks and intimidating narrow walkways, surrounded by boarded-up, graffiti-covered flats, some of which show the smoke staining and damage that results from arson. The estate is part of Canning Town (South) electoral ward. In 2000 and

2001 government surveys which examined indicators such as health, life expectancy, housing need, crime levels, and educational attainment ranked Canning Town South as London's most deprived ward and the 35th most deprived in the whole of England and Wales. No-one wants to live there; residents who are allocated housing on the estate will do literally anything to get away. It was and is a hellish place to live.

Logic would dictate, even if common decency did not, that the area should receive assertive and visible policing; sadly however nothing could be further from the truth. People who lived there at the time that Peter was gunned down describe a level of policing and concern about their well-being that almost defies description. Effectively, there was no policing. The estate was abandoned and even when serious crime took place the response by the Metropolitan Police was almost criminally inadequate. It is for this reason that Peter's murder, and the scandal that preceded it, has become an exemplar of the parlous state of twenty-first century policing in London and beyond.

Peter Woodhams was, in every sense, a transparently decent young man working hard to support his partner and child under the most difficult conditions. He did not deal drugs or live on state benefits; he wanted nothing more than to be allowed to live his life in peace and security. His misfortune was that he had been allocated a house on a 'sink' estate which was plagued by gangs of feral youths, some of whom were as young as ten years old. At an early stage, soon after he moved into his house, Peter was identified as someone 'different' to them. Over long months he and his family were subjected to an unremitting campaign of abuse and harassment. His car was damaged on an almost daily basis, stones were thrown at his windows, and his family were threatened. Despite pleas for assistance to the police and the local authority, absolutely nothing was done.

In January 2006, just seven months before his death, Peter confronted a gang of hooded youths who were throwing stones at him outside his house. Outnumbered, he was quickly overwhelmed and knocked to the ground. One of the gang then produced a knife and in an unprovoked attack stabbed him in the neck, before slashing him across the face, opening an eight-inch wound from his forehead to his chin. Drenched in his own blood, grievously injured and in agonising pain, he collapsed outside his own front door and was tended by his partner, Jane, until an ambulance arrived to take him to hospital. His injuries were grave and, on any reasonable assessment, the assault upon him amounted to attempted murder. Any unbiased observer would have expected the police to launch an immediate, detailed, and professional investigation to bring his assailants to justice. What actually happened however was very, very, different.

After a lengthy delay, a number of plainly disinterested police officers attended the scene. According to local people who remember the incident well, the police gave the impression, without actually saying so, that *'this is what you expect from the scum who live here'*. Details were taken, the allegation was recorded, and they departed the scene to return to the borough police HQ at Forest Gate, where the information was logged onto the computerised crime recording system and then 'booked out' to a Detective Sergeant for investigation. As a subsequent enquiry by the

Independent Police Complaints Commission (IPCC) was to establish, the criminal investigation, if it can be graced with that name, plumbed new depths of inefficiency. From the outset every rule of procedure and practice was either broken or ignored. Even though two supervising officers subsequently attended the scene of the attack, neither made any attempt to take the most basic steps to 'preserve the scene' for forensic examination. As a result, vital DNA and forensic evidence was lost forever. No-one thought the assault serious enough to call out a police photographer to capture the scene. No-one kept a written record of the attack. However, much worse was to come.

People on the estate clearly felt that they, and the Woodhams, had had enough, but were too frightened to come forward and name names publicly. Over an extended period of time a number of anonymous calls were made to the police identifying the assailant and his accomplices. Despite the fact that it was confirmed by the IPCC that the police had indeed received such calls, the leads were never followed up and absolutely nothing was done. Months passed, without any sort of meaningful contact with the Woodhams family. Investigators ignored them and it was abundantly clear to all concerned that an enquiry which could have been solved by any half-competent trainee detective in a few days was completely beyond the ability of Newham Police, from the borough commander to the newest recruit. Peter's partner Jane had carefully preserved all his blood-stained clothing so that it could be forensically examined. For the next seven months she repeatedly contacted the police to ask if they would collect the items for evidential analysis, but on every occasion, she was met with excuses or ill-concealed disinterest. She phoned the police every day for five weeks following the knife attack, but officers never even bothered to take a statement from her.

The failure to investigate the attempted murder of Peter had an effect that could so easily have been predicted. The campaign of intimidation against the Woodhams, and other residents of the estate, was renewed with even greater vigour because the gang firmly believed that they had 'got away with it'. They took to taunting Peter and Jane, telling them that the police could do nothing and that they were untouchable. Whenever the couple emerged from their home, even with their three-year-old child, they were met with obscene abuse and their car would be showered with a hail of stones. The family were terrified. Whenever Peter left for work he lived with the constant nagging worry that something might happen to Jane and his son whilst he was away. When they were together in the house at night, they knew no peace or security. They had nowhere to turn for help. The police, in their view and that of many others, had demonstrated their inability or unwillingness to protect them or bring the offenders to justice. Eventually, on 21st August 2006, the dam burst. Peter had just returned from work and following an incident at a nearby shop, confronted the gang that was making his life a misery. Their leader was an eighteen-year-old thug named Bradley Tucker. Calmly, he produced a handgun from his pocket and, in full view of an army of witnesses, shot Peter four times at close range, and then casually walked off. Peter died on his doorstep in front of Jane and his son.

The Metropolitan Police serious crime team swung

into action and in short order had identified Tucker and the other members of the gang. Arrests followed but even in such a high-profile case incompetence continued to be the order of the day. A neighbour found one of the spent bullets, a vital piece of evidence, and handed it to a police officer, who promptly mislaid it – it was never seen again. On 27th March the following year, Tucker and another youth were convicted of murder, with Tucker being sentenced to life imprisonment with a minimum tariff of 25 years. Immediately thereafter, the Metropolitan Police grandly claimed that their enquiry was yet another victory in their ongoing fight against gun crime. A self-serving press release was issued by Scotland Yard on the day of Tucker's conviction, in which the senior investigating officer was quoted as saying,

> '...This was a meticulous investigation and my team worked tirelessly to achieve this result... The Metropolitan Police refuse to tolerate gun crime and remain committed to robustly investigate offences to bring offenders to justice.'

Unsurprisingly, however, no mention was made of the comprehensive failure to prevent Peter's murder by taking effective action to 'robustly investigate and bring to justice' those responsible for the earlier knife attack on him. The borough commander, a Chief Superintendent, who held ultimate managerial responsibility for the entire debacle, allegedly apologised to the Woodhams family in a private meeting shortly after Peter's murder – a claim disputed by Peter's relatives. Within a few months he was replaced as borough commander and quietly moved on to pastures new and a comfortable job at Scotland Yard. Clearly, Peter's death did not adversely affect his career, because by 2011 he had been appointed as the officer in charge of the Territorial Support Group – the 'riot squad' for London, with a senior role at the 2012 Olympics.

The final insult to the Woodhams family came at the end of the IPCC enquiry into the incompetent handling of the first attack on Peter. The original investigating officers, Detective Constable Adam Suett and his supervising officer, Detective Sergeant Darren Case, were directed to appear before a disciplinary hearing and were found guilty of gross misconduct. Both were required to resign. That seemed to be an appropriate and just end to the sorry business, but in what was interpreted by many as an outrageous decision, the case was reviewed by Assistant Commissioner Tarique Ghaffur at Scotland Yard, and the penalties were declared to be 'disproportionate'. He directed that the officers be reinstated and downgraded the punishments. Case was reduced in rank to Detective Constable whilst Suett was docked a few days' pay and permitted to transfer to the Derbyshire Constabulary, where he continued his career with the active and vocal support of local officers. Indeed by 2016 Suett was back in the CID in his new force and had been promoted to Detective Sergeant. The family challenged the decision at the High Court in 2008, labelling it 'perverse', but lost. So far as the Metropolitan Police Service is concerned the matter is now closed. Speak to people on the estate, however, years after the event, and the matter is far from closed.

It would be tempting and reassuring to assume that

what happened to Peter was an aberration, something that occurred as a result of a couple of rogue officers breaking rules without regard for the consequences. In fact, the exact opposite seems to be true. For in the four decades from 1969 the way in which Newham, the rest of London, and the whole of the United Kingdom is policed has changed fundamentally.

There are no longer five police stations in the borough, and where once there were readily accessible points of contact open around the clock, every day of the year, that is no longer the case. Only Forest Gate is open 24 hours a day, the others have been sold and disposed of to developers with little thought of the impact on or needs of the public. Even busy centres of population such as the Olympic Stadium complex, and Stratford, which has a vast shopping centre and busy night-time economy, do not justify a permanent police presence of any sort. If Peter Woodhams had wanted to seek assistance at his local police station, North Woolwich, after he returned from work in the evening, he would have been unlucky – it no longer exists and Tallis Close is a seven-mile drive from Forest Gate. The closures and gradual withdrawal of station facilities have been achieved by stealth over a number of years, always following much-heralded periods of consultation in which concerned senior officers, locked firmly in 'we are listening' mode, purport to come at the problem with an open mind. In fact, decisions have usually been made long in advance and consultation is little more than cynical window-dressing. Closures, and limited opening hours, are presented as if they are taking place in some sort of parallel universe, where not having a station open its doors at weekends, or at all, represents 'enhanced customer service'.

Figures for England and Wales published in 2009[7] revealed that 880 police stations had closed since 1992 whilst 376 new ones had opened, leaving a net loss of more than 500. It was also shown that of those that remained open, fewer than one in eight were available to the public 24 hours a day.

The issue became the subject of national debate shortly before Christmas in 2006 when Stephen Langford, a middle-aged businessman, died following a violent incident when he was set upon by a gang of youths just yards from the police station in Henley-on-Thames, which was closed to the public at the time. Officers were working inside but claimed not to have heard the commotion taking place directly outside their door.

Since 2010, with the election of the Coalition Government and the onset of the austerity-era cuts, at least 663 further police stations in England and Wales have closed. This equates to approximately four-in-ten stations closing over this period. Alarmingly, despite this sharp decrease in the number of police stations across the UK, the Home Office appears to be wholly unaware of the scale of the issue. When approached under Freedom of Information legislation about the number of stations to have closed over the decade since 2010, the Home Office admitted that it 'does not centrally hold or collect the information requested'. Yet analysis of open-source data casts an alarming picture about what is happening in some of Britain's largest and most scrutinised police forces.

---

7   Tom Whitehead, Daily Telegraph 28.9.2009 (Home Office data)

The Metropolitan Police, the pre-dominant police force in England and Wales, has seen the closure of 106 police stations and police offices with public access – around 75% of the total operational estate in London in 2010. Whilst some of these stations lay disused, others have been put to good use by those with criminal intent. In 2022 a large cannabis farm was uncovered at the Isle of Dogs Police Station on Manchester Road, in Docklands, a mere five months after its closure. Meanwhile, West Midlands police, which covers an area with the country's highest rate of knife crime per capita in 2020/21, has seen almost 80% of its stations with a public counter close; Greater Manchester Police shut ten but opened seven new buildings, only one of which will provide a 24-hour service. In Scotland, a further 140 were disposed of in the same period.

So how is Newham policed in the twenty-first century?

On the face of it, all the advantages would seem to be with the police. The population of the borough is only marginally greater than forty years ago, and overall police numbers have increased by some 20%, although the proportion of uniform officers posted to boroughs is less than in 1969, at just 20,000 (55%) of the force total of 36,000[8]. Survey after survey however exposes the fact that when asked, the public's greatest complaint is the almost total lack of visibility of police and their proven inability to deal with the low-level crime and anti-social behaviour which blights their lives on a daily basis. The clamour for real 'Dixonesque' policing became impossible to ignore during the dogdays of the last Conservative government

---

8   Metropolitan Police Annual Report 2009

in the mid-1990s. Despite the fact that official figures seemed to show that crime was in the process of falling to historically low levels compared with the decade before, no-one believed the data. The experience of the man and woman in the street was that crime and criminality was rife. Everywhere, so the press and media would claim, drug dealers held sway and knife-wielding thugs ruled the streets. The Sheehy Inquiry, which reported in late 1993[9], identified management weaknesses in the police and made some radical recommendations for change, many of which were conveniently forgotten as New Labour wrested the law-and-order policy agenda from the Tories. Two key elements survived beyond 1997 however; one was the need to build a performance regime for the police at the heart of which would be a series of targets; the second was a commitment to introduce real community policing. It seemed that George Dixon was about to rise, like Lazarus, from the grave.

As the millennium celebrations came and went, the solution for Newham and the Metropolitan Police was 'Safer Neighbourhoods', driven through by the new Metropolitan Police Commissioner, Ian Blair, with the active support and encouragement of the Mayor of London, Ken Livingstone. The plan was ambitious – teams of police officers would be posted to every local authority ward to patrol, to get to know the people again, and to deal with their problems. With fanfare publicity it was heralded as a triumph for the police and the people of London (nor was New Labour slow

---

9 'Inquiry into Police Responsibilities and Rewards', June 1993 (HMSO Cm 2280.I)

to bathe in the reflected glory of the Commissioner, or to stress the extent to which they were funding the initiative).

Everyone wants to live in a safe neighbourhood, so the choice of name for the new strategy was inspired. Some years ago Alan Coren, the much-missed columnist, wrote that the nuclear power industry in this country could have avoided much of the bad press it has had over the years if it had only referred to radioactivity as 'magic moonbeams.' So it was with Ian Blair's new policing model. 'Safer Neighbourhoods' promised everything whilst simultaneously promising nothing at all. The title was warm and fluffy, it was reassuring, it implied (but did not actually state) that every street would have its own 'bobby' back on 'the beat'.

In those far distant days when money was no object, it was intended that the personnel levels of the Met would be increased, part-funded by the Greater London Council, to meet the requirement to man the new posts that would be created. There are 624 local authority wards in Greater London, 20 of which are in Newham. If just five full-time officers (not an overly ambitious number) were to be posted to each ward then over three thousand would be needed to service the commitment across the capital. It was soon realised that this was an unsustainable number, equivalent to the creation of a provincial police force the size of the Hampshire Constabulary. Ambition had to be diluted with a strong dose of realism. In addition, events in the real world beyond Scotland Yard and the Home Office would have a bearing on the way in which 'Safer Neighbourhoods' was implemented. The post 9/11 and 7/7 environments forced a reappraisal of the way in which trained personnel were used. Priorities changed as counter-terrorism, security and protection duties swallowed armies of officers, taking them away forever from the core policing which should have been their principal purpose.

A solution to the problem was found by 'killing two birds with one stone'. Ever since he had been Chief Constable of Surrey, Ian Blair had argued for the creation of a lower-tier, lower-paid and lower-skilled police body, to replace expensive trained police officers on the streets, in order to give the impression of a police presence, whilst the fully warranted officers were used for other duties. As Deputy Commissioner and then Commissioner, he had the ear of the then Home Secretary David Blunkett who warmed to the idea, largely because it was cheaper and easier than going to the Treasury and asking for funding for a lesser number of 'real' police officers. So it was that Police Community Support Officers (PCSOs) – known disparagingly as 'Blunkett's Bobbies' – arrived upon the scene untested, to fill the gaps in the shiny new 'Safer Neighbourhoods' model. There is now much evidence to show that the introduction of PCSOs has not been garlanded with success, and their impact and future will be discussed in greater detail later. Suffice to say however that the knock-on effect of their introduction in boroughs such as Newham and elsewhere has not been wholly beneficial.

Canning Town (South) Safer Neighbourhoods Team (SNT) is typical of those across the rest of the borough, and most other areas of London. To provide day-to-day policing for the entire ward, with its sink estates and myriad social and economic problems, there were just two junior constables and three PCSOs under the SNT model. None of them worked at night and seldom at weekends or in the evenings. In addition they were entitled to two days off each week, holiday leave and training; none of which is covered by replacement personnel. The team claimed to be contactable by telephone and e-mail, but it was difficult to know how to achieve this as their telephone numbers and e-mail addresses appeared to be a state secret – as now, they are difficult to find on the Newham Borough Police website, or indeed anywhere else. It is also difficult to know what they achieved, beyond posing for the occasional group photograph. It is however instructive to walk, as I have done, around the ward and speak to people in Victoria Dock Road, or Tarling Road, or Butchers Road, and ask them about policing. Liberally spiced with East-End slang and a few expletives, the most common response is, '*What f***ing police? You never see 'em round here!*' Questions about the Safer Neighbourhoods Team and community policing in general elicit an equally robust response. No-one was even aware of the existence of such units and had certainly never seen them patrolling. A few mentioned that they had seen, '*those yellow numpties*' (PCSOs), '*hanging around in twos and threes on the estate*', occasionally. Beyond Canning Town, one experiences a similar reaction after a few brief conversations with ordinary people elsewhere in the borough, and indeed across the capital and in provincial forces. The enduring impression is that the much-vaunted Safer Neighbourhoods model in London, which was rolled out as 'Neighbourhood Policing' across the rest of England and Wales, is little more than a masterpiece of spin. Around 16,500 officers are ostensibly, but seldom actually, committed to neighbourhood policing – just 11% of the total in all forty-three forces. On the back of this ill-starred experiment, however, changes have taken place that affect everyone who lives and works in Newham and elsewhere; changes which have undermined the effective and trusted model of policing in our communities that was developed over many decades.

The concept of dedicated police officers reassuring the public by walking preventative patrols on beats, alone, in uniform, has been comprehensively abandoned. There are no beats anymore – there are no 'bobbies on beats' anymore, neither have existed for most of the first two decades of this century anywhere in the country and no-one in government or the police establishment is in any hurry to bring them back.

Beware of any politician or senior police officer who speaks soothingly of his or her intention to move 'bobbies' out from 'behind their desks', so that 'they can get back on their beats'. They do not mean it. There is a limited and essentially artificial police presence on the streets of Newham and beyond, provided by PCSOs, which has allowed today's young officers to escape from what they never really wanted to do in the first place – visibly patrol the streets in all weathers, on their own, providing a service to the public. Home Office figures showed that in 2007/08 officers spent just 13.8 per cent of their time on patrol, which does not include attending incidents, down from 15.3 per cent in 2004/05[10]. By 2019[11] this already low figure had fallen still further to little more than 10%, to the equivalent of one hour in an average eight-hour shift or less

---

10 Hansard, 10 December 2007, Col. 91WA

11 Home Office, Police Workforce Statistical Bulletin, March 2019

than six in a 40-hour week, and these are generous figures. Reality 'on the ground' according to many officers is that the amount of time actually spent patrolling may even be half of this figure. This is reduced yet further by the fact that officers almost always patrol in pairs, effectively halving the cover on the streets. Supine management and non-existent supervision over the last two decades has compounded the problem.

For, as their senior managers are fully aware, there is no shortage of 'real' police officers in Newham – they just busy themselves doing things that are largely unrelated to what the public wants and expects.

Newham borough headquarters is situated in a relatively new complex on the main road that runs through Forest Gate and then on, after four or five miles, to the City of London. In common with almost every major police station in London and beyond, it bustles with activity. Cars and vans pass in and out of its gates, full of hard-faced young men, very often crop-haired, in earnest conversation with their colleagues. The station is home to a dozen or more squads and units, all of which employ officers who, when asked, argue strongly that what they do is vital and is 'real' policing.

There are personnel designated solely to deal with 'hate crimes'; others who deal exclusively with burglaries; yet more who focus only on street robbery. There are officers whose sole function is to draw up plans and duty rosters, to liaise with minority groups, or to sift intelligence. Yet more are involved in 'community liaison' and servicing ongoing relationships with the local authority. Other officers, who are ostensibly attached to Newham, actually serve on discrete and separate teams elsewhere in East London and beyond, such as 'Sapphire' dealing with rape allegations, or on Forward Intelligence Teams (FIT) with the Public Order Branch at Scotland Yard. There is a 'Safer Transport Team' which deals with the policing of the bus network. At least ten officers are referred to as POLSA trained (an acronym for 'Police Search Adviser'), which qualifies them to take part in expert search operations at scenes of crime, but also means that they are regularly absent from the borough on operations and training. Everyone seems to have a specialism and with such a range of supposed expertise at their disposal, it is frankly astonishing that those responsible for the investigation of the knife attack on Peter Woodhams performed so incompetently.

So, as darkness falls in the early evening, and the Safer Neighbourhood Teams return to their homes in the far distant suburbs; as the PCSOs book off duty having spent another shift 'walking with a purpose' in pale imitation of patrolling the streets, who is left to police a London borough with a crime level which rivals that of the entire county of Surrey? Frankly, not many officers at all. Coverage at such times is provided by Response Teams, all of whom are mobile and operate in pairs, two officers to a vehicle. They dash from call to call on 'blues and twos', providing what is effectively a fire brigade service. Hedged around by performance targets linked to arrival times and robbed of any discretion by a library of instructions relating to how they should or should not deal with various offences and offenders, they have little time or inclination to provide a service in the way that their predecessors did forty years before.

The target-culture in other parts of the public sector abounds with in-built perversity, and so it is with the police.

Officers will be praised for having succeeded to meet a target if they drive to an incident at breakneck speed which endangers their lives and that of others, yet will be criticised if they arrive a minute later, having driven there safely but under the target time.

There are only two custody suites in Newham, at Forest Gate with an overflow unit at Plaistow (which is not always in use), whereas forty years ago there were five. Newham is a large borough with a network of busy streets and arterial roads, which means that when officers make arrests, they, and their prisoners, often have to be conveyed considerable distances before the offender can be booked in, and an investigation can start. Even a simple and straightforward case might mean that officers become unavailable for three or four hours, their vehicle off the road, miles from where they should be patrolling. Far from seeing this as a problem, the Metropolitan Police and the senior officers at Newham have come up with a solution.

In their 'Asset Management Plan' published in 2007, following a public consultation meeting attended by just twenty people, Newham Police announced that they intended to rationalise all their current police buildings, and move to a model which would signal their final departure from any meaningful contact with the public. Of course they did not admit that that was the case, and would never describe it as such, but retrenchment was implicit in everything set out in the strategy. Whilst 'Safer Neighbourhoods' PCSOs and a few junior constables would operate from shop-front premises dotted across the borough, the remainder of the policing effort, in excess of 500 police officers, would stay hidden behind the walls of two purpose-built redoubts – with the Orwellian titles 'patrol base' and 'custody facility'. The way in which this new operational approach is described and justified in the published document is set out below. There is no suggestion of anything being lost, no admission of a withdrawal of service. The tone is quietly authoritative, suggesting that there is no option other than radical change. In truth, this is almost certainly the case because the powers-that-be at Scotland Yard had directed that this template would be applied in all of the thirty-two London boroughs as a further programme of borough amalgamations was rolled out after 2016.

Our future plans: new custody provision in Newham

The MPS has recognised that it is no longer necessary or appropriate to have custody cells in high street police stations and that locating these at a strategic point in the borough will save money, improve efficiency and enable more frontline policing.

We are now looking at developing specialised custody facilities, known as Custody Centres in each borough in London. The concept of a Custody Centre is grouping between 20–40 cells in one location along with related facilities such as interview rooms, consultation rooms and a search suite. A Custody Centre would offer more cells that meet modern standards and provide more suitable facilities for officers, lawyers and other visitors.

We are now in the process of looking at options

> *for a Custody Centre in Newham at the Forest Gate police station site or an alternative location and we will continue to keep you updated on our plans.*[12]

It is patently obvious that the good people of Newham are hardly acknowledged as players in the decision-making process. The opening paragraph has the tone of holy writ. *'The MPS has recognised'* that change is required, without offering a shred of supporting evidence and has decided that *'...it is no longer necessary or appropriate...* to deal with custody of prisoners at a number of convenient locations. The implication is that bigger is better for the benefit of *'...officers, lawyers and other visitors...'* The plan is effectively offered as a *fait accompli* with no reference to any advantage or otherwise that might accrue for the public. The section dealing with the proposed 'patrol base' is even more telling,

> **Our future plans: improved patrol facilities in Newham**
> *Operational officers currently patrol the borough from Forest Gate police station. However as policing demands in the borough increase operational officers will need more space and updated facilities to ensure sufficient lockers for uniforms, equipment, clothes-drying facilities; larger briefing rooms so teams can be briefed together; and sufficient parking to allow all patrol vehicles to be in one location.*

---

12 MPS Asset Management Plan 2007 (Newham Borough Command Unit)

Therefore in order to develop a better service in the borough it is our intention to develop a single facility known as a Patrol Base.

A Patrol Base is a flexible warehouse-style building that will accommodate the majority of operational police officers and resources for the borough in one main building. It will also provide garaging for police vehicles and operational parking, allowing a large number of vehicle movements with minimal disruption and enabling faster response times. **These bases will not be open to the public** *but will bring officers and vehicles together at a single location with faster access to all parts of the borough.*

This would be a new style of police base for Newham and central to the requirements of a possible location will be excellent 24/7 transport accessibility and vehicular access, together with a high level of operational parking availability. The building will need to be as flexible as possible so that internal layouts can be adapted as necessary to suit changing police requirements. Our preferred areas for this kind of facility include East Ham or the Barking Road and we will continue to keep you updated on our proposals.[13]

This vision for the future, described without any justification or indeed embarrassment, as an *improvement*,

---

13 Ibid

is set out by those responsible for policing Newham in 2009 as being a path to the provision of a better service, but the lie is given away in the third paragraph. Officers would patrol in vehicles from a 'warehouse-style' building located at some distance from the main residential areas. Foot patrols, so reassuring to the public, appear not to be an option. Most significantly, the base would not be open to the people of Newham, who presumably would only be able to speak to officers at the one remaining police station, or via the telephone. The service ethos has been redefined for the twenty-first century. The 2007 strategic plan has been superseded by even more radical change as Newham has been amalgamated with neighbouring boroughs for policing purposes, so that by 2019 the original, locally based, model had ceased to exist.

Newham has changed in many ways over the past forty years, but in some respects, it has hardly changed at all. It is now London's second most ethnically diverse borough, according to the Office for National Statistics' 'league table'[14]. It is also one of the most deprived, along with neighbouring Hackney and Tower Hamlets. Only a third (33%) of Newham's population of 244,000 is White British. This is the second-lowest proportion of all London boroughs. There are nearly as many Asian people living in the borough as White British (79,000 compared with 82,000). Newham has the largest Pakistani population of any borough in London and its proportion of black residents is one of the highest of all London boroughs, at almost 22%. There are nearly twice

---

14 Office for National Statistics (Neighbourhood Statistics) retrieved 31st May 2018

as many Black Africans as Black Afro-Caribbeans (32,000 and 18,000), and the former group includes more than 800 people born in the Democratic Republic of Congo – the largest such population in England. Interestingly, however, there is little evidence of racial tension, certainly not to any extent that would require active police involvement. Most, if not all, of the people who form these disparate ethnic and social groups want nothing more than to open their small shops, run their businesses, bring up their children, and live in peace and security. To that extent they are no different from the Eastenders who emerged from Whitechapel to settle in Newham a century before, or the dockworkers, shop assistants, and labourers of forty years ago. They are also no different from Peter Woodhams, who wanted the same things but was so cruelly let down.

The challenge for modern policing, in Newham, which hosted the Olympic Games in the summer of 2012, and everywhere else in the UK, is to meet those needs. On current evidence however there is little to suggest that those needs will be met. When you cast a sceptical eye over each so-called 'ground-breaking' but quickly forgotten initiative; after you cut away the presentational hyperbole and self-congratulatory spin which is generated by every police force in the land, and when you look beyond vision statements and each 'Policing Pledge', you see very little of real substance.

CHAPTER 2
'CITIZENS IN UNIFORM?'

HOW IT LOOKS TODAY

There is never a good time to criticise the police. Just as all nurses are 'angels', and all soldiers are 'our boys', so all police officers are 'heroes' and woe betide anyone who has the effrontery to take a contrary view.

We have the best police in the world, don't we?

Until the tragic kidnap, rape, and murder of Sarah Everard by PC Wayne Couzens in 2021 that is what the popular press and producers of 'fly on the wall' TV documentaries would have us believe. However, in order to accept the statement at face value there would need to be a lengthy debate on whether or not we really do have a system to be truly proud of, and much would turn on precisely what is meant by 'best'. Does the best police service catch more criminals, or prevent more crime? Should it make the honest citizen feel safer in his bed, or make the criminal lie awake in his, fearing a knock on the door and summary arrest? Is it any or all of these things?

The Venezuelan Police, acknowledged to be the most

corrupt in the world, are remarkably good at terrifying drug dealers in the shantytowns of Caracas. The Amsterdam Police are noted for their liberal attitude to the sale of marijuana in city centre 'coffee-shops', but heaven help anyone found in possession of a 'spliff' in the suburban areas of the city. The value and efficiency of any police force must be measured within the context of where it operates, and the political and economic system under which it is required to deliver a service. In this connection the single feature which makes the police system in the United Kingdom stand out as different to, but not necessarily better than, others in the world is its constitutional position.

All police officers serving within the four nations in these islands are theoretically, legally, and actually accountable to the law, and to the law alone. Whereas brother and sister officers across the globe swear loyalty to Presidents, Ministers of the Interior, Constitutions or even flags, those in Britain swear an oath of allegiance to the Crown as the embodiment of the rule of law. The implications of this are profound when examined in detail. No police officer, from newest recruit to Commissioner or Chief Constable, can be ordered, by anyone, to do anything that might conceivably conflict with his oath. No Home Secretary or government official can direct a senior officer to arrest that person or this person. The decision to arrest, or even investigate, is something that rests entirely with the discretion of the individual officer. All police officers, no matter how senior or junior, have unrestricted 'operational independence' and complete freedom in the exercise of their powers. However, with such freedom comes great responsibility and a whole raft of legal sanctions if any officer abuses his position.

Malfeasance in public office, or official misconduct, is the commission of an unlawful act, done in an official capacity, which affects the performance of an individual's official duties and is often applied against police officers who act beyond their oath and outside the law, whilst ostensibly discharging their duties. The offence is punishable with a lengthy term of imprisonment. Thus police officers in this country work within a markedly different regime to that which governs colleagues elsewhere.

Policing in the United States, for example, is fundamentally different in form and function to that delivered in Western Europe, which in turn bears no close relationship to the way it is done in the UK. However, because of the impact of the US entertainment industry on media and popular culture, the average man in the street in this country expects crime to be tackled and policing delivered as per the latest Hollywood crime show and considers himself to be a lay expert on forensic science, having seen the current series of 'C.S.I.' There are currently 4687 separate police departments in the United States, most having no more than five or six officers. Every state, county, city, town, village and hamlet is entitled under US federal and state law to elect a police chief and establish its own police force, with officers having the full range of powers shared by all other officers across the country, up to and including the right to use lethal force. Add to this the 236 US-based international law-enforcement agencies, the 10 Federal and Military investigative bodies and the 50 State Police and State Trooper outfits, and what you have is a recipe for confusion and petty corruption. Whilst the FBI and the big city forces, such as New York and Los Angeles, are models of efficiency and very often exemplars to the world, the US policing system is not one that we should seek to emulate. Sadly, however, life imitates art and many of today's young British officers, in the way that they conduct themselves, in the way that they regard the public, and in their desire to always patrol with a 'partner', clearly believe that what is acceptable in downtown Baltimore should be the norm in Newham or even Chipping Sodbury.

So should we look to the European mainland for guidance? Probably not, for the way that policing has developed on the continent is very much a legacy of the past two hundred and fifty years of conflict and history. It is fascinating to note that in all the countries where Napoleon's *La Grande Armée* established French power in the nineteenth century, each has a model of policing that is still based upon that imposed by France. Thus in France, Spain, Portugal, Italy, The Netherlands, Federal Germany and even Poland, there was and is a dualism to the way the people are policed, born of a philosophy which is markedly at odds with the way we do it (at least until very recently).

In mainland Europe, policing is 'top-down'. The role of the police is to watch the people in case they should present a threat to the well-being of the state. Community policing as a concept is largely alien to their experience. That does not mean that they do not offer a fair and measured service – in most places in Western Europe policing is excellent – but in the final analysis they do not consider themselves to be 'of' the people. They are loyal servants of the state and are there to ensure that state power is maintained and upheld. For this reason policing is shared between the military arm of government and the Ministry of the Interior. This often leads to overlap of jurisdictions and 'turf wars' about which agency should take responsibility for an investigation or an incident.

In France, the *Gendarmerie Nationale* – a military institution with national responsibility for public safety and police duties amongst the civilian population is often at odds with the *Police Nationale*, whose 155,000 members come under the wing of the Ministry of the Interior in Paris and provide the primary, but not exclusive, policing presence in all major cities and towns. All of this is yet further complicated by the existence of the *Police Municipale*, who have limited, but important, enforcement powers in many French towns and cities. Italy has the same problems of co-ordination between the military *Arma dei Carabinieri* and the two main civilian uniformed police forces, the *Polizia di Stato* and the *Guardia di Finanza*. Likewise, in Spain the military *Guardia Civil* vies with the Ministry of the Interior's *Cuerpo Nacional de Policía*. In the Netherlands the *Koninklijke Marechaussee* (Gendarmerie) has national responsibility superimposed upon 25 regional police forces and a national police agency. The favoured model across Scandinavia is national policing under the direct control of central government. No-one has ever argued that policing in the UK should adopt the dual military/civil style that is the main feature of European policing. Our history is different; our constitutional position bears little similarity to that of many of our neighbours. Our roots were planted in different soil and have produced a markedly different tree, one which has always (until recently) had the distinct advantage of drawing its strength *from* the people as their protector, whilst simultaneously maintaining an arm's length relationship with government.

T A Critchley, the eminent historian, wrote that what makes police officers in the United Kingdom different from those elsewhere is that the former are 'citizens in uniform'[15]. Captured in that phrase is the essence of what most people recognise, often unconsciously, as the key element of value in our system. For all of the last century, and for the early years of this, no matter how strained relations became over the occasional scandal or over-zealous exercise of power, the public never regarded the police, as an institution, as anything other than a body that was committed to their protection. The British police were never spoken of in the same breath as the pre-Apartheid South African Police, the Stasi or the French CRS. Newsreel images of US police officers clubbing and shooting peaceful protesters during the civil-rights protests in the American south in the 1960s were all the more shocking to British eyes because we knew that such things could not possibly happen here. British bobbies just did not behave in that way. Such a relationship has value beyond gold but is fragile and because of that fragility needs to be safeguarded and nurtured.

Everyone today believes that they know about the police, how they operate, how they think, and what motivates them. Popular culture, TV, the press, media and particularly social media, have made experts of us all, but when you scratch below the surface you rapidly discover that this expertise is flawed. As a result people too often accept, without question, what they are told by police leaders and policy makers and seldom demand, as responsible citizens should, that policing be accountable at all times and at every level of

---

15   'A History of Police in England and Wales' T A Critchley (1972)

interaction. Too often the prevailing attitude reminds one of the trusting view of government that many held in the 1940s and 1950s that was summed up in the phrase, 'The man from Whitehall knows best', only now it has become, 'The man from Scotland Yard knows best'.

There is a need to explode a few myths.

Ask the average man in the street how policing is organised in the UK, and he will confidently tell you that everything is run from Scotland Yard – which is, of course, completely wrong. Scotland Yard is the name for the somewhat drab headquarters of the London Metropolitan Police on Victoria Embankment. It is not an operational building; it never has been and is no more significant to national policing than any other corporate HQ. The Met has a number of discrete and quite specific responsibilities that have national significance, such as the protection of the Royal Family, royal palaces, and foreign diplomats. In addition the Metropolitan Police Service has the duty to co-ordinate the UK counter-terrorism effort domestically and overseas, by assisting the Security Service and Secret Intelligence Service (SIS) in fulfilling their statutory roles, and by providing a senior officer (usually an Assistant Commissioner or Deputy Assistant Commissioner) to act as National Co-ordinator of Terrorist Investigations. Beyond these admittedly vital functions, the writ of the Metropolitan Police only runs in the 32 London boroughs that comprise the Greater London Area, and the City of Westminster.

Since 1839, the 'Square Mile' of the City of London has maintained its own separate police force independent of the Met, employing just under 900 officers, a large proportion of whom are engaged on fraud investigation as the City Police are the national 'lead' force for such crimes. Thus, the City aside, the Met is the force that polices London and nowhere else. The days when provincial forces in the 1920s and 1930s, way out of their depth with a murder or some other serious enquiry, would 'call in the Yard' are now long gone. Expertise in most things is now spread evenly across the country and except for terrorist outrages, all forces would deeply resent any suggestion that they cannot cope and would not welcome interference from the 'Yard'.

The rank structure and organisational makeup of the police confuses many because they try to equate it with the military but unfortunately there is no direct 'read across'. There are only two forces that are headed by 'Commissioners' – the Met and the City Police. The title is an accident of history linked to the fact that the designation was cited in the original legislation establishing the Met but was not used by the officeholder until 1839. Whilst admittedly running a very big operation, with a grand total (police and support staff) of 55,000 personnel, making it second only to the National Health Service as the biggest employer in London, the Commissioner is merely *'primus inter pares'* in terms of all the other chief officers across the country. The post is and always has been influential, but the Commissioner cannot, as many assume, direct what goes on elsewhere in the UK and to that extent he is not, as the press are wont to describe him, 'the most senior police officer in Great Britain'.

Across the rest of England and Wales (disregarding the Met and the City Police) there are an additional 41 separate territorial police forces which come under the umbrella of the Home Office in terms of funding and policy. Prior to 2013 there were a further 8 police forces in Scotland, but all have now been amalgamated into a single unitary force, Police Scotland, for which the Scottish Parliament has devolved responsibility. Finally, there is the Police Service of Northern Ireland (PSNI), formerly the Royal Ulster Constabulary, which for obvious reasons is very much a special case, although since the Good Friday Peace Agreement in April 1998 it has tentatively moved from being on a full-scale 'war footing' to something almost approximating ordinary policing.

For the sake of completeness it should be noted that there are, in addition, separate police forces for Guernsey, Jersey, and the Isle of Man, which are technically not part of the UK policing effort at all, as they were never part of the European Union and are managed and directed by their own legislatures and officials – Bailiffs in respect of the Channel Islands, and the Tynwald for the Isle of Man.

Thus, core policing in the United Kingdom is delivered by forces which have a territorial responsibility for the area in which they are established. This can range from the Met, with its 36,000 sworn officers, through to the tiny Warwickshire Constabulary, with just over 900. The largest forces outside London are those based upon the conurbations around other major cities, such as the West Midlands Police (8,400 officers) based on Birmingham, and the Greater Manchester Police (8,200 officers). The vast majority of the rest are 'county police forces' which have co-terminous boundaries with local authority counties, such as Dorset, or Norfolk, or Derbyshire. Since 1965 there has been pressure for such forces to amalgamate in the interests of efficiency and, over the years, this has produced such hybrids as the Thames Valley Police (Oxfordshire, Berkshire, Buckinghamshire), and West Mercia Constabulary (Shropshire, Herefordshire and Worcestershire). The unifying factor, governing the way in which all of them operate, is that large or small, rural or urban, individual Chief Constables have total responsibility (and legal liability) for everything that occurs within their span of command. For example, as has happened, if the Chief Constable of Sussex Police seeks 'mutual aid' from half a dozen other forces to assist him to police an environmental or animal cruelty protest, and he is 'lent' five hundred or a thousand officers from elsewhere in the UK, he is personally liable for their conduct and responsible for their effective deployment. Quite literally the 'buck stops' with him, as it would for any other Chief Constable in the land, because the operation is taking place in 'his' county.

ALMOST POLICE FORCES - BUT NOT QUITE!

In addition to territorial police forces, there are several other uniformed law enforcement bodies whose activities often impinge upon the lives of ordinary people. The best known of these is the 3,000 strong British Transport Police which is responsible for policing the whole of the rail network in England, Wales and Scotland (but not Northern Ireland). Born of an amalgamation of the various railway company police forces that had existed for decades prior to nationalisation at the end of the second world war, the British Transport Police (BTP) was, until twenty to thirty years ago, regarded as something between a joke and an embarrassment in policing circles. Ill-equipped, badly trained, poorly supervised and led, the force added very little value to the protection of passengers and employees on the railways and might not have escaped being disbanded in the 'run-up' to rail privatisation in the 1990s, had it not been for two things.

Firstly, the IRA mainland bombing campaign with the threat it posed to the rail and underground network, concentrated the minds of a few forward-thinking BTP senior officers who decided that security of the rail network would become (as perhaps it should have been all along!) their 'USP – unique selling point'. Accordingly they began to develop expertise in specific areas such as explosive 'sniffer' dogs, fast-response teams with mobile scanners that could race from station to station to examine suspicious packages in double-quick time so that minimum disruption was caused to the system, and sophisticated use of CCTV. This latter was the second and arguably more significant reason for the operational renaissance of the BTP. Throughout the 1980s and early 1990s the level of violent crime, muggings and assaults on the rail network, particularly the London Underground, approached epidemic proportions and became something of a national scandal. These were also crimes that touched upon the racial sensibilities and stereotypes of the period, because many of the offences were committed by gangs of young black men using extreme violence. The Met could do next to nothing to curb the problem, as they were above ground and could not communicate with the BTP officers below ground because their radios worked on different frequencies and in any event went dead in the tunnels and on the platforms of the Tube system.[16] The solution was CCTV. Using funding from the GLC, Home Office, Department of Transport and the Train Operating Companies (TOCs), the British Transport Police and London Underground Ltd (now TFL) installed a state-of-the-art system which now has over 8,500 cameras recording 24 hours a day on the system, and on platforms and trains. There are a further 2,000 on the above ground Network Rail system, and yet more on stations and systems across the land, from Inverness to Penzance[17]. The whole project has been a stunning success, with crime driven down to historically low levels. Detractors will claim that much of this has been bought at the expense of all our civil liberties and has been used by the TOCs as a means to reduce staffing levels at stations, which, it is argued, would be a greater deterrent. There is some truth in this, but the advantages for the BTP have been profound. From being regarded as something of a 'basket case' nationally, they have transformed themselves into a modern well-equipped and highly professional organisation. Indeed so well regarded have they become that they were given the lead role in the delivery of security for all aspects of policing transport arrangements (road, rail, aviation, and maritime) for the 2012 London Olympics. The then recently retired Chief Constable of the BTP, Sir Ian Johnston, was appointed as Head of Security for the

---

16 As is still the case, despite the investment of millions of pounds in the police 'Airwave' radio system provided by the Home Office, and the salutary lessons of the 7/7 terrorist outrage in London.

17 'Playing Our Part – Corporate Responsibility Report 2006', Network Rail 2007 (updated 2019)

Games as a whole – quite an accolade for someone was nearer seventy than sixty when the Olympic flame was lit.

There is however a darker side to the BTP, which has emerged as the force has become more professional. Logic dictates that the *raison d'etre* of any police force concerned with the protection of a transport system should be to devote the majority of its effort to that purpose. Increasingly however the BTP has trained and equipped significant numbers of its officers for advanced 'public order' duties complete with shields, batons, and riot-protected personnel carriers. One could possibly argue that such officers might occasionally be needed to deal with problems such as the reception of unruly football hooligans on stations etc., but it is difficult to see a role beyond that for the Transport Police. Since 2001 however the real reason has become increasingly clear. Protocols have been agreed between the Met and the BTP, whereby the latter's public order units (known as 'serials') are regularly deployed as front-line elements in major operations which have no connection whatsoever with the transport system. They are, in effect, a reserve riot squad available for use across London and presumably beyond. The use of a non-Home Office police force in such a way is unprecedented, largely because part of their funding comes from the private sector (i.e. the TOCs) and there are real constitutional issues, as yet unexplored, about their accountability. It is worthy of note that they were very much to the fore during the 2009 'G20' disturbances and attracted a number of complaints of violence and misconduct.

The Ministry of Defence Police is another force that has enormous power and influence in terms of its potential impact on the ordinary man in the street, but about which the public know very little. The MoD Police or, to give it its correct title, The Ministry of Defence Police and Guarding Agency, is an executive agency of the Ministry of Defence and was formed in 2004 from an amalgamation of the MoD Guard Service – a civilian body – and the MoD Police Agency, which used to provide limited policing services within military sites such as Faslane, where the UK's Trident submarine fleet is based, and the Atomic Weapons Research Establishment at Aldermaston. It is headed by a Chief Executive, usually a retired Chief Constable or Deputy Chief Constable from a provincial police force, and has around 3,400 officers located in over a hundred locations throughout the UK and overseas. All MoD officers undergo firearms training and at any given time, over three-quarters of the strength of the force, some 2,500 officers, are posted to duties where they are armed on duty in uniform, carrying handguns, or Heckler & Koch MP5 sub-machine guns. Under what are grandly called 'Concordats' with Home Office forces such as the Met or provincial county forces, MoD officers are allowed to conduct vehicle patrols beyond military establishments at many places up and down the country. Again, as with the public order role of the BTP, there has been no public debate about the deployment of heavily armed MoD Police officers outside military establishments.

For example, the Wiltshire Constabulary, a small rural force which has responsibility for over thirty army and air force bases, relies upon the MoD police in ways that were never intended and have never been the subject of public scrutiny. Early in 2009, PC Stephen Porter of the

Royal Wootton Bassett Neighbourhood Policing Team announced proudly in a newsletter to local residents that his force had a 'close working relationship with the Ministry of Defence Police'; undertaking joint patrols with them, and that MoD officers had been 'moving on youths hanging around in Lyneham'[18]. This is happening in communities across the county and indeed in many other places across the UK. It is highly unlikely that the MoD officers surrender their weapons as they leave military premises, so the assumption must be made that by default, and with little or no management intervention, junior officers are making decisions about how they should be employed whilst armed. In addition MoD officers are not trained to the same level of competence as their colleagues in Home Office forces, nor do they fall under the same chain of command. It therefore follows that were a tragedy to occur in which MoD officers were to discharge their weapons in an incident 'off base' – whilst conducting some sort of 'joint patrol' in Lyneham for example – the accountability and legal liability would be ill-defined. What is beyond doubt however is the clear moral responsibility of the hapless Chief Constable of Wiltshire for failing to ensure that the relationship was scrutinised at an executive level, rather than leaving matters to junior constables in the rural fastnesses of the county.

The last, little known and perhaps most intriguing, non-territorial police force in the UK is the Civil Nuclear Constabulary, which has 750 officers stationed in England, Scotland and Wales. It is a highly specialised police force responsible for providing law enforcement and security

---

18   Wiltshire Police Website – Wootton Bassett (Rural) NPT

at civil (as opposed to military) nuclear installations throughout the United Kingdom. It also has a wider remit to provide security for nuclear substances, such as high-grade radioactive waste, nuclear fuels in transit and plutonium. The force has no responsibility for guarding Britain's nuclear weapons, which is clearly the duty of the military and the MoD Police.

Established in 2005 it replaced the former Atomic Energy Authority Constabulary which had been set up at the dawn of the nuclear age in the early 1950s. Under the Energy Act 2004 it was specifically not placed under the control of the Home Office but was instead made an executive agency of the Department of Energy and Climate Change, which at the first opportunity did something that raised eyebrows in policing and civil liberties circles. The Minister appointed a former senior diplomat, Richard Thompson, as the first Chief Constable anywhere in the country who did not have a prior police background. No-one had ever heard of Thompson and his inclusion on the shortlist for the post was baffling, but since his appointment in 2007, information has trickled out that makes matters much clearer. In a vitally important but little read article in the 'Guardian' in October 2009[19], columnist Rob Evans pointed out that Sir Christopher Rose, the UK Chief Surveillance Commissioner, had said of Thompson that, 'he has extensive experience in the intelligence world, but has no previous police background'. Suggestions have been made that he was in fact a former senior MI6 officer. At

---

19 'Secret files reveal covert network run by nuclear police' Rob Evans, 'The Guardian' 20.10.2009

a time when government concern about environmental protest and the security of energy supplies is paramount, any police and security service links need to be examined closely. As Evans observed, the nuclear industry pays around £60 million a year to finance the force which comes from the companies who run the remaining 17 nuclear plants in the UK, including Dounreay in Caithness, Sellafield in Cumbria and Dungeness in Kent. Around a third is paid by the private consortium managing Sellafield, which is largely owned by American and French firms. Nearly a fifth of the funding is provided by British Energy, the privatised company owned by French firm EDF.

Alone amongst police forces in the United Kingdom (with the obvious exception of the PSNI), all CNC officers are routinely armed when on duty. Indeed the CNC spent £1.4m on weapons and ammunition between 2006 and 2009 and continues to resource its armoury at this level to this day. The CNC also operate the heavy armament on board the ships of a private company, Pacific Nuclear Transport Limited, which specialises in transporting spent nuclear fuel and reprocessed uranium around the world on behalf of British Nuclear Fuels. Such ships have an onboard escort of armed CNC officers, in much the same way that Royal Naval vessels carry Royal Marines. CNC personnel have the same powers as regular police officers, when within civil nuclear sites, but their powers were extended by the 2004 Act so that they could have jurisdiction in any place up to 5 kilometres from the boundary of a civil nuclear site, and *anywhere in the UK* when investigating offences.

Clearly the nuclear industry does not fund a specialist armed police force out of a sense of altruism. As with any private company they are driven by the bottom line, which in their case is the level of profit they can make from the government for building and running, in an uncertain world, the next generation of nuclear power facilities. It is beyond doubt that they see distinct advantage in a situation in which 'their' police have powers that are not available to civilian security officers. The relationship that the industry has with the force is close (some would say too close), and borders on the unconstitutional. In papers leaked to Evans in October 2009 there was private correspondence which showed that in June 2009, EDF's head of security complained that the force had overspent its budget 'without timely and satisfactory explanations to us'. The industry readily acknowledges it is in regular contact with the CNC and the security services, and this goes to the heart of why the CNC is structured in the way that it is. Police officers, unlike security companies, have unrestricted access to intelligence and surveillance databases. They also have tacit authority under the Regulation of Investigatory Powers Act 2000 (RIPA) to conduct intrusive surveillance, something denied to EDF or any other private company. As pressure grows for nuclear power to become a larger element in our power generation mix, the level of environmental protest will increase. The value to the nuclear industry of access to full police powers, and the ability to use informants, phone-tapping etc, through their surrogates in the CNC, will then be at a premium.

Indeed the CNC has already started. In papers disclosed by Evans following a Freedom of Information request by the 'Guardian', Sir Christopher Rose the chief surveillance commissioner, noted in 2010, 'The strategic aims of the constabulary remain on the threat from terrorism and public disquiet over nuclear matters, including demonstrations/protests and criminal offences towards nuclear movements/installations.' In July 2009 Rose said the CNC's 'approach to covert activity is conspicuously professional'. He found that the system for storing the intelligence gained from informers was 'working well' and added that he had been told during inspections that 'senior officers regard covert surveillance as a long-term requirement'.

It is also significant that the body that is intended to provide oversight of the CNC's activities, to act as an independent regulator in the *public* interest, is firmly in the hands of the nuclear industry and the Department of Energy and Climate Change. The Civil Nuclear Police Authority is funded by the industry. Four of the eight members of the Authority are nominated by the nuclear industry as its representatives; all four are employed in the industry and a fifth has close links to the industry. Of the remainder, two are retired Chief Constables and the other is a former senior prison Governor. These three, all of whom were appointed by the Energy Minister, are apparently regarded as the 'independent' members.

Thus we have a situation in which two police forces, the MoD Police and the CNC, neither of which is accountable to parliament in the same way as territorial forces, have been given wide powers to operate beyond their authorised places of duty. Both can conduct intrusive covert surveillance and, furthermore, are permitted to carry and 'in extremis' use firearms. Their uniforms, vehicles, insignia etc., are all exactly the same as that of Home Office forces. It would be reasonably safe to wager a large sum of money that less than one person in a thousand is even aware of their existence, or would know the difference between either of them or their local police – they would just be regarded as 'cops'. Whilst their core tasks are clearly necessary – there is an obvious need to protect nuclear sites – do these functions have to be performed by police officers? The compelling answer is almost certainly 'No'. The BTP can at least claim that their existence is justified by the fact that they deal with millions of members of the public every day as travellers on the transport system. The defined roles of the MoD Police and the CNC place them in an altogether different category. Both effectively operate as high-level security guards, the former as the agent of the Ministry of Defence, the latter as an in-house security firm for private companies, BNFL, EDF, etc. It is therefore difficult to accept that a policing role exists or is appropriate.

Sadly, the establishment of such forces, their functions and accountability have never engaged the attention of our elected representatives to the extent that they should. To the average MP, one policeman looks very much like another and discussion of the byzantine complexity of enabling legislation such as the Energy Act 2004 with its 198 sections and 23 schedules, or indeed the Ministry of Defence Police Act back in 1987, clearly never extended to asking the fairly basic question – why do we need police officers at all on military or civilian nuclear sites? The continued existence of these forces, and to a lesser extent the 'mission creep' of the BTP with its illogical decision to establish a fully equipped riot squad at the expense of the travelling public, are yet further examples of the direction in which twenty-first century policing is moving.

It is fairly obvious that citizens in uniform, in the way that Critchley described them, are no more. The implied contract between the police and those on the receiving end of their service has been breaking down with accelerating pace since the 1990s. Spurred on by the actions of government, often in 'knee-jerk' reaction to the latest tabloid headline, or by one of the host of ill-thought-out initiatives cooked up by police leaders, this is the 'cock up' theory of history. Indeed it would be difficult to find any evidence of broad strategy in police policy over the last twenty years, and certainly not since 1997. Sadly, the enduring theme has been the inexorable withdrawal of service. However, as the new millennium dawned little did we know that one of the largest in a whole boxful of nails that would be produced in the first decade of the twenty-first century, was about to be driven into the coffin of policing.

PLASTIC POLICE

Until 1997 there was a fine tradition in the public sector which basically said the following – *'If you want to spend public money on something new, make sure that you comprehensively test the idea first'*. Ministers and officials across the whole of Whitehall were well aware of the rules of the game, because they knew that unless they could prove that a concept had been road-tested and found to be fit for purpose, the Treasury was very likely to slam the door in their face when they asked for a pot of money to fund it.

Then along came Police Community Support Officers

(PCSOs), otherwise known as the 'Plastic Police', 'Blunkett's Bobbies', or 'Yellow Numpties', and everything changed.

Ask any senior police officer if we really, honestly, truthfully need PCSOs as part of the policing effort, and he will cast a suspicious glance over his shoulder to make sure that the Home Secretary is nowhere near before answering *sotto voce*, 'Of course not, they are a complete and utter waste of time and money. What we need are real cops'. Put the same question to junior officers at police stations, as I have done, and you will get exactly the same answer, although emphasised with the use of more colourful language. PCSOs were foisted upon the police service and the public without any debate as an ill thought-out and untested scheme. The concept has never been independently evaluated and there is a growing body of evidence to show that far from improving the quality of service to the public, the very existence of PCSOs is having a profoundly damaging effect. Their genesis is an object lesson in how to make the wrong decisions for the right reasons whilst ostensibly trying to remedy something else.

Sir Ian (now Lord) Blair's intellectual credentials have never been in doubt; he is an accomplished individual. On a personal level he is urbane, charming and articulate. He has skills aplenty that marked him out early on as someone destined to occupy the soaring heights of the police service. Every organisation needs people like him, but it is vital that leaders spend a little time each day in quiet reflection, so that they can examine the world that they are creating. The best such people surround themselves with a team of bright iconoclasts whose sole function is to challenge the thinking of the top man as it develops – to act as his critical conscience. Ian Blair was never short of advice.

Ian had a gilded career in the Met before he went to Thames Valley Police where he distinguished himself as an innovative Assistant Chief Constable. After a comparatively short time he moved onward and upward and was soon appointed as the Chief Constable of Surrey Police, arriving in January 1998. His brief time in Surrey can best be described as 'challenging'. Within the first year he had the distasteful task of suspending his own Deputy Chief Constable, Ian Beckett, who was charged with indecently assaulting female members of staff at the force HQ (offences for which he was subsequently acquitted at trial). It was whilst in Surrey that he started to develop his concept of the 'wider police family', a deceptively gentle description of a system whereby each street warden, town centre security guard, and shopping mall custodian would be examined, briefly trained, and then accredited and 'licensed' as someone who could be factored into the policing of a local area.

The original intention was that such individuals might be allowed access to the police radio network to pass on information about suspects or matters of concern, anti-social behaviour etc. They could conceivably be drawn into police briefings and might even have access to intelligence databases under controlled circumstances. This 'wider police family' would, it was claimed, bridge the gap between the police, who could not possibly be everywhere all the time, and activity on the streets. Ian Blair held a series of seminars at Surrey Police HQ at which the views of invited representatives of other forces were canvassed. He then went on to expand his concept in speeches and at conferences. It was at this point that he came to the notice of the 'movers and shakers' at the Home Office and the No 10 Policy Unit.

New Labour liked the cut of Ian Blair's jib. In 1997, Jack Straw had arrived at the Home Office with a stark agenda. In the view of the government, the police were in dire need of 'modernisation', along with those other behemoths of the public sector, health and education, and this could only be achieved by 'new thinking'. The key driver for police reform was, and remains, the exorbitant cost of paying and equipping police officers. Linked to this was the pensions 'time bomb' which was driving up personnel costs at an almost exponential rate. The Home Office recognised that something had to be done; because the public hunger for effective policing was almost insatiable, but its policy options were constrained. New Labour, elected on a strong law and order ticket, could not reduce police numbers – that was unacceptable in presentational or electoral terms. There had to be another way which would meet the implied and expressed commitments that had been made by New Labour in opposition to challenge the 'yob culture' and anti-social behaviour, whilst simultaneously avoiding the need to seek extra funding from the Treasury for a major round of police recruiting. The 'wider police family' was the answer to a maiden's prayer.

Ian Blair with his propensity for 'new thinking' rapidly became New Labour's favourite senior police officer. Young, intelligent, media-savvy and possessed of ideas which had the smack of modernisation, he was just the sort of thinking policeman that appealed to the bright young PPE graduates in the No 10 Policy Unit, busy building their version of the 'West Wing' during the initial two years of the first Labour Government after the 1997 landslide. Peter Hennessy, the noted academic and historian, commenting on those times, has described the way in which delegated power was deployed to advance policy[20]. All that a special adviser from No 10 had to say to a minister or an official was, 'Tony wants...' and, miraculously, it happened. Tony Blair had been well briefed on what Ian Blair was proposing and as a result the concept had a following wind – Tony wanted!

In January 2000, following the departure of Paul Condon from Scotland Yard under the glowering cloud of the Stephen Lawrence affair, vacancies appeared at the top of the Met. John Stevens (now Baron Stevens of Kirkwhelpington), a natural and charismatic leader, took over as Commissioner and needed a Deputy. So far as the Home Office was concerned (for which read No 10 Policy Unit), Ian Blair was the obvious choice from a succession-planning point of view so that he could be in place to take over from Stevens, who would be due to retire at the end of his contract in 2005.

Ian Blair arrived as Deputy Commissioner at the Yard in February 2000 and within a matter of a few months, Police Community Support Officers were ready to spring, fully formed, from the womb of the 'wider police family', for deployment on the streets of London. The Police Reform Act 2002 gave legal authority for their recruitment and the pace quickened. At the 'Future of Policing Conference' in October 2003 Ian Blair spoke to an audience of Chief

---

20 Quoted in *The secret world of Tony Blair*, Michael Cockerell, New Statesman, 14.2.2000

Constables about the strength and value of his vision[21], and gained their tacit support for expansion of the programme as a result of what could be construed as collegiate loyalty. There had not been any real attempt to properly pilot or validate the concept, because PCSOs continued to be 'a work in progress', and there was no settled view on how they might look or how they might operate even in London, let alone elsewhere. It had always been intended (but never openly admitted) that this new body would give the *impression* that there was a police presence on the streets, whilst a smaller core of fully trained officers would provide a response service. With minimal training, minimal pension entitlements, and salaries set at a low proportion of a Constable's starting wage, PCSOs were in every sense 'policing on the cheap' despite vehement denials by their proponents and the then Home Secretary, David Blunkett, who became one of their most ardent supporters. Uniforms were designed which made the wearer look like a police officer from a distance, and from 2004 they became an integral part of the Met's ward-based Safer Neighbourhood Teams (see Chapter 1). Indeed, without PCSOs the Safer Neighbourhoods initiative would have sunk without trace because they formed by far the largest element in each team *vis-a-vis* real police officers.

All security patrols in Whitehall and its environs, target-rich from the point of view of the terrorist threat, were handed over to PCSOs whilst simultaneously real police officers withdrew from any pretence of patrol. Where once, in the beating heart of London, it was possible to encounter

---

21 'Leading towards the future', Keynote speech, Sir Ian Blair 10.10.2003

patrolling police officers in most of the main thoroughfares, it is now impossible to do so. Nor is this just a feature of Central London. As Safer Neighbourhood Teams were rolled out across the capital from 2004, the arrival of PCSOs in the inner boroughs and then in the suburbs was the signal for fully warranted police officers to abandon all forms of preventive patrol. Beats became a thing of the past and since 2004 no longer appear on borough divisional maps. Any appearance on the streets, even by PCSOs, was governed by so-called 'Intelligence-led Policing', introduced as a result of yet another central diktat, the National Intelligence Model (NIM) which grandly sought to provide, '...a business process to provide focus to policing... within a framework of information and intelligence allowing a problem-solving approach to law enforcement'[22].

Ian Blair knew very well that Tony Blair was behind him every step of the way. In his memoirs, published in 2009[23], Ian Blair describes an incident in 2004 whilst he was still Deputy Commissioner, when he travelled down on a train to Bexley in South-East London with Tony Blair and the then Home Secretary David Blunkett, enjoying the sort of easy access to power that was and is denied to most senior police officers. The anecdote Ian Blair relates is fascinating for the fact that it highlights the *real* reason why New Labour hitched its wagon to PCSOs and Safer Neighbourhoods, and confirms that Ian Blair, ever the pragmatist, understood only too well that decisions

---

22 Guidance to Police Reform Act 2002 (published by the National Policing Improvement Agency 2005)

23 'Policing Controversy', Sir Ian Blair, Profile Books (2009)

were being made for reasons of electoral advantage, not commitment to policing.

> *'The Prime Minister was clearly tired: the invasion of Iraq and its aftermath were becoming poisonous issues. He warmly shook hands with various people and listened for a moment or two to the officers from the Safer Neighbourhood Team explaining what was going on, but I could see him drifting into automatic mode.'*

At this point he was introduced to some no doubt carefully selected local residents who sang the praises of the Deputy Commissioner's initiative, and Tony Blair started to take interest.

> *'...I could see Tony Blair's electoral instincts come straight on alert. He listened, he thanked them, he took David Blunkett to one side and said: "This we must have – everywhere – as soon as we can".'*

Between 2002 and 2005 the Home Office, in order to force the pace of adoption of PCSOs across the rest of the country, made an offer to provincial police authorities that they could not refuse. They indicated that they would fully fund the capital and revenue costs of initially recruiting PCSOs as part of a nationwide programme of ward-based neighbourhood policing, closely modelled on the Met's 'Safer Neighbourhoods'. Whilst, theoretically, individual Chief Constables could stand on their independence and choose not to have anything to do with the concept, none actually did (although at least two that I have spoken to came very close to doing so, and only changed their minds after being on the receiving end of robust discussions with senior Home Office officials). Basically, the issue for Chiefs was that the introduction of Neighbourhood Policing was stated government policy and therefore mandatory. They knew from the experience of the Met that the concept could not operate without PCSOs (there were just too few real police officers available to make it work), and that Her Majesty's Inspectorate would penalise them if they lagged behind. In the final analysis, it was obvious that the offer had to be accepted – the Home Office was offering 'new' money which was contingent upon doing something that the Chiefs were required to do in any case.

By April 2009, every force in England and Wales had introduced ward-based Neighbourhood Policing. The eight forces in Scotland, however, decided to have nothing whatsoever to do with PCSOs, preferring instead to opt for an increase in the numbers of real police officers, supported by the Scottish Parliament, and Her Majesty's Chief Inspector of Constabulary for Scotland, Paddy Tomkins, based in Edinburgh. This was the first time that anyone could recall the Scottish Inspectorate departing from the Whitehall 'line' on a matter of stated government policy, and (it is whispered) is probably the reason why Paddy never received a knighthood as most of his predecessors had.

The makeup of the ward-based 'policing teams' across England and Wales is disproportionately biased towards PCSOs rather than real police officers, despite the fact that all forces presented Neighbourhood Policing as a return to the active involvement of police officers in communities. It is difficult not to see the whole thing as yet another 'dodgy dossier' being sold on a false prospectus. Confirmation of the extent to which day-to-day 'policing' has been handed over to PCSOs can be found by reference at random to any police force website. For example, in the Cambridgeshire Constabulary, Linton Neighbourhood Policing Team, covering seven large villages within an area of forty square miles south of Cambridge, has just one WPC and four PCSOs who patrol in a vehicle, never on foot. The Letchworth (Southwest) and Wilbury wards in Hertfordshire – part of a busy dormitory commuter town just outside London – have just one PC and four PCSOs between them. In the Met the ratio can be considerably higher; sometimes as high as eight PCSOs to each PC on a Safer Neighbourhood Team or on one of the new Safer Transport Teams which are supposed to lend some sort of security to the bus network.

London has also led the way with a form of 'mission creep' in the way in which PCSOs are deployed, with an increasing proportion being employed on duties for which they were never intended. The original argument for their use was that they were 'the eyes and ears of the bobby on the beat', which pre-supposed their exclusive deployment on foot patrol duties. Whilst this may still be the case in a few central London locations, it is far from the case elsewhere. Recent research[24] has confirmed that in twenty-one London boroughs surveyed (out of 32), PCSOs have access to and are regularly deployed in patrol vehicles, which makes a

---

24 Author's questionnaire research, Sept/Nov 2009

nonsense of greater community involvement. It is difficult to be the 'eyes and ears' of anything as you speed along at thirty miles an hour chatting to your colleague.

In at least three boroughs, PCSOs are used on plain-clothes duties that have nothing to do with their core function, such as performing enquiries for Missing Person Units and taking statements. During 2008 the Met took a policy decision to withdraw police officers from the front counters of the few police stations where they were still employed, and replace them with a new variant of PCSO, the Station PCSO. To the uninitiated this might seem to be a fairly innocuous change but in fact the expertise required by an officer at a station counter is of a high level. He or she is the first point of contact for a whole range of concerns that members of the public have, from mundane issues such as noisy neighbours, through production of driving documents, to advice on crime and even more. In 1997, before PCSOs were even thought of, a clearly agitated man attended a north London police station and sat in the foyer until a constable at the front desk was free to see him. He then stepped forward and calmly announced that he had murdered an acquaintance some days before, and wished to give himself up, before casually adding that the dead body was in the boot of his car parked outside. The constable, trained and confident, was in a position to take charge of the situation, preserve evidence, make a record of the statements of the offender and, most importantly, arrest him for murder and place him in custody. No PCSO as currently recruited and deployed would have been equal to that task.

A document prepared by Kingston-upon-Thames

Borough Command Unit in February 2009 gives a fascinating insight into the broadening of the role of PCSOs, way beyond the original concept of being a visible presence on the streets. Clearly, in the view of this Borough commander (and no doubt others), PCSOs are central to meeting a whole range of government performance-indicators, in areas as diverse as counter-terrorism, drugs, domestic violence and the collection of intelligence. Under a sub-heading entitled 'The Issue', the author states;

'A key part of any PCSO's role is to gather community intelligence about local problems in an area. Community intelligence is information gained through any form of engagement with the local community such as meetings or conversations on the street as part of a PCSO's routine patrolling. This community intelligence can be fed into the National Intelligence Model which is the business model the police service uses to ensure that policing is delivered in a targeted way.'

It is therefore clear that intelligence-gathering is about rather more than neighbour disputes and local gossip; the intention is to seek and use actionable intelligence within the NIM. When this is read in the context of the performance indicators below, particularly NI 35 which deals with domestic terrorism, it can be seen that the new role of PCSOs seems to have been expanded beyond the model originally proposed in 2002.

'Work to tackle public reassurance is exactly the

sort of cross-cutting initiative that fits well within the structure of the local area agreement (LAA) framework.

The effective use of PCSOs can contribute to the following national indicators that focus on public reassurance, domestic abuse, drugs and community cohesion:

- **NI 15** *serious violent crime rate*
- **NI 17** *perceptions of anti-social behaviour*
- **NI 20** *assault with injury crime rate*
- **NI 21** *dealing with local concerns about anti-social behaviour and crime issues by the local council and police.*
- **NI 24** *satisfaction with the way the police and local council dealt with anti-social behaviour.*
- **NI 32** *repeat incidents of domestic violence*
- **NI 35** *building resilience to violent extremism*
- **NI 38** *drug-related (class A) offending rate and*
- **NI 42** *perceptions of drug use or drug dealing as a problem'.*

Despite protestations to the contrary, standards of education, ability, physical fitness and, in some cases, prior criminal conduct were greatly relaxed in order to attract the maximum number of recruits. In excess of £3 million (the actual figure is 'commercially sensitive' and thought to be considerably higher) was paid by the Home Office to advertising agency Manning and Gottlieb in order to sell the concept to the public and attract applicants. Many forces, including the Met, took the conscious decision to actively discriminate in favour of ethnic minority candidates in order to enhance their diversity credentials – something that was deeply patronising to able candidates from diverse communities. Not even those responsible for recruiting PCSOs seemed to fully understand what they should be doing. In the Thames Valley Police area, three 16-year-olds were appointed as PCSOs even though they were still legally children and too young to perform many of the duties required of them, such as to seize alcohol! This was too much even for the Home Secretary, who intervened and compelled the Chief Constable to come to her senses. The force apologised and changed their policy. In 2004 a Met PCSO was suspended when it was discovered that he was actually an illegal immigrant who had no right of residence in the UK– no background checks had been made.

When asked, the public have an overwhelming preference for real police officers on their streets and do not want PCSOs. Research carried out by Manning and Gottlieb[25] showed that over 80% of people saw the role of a police officer as having 'value', yet only 28% felt the same about PCSOs. Much of this animosity is due to the fact that the public were quick to realise that PCSOs do not do very much, largely because they have not been given the powers. The powers that *all* PCSOs have at present (in addition to common law powers of arrest that all citizens have) are:

- *To issue fixed penalty notices for traffic offences, littering, breach of dog control orders and cycling on a footpath.*

---

25 Manning and Gottlieb (PCSO Case Study 2006)

- *Require name and address where they have reason to believe a person has committed a road traffic offence, a 'relevant offence', a licensing offence, an act of anti-social behaviour or is in possession of a controlled drug.*
- *Confiscate alcohol from people in designated places and from youngsters under the age of 18 or anyone supplying such young people with alcohol.*
- *Seize and dispose of tobacco from anyone under 16.*
- *Seize (controlled) drugs under the Misuse of Drugs Act 1971.*
- *Enter and search premises to save life or prevent serious damage to property.*
- *Seize vehicles used to cause alarm, distress or annoyance ('boy racers' etc.).*
- *Remove abandoned vehicles.*
- *Stop bicycles.*
- *Control traffic.*
- *Carry out road checks.*
- *Place traffic signs.*
- *Enforce cordoned areas under the Terrorism Act 2000.*
- *Photograph people away from a police station.*
- *Stop and search in an authorised area under the Terrorism Act 2000 if authorised and supervised by a police officer.*

In addition there are powers which may be assigned to PCSOs by the Chief Constable (or Commissioner in London). They vary from force to force but in fact very few forces have permitted their PCSOs to have these enhanced powers. The right of detention is controversial and there is a consensus that PCSOs do not have the training, judgement, or ability to exercise such a power, but they can be authorised to do the following:

- *Detain a person suspected to have committed an offence or an act of anti-social behaviour.*
- *Detain a person who does not provide their name and address when required.*
- *Detain a person who fails to provide details or complies with orders of a PCSO.*
- *Use reasonable force in relation to a detained person or to prevent a detained person making off. This may involve the use of handcuffs if the PCSO has been issued with and authorised to use them.*
- *Issue fixed penalty notices for disorder, truancy, excluded pupils found in public places, dog fouling, graffiti and fly-posting.*
- *Enforce byelaws.*
- *Deal with begging.*
- *Enforce certain licensing offences.*
- *Search detained people for dangerous items.*
- *Disperse groups and remove under 16s to their place of residence.*
- *Remove children contravening bans imposed by a curfew notice to their place of residence.*
- *Remove truants to designated premises.*
- *Search for alcohol and tobacco.*
- *Enforce park trading offences.*
- *Enter licensed premises (limited).*
- *Stop vehicles for testing.*
- *Direct traffic for the purposes of escorting abnormal loads.*

Police forces always describe them as 'the eyes and ears' of the 'bobby on the beat'. This is, of course, arrant nonsense, even when one disregards the fact that 'bobbies on the beat' do not exist anymore. PCSOs generate very little in terms of intelligence reports or enforcement. In 2008 the Kent Police Authority, concerned at the level of expenditure on PCSOs, researched and produced a report which showed that in several areas of the county PCSOs had failed to issue a single fixed penalty notice in an entire year. The report went on to say that '...*there appears to be little relationship between the presence of a PCSO and a reduction in crime*'. Furthermore, of members of the public who were questioned, '...*only about four in ten felt that PCSOs represented value for money... they do not appear to be the best option currently for reducing negative perceptions of anti-social behaviour.*'

In February 2009 a Freedom of Information Act request by the Tax Payers' Alliance revealed that in Lincolnshire the force's team of PCSOs, which cost almost £10 million in salaries and other expenditure since they were established, had generated enforcement activity totalling just 15 fixed penalty notices. On a rough calculation that means that each ticket cost more than £650,000 in public money. Ten of them were for one of two offences – having a dirty bicycle light or riding a bike on a pavement. Susie Squire, campaign manager for the Tax Payers' Alliance, commented at the time, 'There is a huge sum in taxpayers' money being spent on PCSOs, but these figures show that they are just a PR stunt. They don't provide value for money at all, you cannot compare them to beat bobbies – they are no substitute. People do not want cardboard cut-outs – they want real police.' Lincolnshire, a large and predominantly rural county with very low crime levels, has the lowest level of funding of any police force in the country. Their total establishment of PCSOs grew from 114 in 2006 to 159 in 2009, increasing the annual wage bill from £2.63 million to £3.79 million (although it has been drastically reduced in the years since due to austerity). An FoI request revealed that Lincolnshire's entire strength of PCSOs issued just four fixed penalty notices in 2006, one in 2007 and ten in 2008. The Police Authority, clearly unaware of just how ineffective their PCSOs really were, expressed genuine outrage. Councillor Chris Underwood-Frost, a member of the Authority, went on record in trenchant terms, pointing out that the £10 million spent on the county's PCSOs could have paid for 70 full-time officers. In a statement to the press he angrily said, 'People aren't daft – the public know that this is just policing on the cheap.'[26]

Admittedly, enforcement is just one part of what PCSOs are intended to do, but all evidence seems to point to the fact that the public regard it as a crucially important element, nonetheless. To them it is quintessential policing; it is what they expect from a policing presence in their community – that, and an assertive and visible patrol presence. Visits to toddler groups, group photographs, and self-congratulatory hand-produced newsletters offer no substitute. As Manning and Gottlieb observed – it is all about the extent to which the role is 'valued'.

Apart from their lack of efficiency, and the well-reported examples of PCSOs refusing to intervene when

---

[26] 'PCSOs issue only 15 fines in three years' This is Lincolnshire (17.2.2009)

assaults were taking place in front of them or failing to go to the aid of a child drowning in a pond, there is a burgeoning problem of misconduct and indiscipline. In February 2009, Martin Tiplady, the Director of Human Resources for the Met, delivered a report to the Metropolitan Police Authority which was a stunning indictment of the conduct of PCSOs in London. Even though they represent only 20% of the non-police workforce of the Metropolitan Police, they accounted for more than half of all gross misconduct cases in 2008/9. PCSOs had been disciplined for a variety of offences including misuse of police computers and databases, and in one case making a false allegation of crime. Twenty of the 35 PCSOs found guilty of gross misconduct, for offences such as assault or drunken driving, were dismissed, with the remainder being made the subject of staff reprimands. There is strong anecdotal evidence to suggest that a similar situation exists elsewhere in the country. The Tiplady review suggested that part of the problem is that PCSOs have an ill-defined function and as a result are bored and lacked motivation.

In July 2009 the Home Office confirmed there were 16,507 PCSOs in England and Wales (reduced to 9,547 in the year ending 2019 due to budgetary constraints), commanding a total salary bill of over £282 million per annum. Since the first PCSOs appeared on the scene in London in 2002, well over £2 billion of public money has been spent on an untried and unevaluated scheme that was originally intended to provide reassurance to the public and assist fully warranted police officers. The result has actually been a mirror image of what was intended. The public do not want PCSOs, they are not taken in by the spin and hyperbole of the Home Office and various force media departments, they know that they are not getting real policing, merely a pale imitation.

However, by far the most important result of this ill-starred experiment has been the damage done to core policing. The status of the ordinary constable has been diminished by the implied suggestion that patrolling the streets is basically a low-skill activity. It is no surprise that as a result police constables have abandoned such activity in their thousands. Police leaders, from Chief Constables to lowly sergeants, have done nothing to arrest this trend and as a result the quality of service provided at street level, where it really matters, is fast receding to the vanishing point.

CHAPTER 3
PC PCs? THE PROBLEM OF RACE AND DIVERSITY

'I have put forward the proposal that the law should be amended to enable us to send back to their own countries certain classes of British subjects who are consistent and flagrant law-breakers. Cypriots, Maltese and coloured British subjects are responsible for a disproportionately large part of the offences connected with gaming, living on immoral earnings of prostitutes, and the sale of drugs and liquor. If they could be sent home on conviction, there would be a distinct improvement in those areas where they are active.'

The above comment was made by Sir Harold Scott GCVO, KCB, KBE in his memoirs, published in 1954[27]. Just the sort of reactionary comment, you might think, that one could have expected from an unreconstructed

---

27 'Scotland Yard' (Page 66–67) Sir Harold Scott. (pub. Andre Deutsch 1954)

'Colonel Blimp' of the time. In fact Scott was one of the most effective and one of the most liberal Commissioners that the Metropolitan Police has had since the end of the Second World War. He served for eight years from 1945 until 1953 and guided the force through its difficult post-war reintegration into civil society, against a background of austerity, soaring crime and major social change.

The early 1950s saw the beginning of mass immigration into the UK. The MV 'Empire Windrush' docked at Tilbury on 21st June 1948 and disembarked four hundred and ninety-two West Indian passengers who had paid the £28.10s fare (*the equivalent of around £900 in today's money*), to come to the UK in search of work. Within ten years over 125,000 West Indians had travelled here. Almost exclusively young and male they settled in London and a few of our other big cities and did what young men do. They worked hard, and when they were not working, they enjoyed themselves; they chased girls and a few of them got into trouble. They behaved no differently to the way that countless generations of newcomers to any land have done. What made them instantly stand out however was the colour of their skin, with the implication that as 'children' of the Empire they should know their place in the social pecking order. In drab, bomb-ravaged and bankrupt Britain, still trying to come to terms with winning the war but losing the status of a great power, the fact that these newcomers were black marked them out for special attention. As Sir Harold Scott was only too aware, the new immigrants almost always came to the notice of police as offenders as they tried to establish themselves in already over-crowded urban settings where there was precious little undamaged housing, or employment available, even for the indigenous white population. In such circumstances the police were the only agency who could hold the ring. The comments that he made in 1954, unacceptable as they are to us over half a century later, were nonetheless made in response to what was to him an almost seismic social and demographic change in the way that Britain looked and felt. His proposal was not born of racism; I doubt that such an unassuming and unfailingly courteous product of the Edwardian upper-middle class had a racist bone in his body. He was however the first of a long line of police policymakers who sought to shape the environment for the benefit of society as a whole. A few were successful, but most were unsuccessful, and one or two did damage to race relations on a majestic scale.

There is no doubt that mass immigration from the New Commonwealth has been appallingly handled by all governments since the end of the Second World War, with no strategic direction of the policy over decades. In the late 1950s ministers in the Macmillan administration were complicit in sending recruiting teams from London Transport to tour the West Indies, virtually press-ganging young men to work on the Underground, without any thought given to where they would live when they arrived here, and the extent to which the host community would or could assimilate them. By 2001, with the twin issues of immigration and the social fabric of Britain identified as key electoral concerns, the Labour Government went to the lengths (it is reported) of striking out any reference to 'Criminal Behaviour' from a Home Office commissioned report, *'Migration, A Social and Economic Analysis'*. A section of the report apparently warned, prior to the words being deleted, 'Migration has opened up new opportunities for organised crime', and that, 'there is emerging evidence that the circumstances in which asylum seekers are living is leading to criminal offences, including fights and begging'. No government, Labour or Conservative, has clean hands on the issue. For over half a century there has been a burgeoning problem associated with mass migration to our islands, but policymakers of every hue have collectively shied away from confronting it. Employment policy has been piecemeal, targeted on the basis of regional aid and party-political constituency considerations. Housing policy has been non-existent, and as a result pockets of residency have emerged which amount to racially exclusive enclaves. Since the days of the Jewish Diaspora in the Middle Ages, it has been a feature of migration that those who are newly arrived cleave to those who are most like them for support and protection; so it is today.

In this context it is worth making the point that the enclaves that have grown up since the late nineteen-forties in London and our other major urban areas are not 'ghettos'. The use of this pejorative word to describe places such as Brixton, Moss-Side, St Pauls, Toxteth, etc, began in the mid nineteen-sixties when Holocaust Studies became a recognised area of academic research in the United States and subsequently in the UK. 'Ghetto' is a mediaeval Venetian word, originally used to describe an island in the Venice lagoon on which Jews had established themselves. By the twentieth century the word had quite specific overtones of oppression linked to the Polish ghettos of 1941 to 1945, residence in which was imposed by the Germans on the Jewish people as part of a policy of extermination.

American sociologists in the nineteen-sixties, during the civil-rights movement, began to refer to places where there were large housing projects with significant African-American populations, such as those in Newark, Gary Indiana, and Pittsburgh, as 'ghettos'. Within a short time academics, and then the media, in the UK had followed suit. If one accepts that a 'ghetto' is maintained by force of arms and oppression from outside – then it would require a real leap of imagination to think of South Manchester in this way, still less the London Borough of Lambeth.

The word reeks of guilt, and places those with power and responsibility in the role of oppressor. Lazy academics, lazier journalists, and senior police officers who should have known better, all stuck to the notion that the majority of our visible ethnic minorities were imprisoned in ghettos. The boundaries of real ghettos were defined by lines drawn on Einsatzgruppen maps but, it was claimed, those in Brixton, Moss-Side, St Pauls etc, etc, were defined by social, economic, and educational forces that were every bit as oppressive. This nonsensical argument has had a profound effect on social policy, and particularly policing in our urban areas, fostering conscious and unconscious guilt on the part of public bodies, and a sense of victimhood on the part of many black and Asian residents of such communities.

The angst generated by such attitudes has likewise had a corrosive effect on the resolve of the police in terms of crime and social disorder, with the result that weak police leaders and poorly led police officers operate a double standard in terms of what they regard as acceptable in such areas, compared with the norm elsewhere. Put simply, to deal drugs openly in a residential street in one of our prosperous, largely white, suburbs is something that would have been considered (at least until recently) as unthinkable. Such activity would have attracted highly assertive and visible policing with the problem being quickly nipped in the bud. However, street dealing on a largely black, sink estate in Brixton or Moss-Side generates an entirely different approach. Hand-wringing senior officers whine about the need to 'consider cultural issues' or their obligation to 'preserve community cohesion', as reasons for holding back from an interventionist policy. Each violent incident when a dealer protects his market is logged and recorded as a 'Tension Indicator', rather than a crime. In such places the police are very good at counting things.

The real losers when such an apologist line is taken are, of course, those that have to live, work and raise families in such areas, exactly the people who deserve the highest level of care and commitment from their local police. They are the ones who are at the mercy of predatory gangs, and whose lives are blighted on a daily basis by drugs and violence. Thus, many decent first- and second-generation immigrant families are not only the victims of a minority who live amongst them and prey upon them, but also the victims of deeply patronising inaction by police, who lump everyone together and regard the situation as a 'community and cultural problem' in what are still referred to as 'Symbolic Locations'.

There are three milestones on the road to the abandonment of common sense and mature judgement by the police in terms of Race, and the policing of those urban areas of our nation where ethnic minorities (and ethnic majorities) have settled. The first marked our farewell to a state of innocence where the received wisdom of the time was that the police, the host community, and the new immigrants would all pull together for the sake of society as a whole, and that racial prejudice did not exist. The second and third were shocks to the body politic which reacted in the way that it always does when confronted with a crisis that it cannot immediately control. Retired judges were called upon to prepare and submit lengthy reports. All three were cathartic and changed the policing environment for ever.

The Notting Hill riots, which broke out in 1958, ostensibly came from nowhere and according to Rab Butler, the Home Secretary at the time, were solely linked to criminality with no evidence of racial motivation behind the disturbances. We now know differently of course; subsequent examination of Home Office papers from the time clearly shows that vital information was never disclosed to him by the police. It is also significant that just one week before the outbreak of violence in Notting Hill, there had been inter-racial tension in Nottingham which resulted in street disturbances that went on for more than ten days. Throughout the 1950s, the white working-class became increasingly disenchanted with their prospects of well-paid employment and housing in London and elsewhere. Macmillan's call 'We've never had it so good!' from the platform of a Conservative Party rally in Bedford in 1957 rang hollow with many such young people. Increasingly they were drawn into the embrace of Sir Oswald Mosley's Union Movement, the League of Empire Loyalists, and other fascist groups, who urged their supporters to 'Keep Britain White'. 'Teddy Boy' gangs who practised extreme violence with bicycle chains and open razors on black immigrants and their homes and families, and indeed anyone else who got in their way, also offered a home to a generation of young men who saw themselves as dispossessed.

The riot started on Saturday 30th August when a gang of Teddy Boys attacked Majbritt Morrison, a white Swedish woman who lived near Latimer Road Notting Hill, with her Jamaican husband. The gang had seen her and her husband the night before outside a local Underground station, having a heated argument. Thinking that she was a white woman being pestered by a black man they intervened and shouted extreme racial insults at him. However, to their surprise she turned on the gang and forced them to retreat. The following night they went looking for her, and eventually found her in Ladbroke Grove, W.11, where they pelted her with stones and bottles and struck her with an iron bar. The police were called by a passer-by but by the time that they arrived the gang had fled the scene, so they took Morrison home and reported the incident. The gang clearly believed that they had a score to settle however and went away to re-group. Later that night a mob of at least 400 Teddy Boys together with other white youths and men (and a handful of young women) went to nearby Bramley Road where they started to attack any houses known to be occupied by West Indians.

The disturbances, rioting, looting, and attacks continued every night for the next ten days until they eventually petered out in early September. Over 140 people were arrested by the police during the disturbances. Most were white youths, but a few black people were detained when they were stopped and found to be carrying weapons, which they claimed were for self-defence. A Scotland Yard report subsequently disclosed that of the 108 people charged with crimes such as grievous bodily harm, affray, riot and possessing offensive weapons, 72 were white and 36 were black.

Notting Hill should have been a wake-up call for politicians and those professionals concerned with social policy and the policing of our urban areas, but after the initial flurry of newspaper headlines, and some soothing words from the government, nothing very much changed. Nothing, that is, that was easily discernible. Below the surface however attitudes were being re-shaped.

The lesson that black immigrants in Notting Hill and beyond drew from the disturbances was that they could not rely upon the police to protect them and that therefore, if they were to adequately protect themselves, they needed to organise and establish an identity. Some amongst them were quick to realise that such an identity would also give them power and influence that they had not, until then, possessed. Within a few years the US civil-rights movement would lend focus and militancy to the philosophy that they were starting to adopt.

The police, as they so often do in similar circumstances, saw the changing environment as little more than an enforcement issue and retreated to a position from which they could claim to act as the neutral guardians of the law. The difficulty with that position however was that they had unfettered freedom to enforce whichever laws they chose, and all too often they chose to enforce those that required least effort. So, during the 1960s and on through the next two decades, street offences became the vogue in

London, with young constables being actively encouraged to cut their operational teeth on arrests for 'Being a suspected person loitering with intent', otherwise known as 'Sus', and after 1971, the myriad offences of possession and obstruction under the Misuse of Drugs Act. This, coupled with the fact that many of the police constables emerging on to the streets from the early 1960s had been born during and just after the War, and had none of the maturity and discipline of the generation of ex-servicemen who had preceded them, created a recipe for confrontation. Street activity bore more heavily on young blacks because like most young men they tended to gather together out of doors in certain areas and because their new-found radicalism encouraged them to challenge, rather than be deferential, to the police. As it was then, so it is now, with street policing in our urban areas being conducted by young men in eyeball-to-eyeball confrontations with other young men, the only difference being that one group is in uniform and the other is not.

As will be discussed in more detail later when we look at the police workforce, the majority of this new generation of young police officers came from the same white working-class roots as the disenchanted Teddy Boys. They had often had the same sort of education in the same schools and had many of the same values, and prejudices, as their peers. It was not until 1967 that PC Norwell Roberts, the Met's first black officer, started at Bow Street Police Station and even in the decade after he first put on a uniform the rate of recruitment of black and Asian officers was miniscule. The police service across the whole of the UK was effectively a white male working-class occupation and therefore it is not very surprising that attitudes towards immigrants from the New Commonwealth were less than enlightened.

The police promotion system operated in such a way that all but a tiny proportion of its leadership cadre was drawn from officers who had served at least two years as a constable, and as a result attitudinal problems of prejudice and lack of imagination were almost guaranteed to be hard-wired into the hierarchy of most forces. The problem became self-perpetuating. Many constables who harboured deep feelings of animosity towards immigrants might have been rooted out of the organisation had the right sort of leadership existed, but in all too many cases their bosses, up to and including the most senior officers, actually saw little wrong with what they felt as long as they kept it to themselves. An officer, who served for thirty years as a constable from 1966, recalled the following incident from the late 1960s:

'My relief were on late turn, when at about 7pm one winter's evening we were taken by van to [a nearby station on another division] where we were told a three-year-old child had been missing for over four hours and we were to form a search party to comb some rough ground and derelict factory sites. We went into the parade room for a briefing by a young Chief Inspector. He stood on a platform, held up an enlarged photo of a young black boy sitting on a sofa, and I'll never forget what he said. "OK gents, this is [name of the child]. As you can see, he's a little n****r kiddy. He wandered out of his flat at about 3pm – probably didn't want Mum to cook him and

eat him". Then he laughed, and so did half the people in the room. Most of us were fathers of young children and yet, to my eternal shame, I never said anything to that oaf of a Chief Inspector and nor did anyone else. Anyway, the boy was found safe and well at a neighbour's house about an hour later. Looking back, I suppose no-one thought the Chief Inspector's comment was all that bad because that was how society was in those days. It wasn't just the police – we were no worse than anyone else. Better in some respects; at least we weren't like the police in South Africa where they wouldn't even have bothered to mount a search. We cared'.[28]

By the late 1970s, the first wave of immigrants from the West Indies, the majority of whom were God-fearing, deferential, and quintessentially 'British' in their attitudes, had become parents themselves. During the decades since they had arrived, as we have seen, attitudes had started to change. They now had teenage children who had been born and schooled in London, Liverpool, or Birmingham, who knew nowhere else, but who talked in the patois slang of islands that they had never seen. It was they who were on the receiving end of the street policing of the seventies and eighties. They were also, being almost exclusively working class, the ones most affected by the Thatcherite economic reforms after 1979. Along with white car-workers in the Midlands, miners in Scotland, and Asian textile workers in Leicester, they were angry.

---

28 Research interview by the author, March 2009

Brixton, in the centre of the south London borough of Lambeth, is just six miles from the Houses of Parliament. Despite some gentrification and the investment of hundreds of millions of pounds of public money in the form of targeted urban regeneration projects over the past three decades, it remains an area with deep social and economic problems. In 1981, in a predominantly black community comprising between 25% and 30% of the population, when national levels of unemployment amongst ethnic minorities were between 13% and 25.4%, unemployment levels for black youths in Brixton was estimated at 55%. In addition crime, particularly street robbery ('mugging'), was out of control with reported crime figures for Brixton being as much as ten times higher than those recorded in comparable areas elsewhere in the capital. Housing was poor – largely what would now be referred to as 'sink estates', with few amenities and a predominance of single-parent families lacking positive male role models. It would be no exaggeration to say that amongst a significant section of the black community, the police were hated. They were not seen to be offering any sort of service and were regarded as oppressive and distant. All the ingredients were in place for a major confrontation which could and should have been detected in advance.

In late March 1981 the Metropolitan Police devised a plan to tackle crime, and launched *Operation Swamp 81* at the beginning of April, aimed at reducing street robbery. Central to the strategy was the heavy use of the so-called 'Sus' law[29], and extensive application of 'stop and search'

---

29 Section 4 of the Vagrancy Act 1824 – 'Being a Suspected Person loitering with intent to commit a felony'.

powers. The Special Patrol Group, an elite body which at that time had a fearsome reputation for 'in your face' assertive policing, were used as a key element in the operation. Plainclothes police officers were infiltrated into the toughest areas of Brixton to act as 'spotters' for crime and criminals in order that uniformed officers could then be called in, in strength, to deal with individuals. In five days in early April almost 1,000 people, the vast majority black, were stopped and searched. There had not been any local consultation in advance about the operation largely because, it was claimed later, there was no proper mechanism to do so, but more importantly because of what the police referred to as 'security considerations'. Community tension rose and the always difficult relationship between the local police and the black population began to fracture. Local community leaders, many of them self-appointed, complained about young and inexperienced police officers being sent on to the streets, provoking confrontation.

During the early evening of the 10th April a black youth who had been stabbed in an attack involving other black youths was discovered by uniformed police officers in Atlantic Road, which is in the centre of Brixton and at the heart of what was regarded as a black 'enclave'. They started to render first aid whilst waiting for an ambulance but as they did so a large hostile crowd began to gather and started to shout insults at the officers. The police could see that it was too dangerous to remain where they were, so they decided to try to take the victim of the stabbing to a police car that was parked in a side road in order to convey him to hospital. As they made their move however the crowd intervened. The officers were attacked, and the assaults only ended when police reinforcements arrived, and the injured youth was taken to a hospital.

Evidence given subsequently to the public inquiry confirmed that witnesses mistakenly believed that the police had stopped and questioned the stabbed youth, rather than help him. Rumour fed on rumour and within less than an hour a story was circulating throughout Brixton that the youth had been left to die by the police, or even that police officers had stood by and looked on as the stabbed youth was lying on the street at their feet, his blood running into the gutter. A crowd of over two-hundred youths, largely black but including a significant minority of whites, then gathered and started to throw bricks and bottles at police patrols. Senior officers were caught completely off guard and did not fully understand the level of disorder that they were about to face. They took piecemeal action, and in response to the initial incidents decided to do little more than increase the number of foot patrols in Railton Road which was one of the principal points of activity.

Notwithstanding the obviously deteriorating situation, a policy decision was made to continue with 'Operation Swamp' throughout the night of Friday the 10th and into the following day, Saturday the 11th of April. This was a disastrous error of leadership and pre-figured much of what followed. Indeed, if the local Chief Superintendent and Commander had taken the advice that a number of experienced junior officers offered, it is possible that the disorders could have been avoided.

During the night of the 10th and into Saturday 11th, police commanders heavily reinforced the area with contingents of officers drafted in from all over London. By now, stories circulating on the street had blown the initial incident up to almost mythical status with claims that the youth had not been stabbed at all but had been beaten to death by the officers. No amount of intervention by religious leaders and others, called upon at short notice in an attempt to calm the situation, made any difference. Tensions rose throughout the day as angry crowds began to gather and then coalesce into larger groups. At 4pm, disorder was triggered when two officers working on 'Operation Swamp' attempted to stop and search the occupants of a mini cab in Railton Road. A fight broke out, the officers called for assistance, but were cut off from aid by the fact that the main thoroughfare through Brixton, the High Road, was filled with angry crowds who started to throw bricks and bottles at the police cars which were attempting to get to the scene of the Railton Road incident. Throughout the rest of the evening and into the night, pockets of disorder broke out all over Brixton. Shops were looted across the borough in what was obviously organised looting of electrical goods and designer clothing. Looting was not confined to any racial group – there were just as many white looters as there were black, with organised looting by white outsiders being reported. By 8pm the police had obviously lost control of the situation. The main command and control complex at Scotland Yard sent out emergency calls to police stations across London, directing that all available officers should be sent to Brixton to assist in curbing what was now being referred to, quite openly, as a 'riot'.

As was grudgingly admitted later, the Metropolitan Police had no strategy for dealing with disorder on this scale, nor had any local planning taken place to meet the possibility that 'Operation Swamp' might produce a reaction. In addition there was a complete absence of protective equipment of the sort that we are used to seeing today. Radio communication broke down on a regular basis and in some respects the rioters seemed better organised than the police, moving from place to place and constantly surprising them with new tactics. The throwing of bricks and bottles was replaced, by the late evening, with the throwing of petrol bombs, something that had only ever been seen in Northern Ireland. The destructive efforts of the rioters reached a crescendo between 8pm and 10pm as all attempts at mediation failed. In all, two pubs and twenty-six shops, businesses and schools were set on fire by rioters. There were reports of violent assaults on whites and at least one allegation that a white woman was raped in her home by a black rioter. There is little doubt that a proportion of the violence was planned and organised with military precision, including the stockpiling of petrol bombs. There is also strong evidence that some of the rioting was quite cynically used as a cover for systematic looting. At the height of the riot over a thousand police officers were deployed on the streets of Brixton in violent confrontation with rioters, eventually calming the area by the early hours of Sunday morning. More than 2,500 police officers were deployed throughout the weekend and for a few days thereafter, but by the following Tuesday the disorders had effectively ceased.

The riot claimed no lives, but nearly four-hundred officers were injured, plus at least one hundred and sixty members of the public. There was damage, arson, and looting on a grand scale and over 320 people were arrested and charged with serious offences. The Metropolitan Police, the media, and Mrs Thatcher's government were stunned by what had happened. The Brixton riots were the most significant street disturbances that had taken place in London for over a hundred years, even more violent than Notting Hill, or the 'Battle of Cable Street' in 1936 when the police had been involved in pitched battles with demonstrators opposing Oswald Mosley's BUF. The events in Brixton proved to be the trigger for serious disorder across the rest of the United Kingdom throughout the early summer of 1981. During the first week of July of that year, there were more serious outbreaks of rioting, generated by racial and economic grievances, in Birmingham, Southall, Liverpool and Manchester. There were even what was referred to as 'copycat riots' in places as geographically diverse as Leicester, Bedford, Bristol and even Edinburgh.

There clearly had to be a reckoning. On the day following the riot Mrs Thatcher, in a combative TV interview, dismissed any notion that the social and economic policies of her government had played any part in what had taken place. As far as she was concerned unemployment was not a factor, nor was racism, social disadvantage, or insensitive policing – it was criminality pure and simple. When Lambeth's Labour council leader, Ted Knight, suggested that the police tactics during 'Operation Swamp' had effectively 'amounted to an army of occupation' thereby provoking the riots, Thatcher became almost apoplectic with rage and responded, 'What absolute nonsense and what an appalling remark… No one should condone violence. No-one should condone the events… They were criminal, criminal, criminal!' She completely rejected any suggestion that investment in urban regeneration in the inner cities would alleviate the problem with the sweeping remark, 'Money cannot buy either trust or racial harmony'. Under her leadership the government set its face against social or economic change but had to be seen to be doing something, so great was the pressure from the public, press and media. William Whitelaw, the Home Secretary, therefore appointed a senior Law Lord, Lord Scarman, to examine the causes of the disturbances. His report[30] is the second milestone on the road to the current uncomfortable relationship that the police service has with anything linked to race and ethnicity.

Even today, almost four decades after it was published, Lord Scarman's report makes fascinating reading. Leslie Scarman, who died in 2004 at the great age of 93, was an accomplished jurist and a liberal of the old school. He had a life-long commitment to civil liberties and a utopian view of the way in which society should function. Critics of Lord Scarman's report (and there are many) cite his personal beliefs as having been too influential on the way in which he framed his recommendations. That is unfair, he was far too experienced to allow such a thing to happen, but his report does disappoint the reader in the sense that it does not reach a satisfactory conclusion about the causes of the riot.

In his introduction he discusses the possibility of the riot having been a spontaneous eruption of anger and resentment aimed at the police by a disadvantaged black 'community'

---

30 The Brixton Disorders 10–12 April 1981, Report of an Inquiry by the Rt Hon the Lord Scarman OBE, November 1981, Cmnd 8427

in protest against harassment and insensitive policing. Elsewhere however he suggests, and never disregards, the possibility that the real motivating factor, far from being some high-flown expression of discontent, was crime. He concedes that there was evidence of organisation prior to the disorders and includes testimony that looting went beyond the opportunistic, with identified individuals (many white) coming from outside Brixton to take part. Almost wholly absent from his report, beyond statements of bland exhortation, is any suggestion as to how the police should police in a high crime area, where the population is resentful and uncooperative because of economic and societal factors that are beyond the ability of any one agency to influence. As Peter Hitchens commented in a controversial and masterly analysis in 2003, '…one senses that Scarman's conclusions were designed to deal with the political aftermath of the riots rather than the riots themselves'.[31]

In the context of subsequent findings over two decades later, it is significant that Scarman rejected the assertion that the police were institutionally racist. He stated in his findings, 'The direction and policies of the Metropolitan Police are not racist… I totally and unequivocally reject the attack made upon the integrity and impartiality of the senior directors of the force… The allegation that the police are the oppressive arm of a racist state not only displays a complete ignorance of the constitutional arrangements for controlling the police, but it is also an injustice to the senior officers of the force.' Notwithstanding, however, he did concede that one of the

---

31 'A Brief History of Crime' (2003) re-titled 'The Abolition of Liberty: The Decline of Order and Justice in England' (2003), Peter Hitchens

triggers for the riots was the '...Ill-considered, immature, and racially prejudiced actions of some officers'. His solutions were set out in a series of recommendations which the Tory government originally indicated it would implement in full, a promise which it subsequently reneged upon. Basically, Scarman's strategy was to enhance the standing of the police amongst ethnic minority communities by a programme of openness, and to foster inclusion across society as a whole. The core elements of his recommendations were more recruitment of black officers, better race awareness training, and the development of a black middle class in the area to act as a buffer to working-class anger. He wrote, '...Our underlying strategy should be to create ethnic minority opportunities in the universities, the professions, the civil service, the police, in politics and public life, in business activities and in industrial management.'

Scarman argued that Brixton was not a 'race riot', but a spontaneous outbreak of disaffection generated by a complex mix of social, economic, and political factors such as the acute levels of disadvantage common to many urban areas at the time. Scarman was naive in ascribing everything that had happened to social conditions, particularly at a time when he was extremely unlikely to garner much support for his views from the incumbent government. Behind the scenes, political advisers and senior members of the police staff associations went on the offensive in the media and the recommendations were gradually watered down. The proposal that 'racially prejudiced or discriminatory behaviour' should become a specific offence in the police disciplinary code was attacked by the Police Federation and was eventually dropped by the Home Secretary William Whitelaw.

Scarman was not holed below the waterline completely, however. Structured arrangements for police/public consultative groups became law, and the system of investigating complaints against police was fundamentally overhauled. The most significant effect of Scarman however was the impact that it had on the mindset of the police establishment and the gradual recruitment of black and Asian officers into the police. No longer was it acceptable for one or two 'token blacks' to be recruited and provided with helmets and uniforms as patronising proof that a Chief Constable had done what was expected of him. From the nineteen-eighties onward, recruitment from ethnic minority groups would accelerate, slowly at first but with gathering pace. This was a sea-change, unwittingly acknowledged by Lord Belstead as he introduced Lord Scarman's report to the House of Lords on 25th November 1981. For the very first time, in any public statement, a government minister made reference to the UK being a multi-racial society, apparently much to Mrs Thatcher's chagrin.

> *'The police have a right to look for action by society as a whole; they must not become scapegoats. As far as the Government are concerned, we accept the responsibility, in which we must all share, to make our multi-racial society work more justly.'*[32]

The last of the three milestones from 1958 to the present was put in place twelve years, almost to the day, after the outbreak of the Brixton riots. On the evening of the 22nd

---

32 Hansard 25th November 1981 Vol 425 cc 769–78

April 1993 a black teenager, a student, was waiting with a friend at a bus-stop at Eltham in south-east London when he was attacked and stabbed to death by three, possibly four, white racist youths. Despite one of the most high-profile and searching murder investigations ever conducted by the Metropolitan Police (plus a series of comprehensive re-investigations), it was not until fifteen years later, in January 2012, that Gary Dobson and David Norris were found guilty of Stephen's murder and sentenced to life imprisonment, with minimum terms of 15 years and 14 years respectively. The original investigation by the Met was shown to be professionally incompetent, and almost certainly tainted by the involvement of allegedly corrupt officers.

The Lawrence case has entered the folklore of race relations in this country and its impact has been out of all proportion to the event itself. There have been murders that were more shocking and more violent; murders in which the quality of the police investigation was even more inept; murders in which the final outcome was an even greater affront to natural justice. However, the murder of this young man in a suburban street acted as a lightning rod for decades of concern amongst ethnic minorities about the sort of service that black citizens of the UK could expect from the police. For those intent upon using his death as a *cause celebre*, Stephen's murder had everything. Here was an eminently decent, hard-working, young man who had done no harm to anyone. He didn't fit any of the racial stereotypes of young black men in the inner cities; he was not a gang member, a drug-dealer, or some 'gangsta' rapper. He was a student who worked hard at his studies and wanted to qualify as an architect. Nor was he the product of an absent 'baby father' and some feckless teenage girl; he lived at home with his mother and father who were themselves models of rectitude and decency. The image of him smiling into the camera at a family gathering a few months before he died has achieved almost iconic status, in the literal, almost religious meaning of the word. Stephen looks out from the photograph and asks, 'Why?'

What is beyond doubt, irrespective of any deeper motives or systemic failings, is that more could have been done within the first few hours after Stephen's murder to gather evidence and drive the investigation forward. Whether this amounts to a comprehensive failure by the police on the grounds of racial discrimination is much more doubtful, indeed there has always been more than a hint of political opportunism about the way in which the case was taken up by politicians on the left and the right. On 31st July 1997 a mere ten weeks after arriving at the Home Office, the new Home Secretary Jack Straw announced that the government had decided to establish an inquiry into Stephen's death, chaired by Sir William Macpherson, *'in order particularly to identify the lessons to be learned for the investigation and prosecution of racially motivated crimes'*. At the time of the announcement the government were aware that the Independent Police Complaints Authority (PCA), which had been directed by the outgoing Tory Home Secretary in March 1997 to re-investigate the original allegations, had not found hard evidence of racism being a factor in the way that the murder investigation had been conducted. This was confirmed on 15th December 1997 when the PCA report was presented to the Secretary of State. The PCA had employed senior officers from the

Kent Constabulary to re-investigate the murder and whilst they found much to criticise – one section of their review described the Met's initial investigation as 'a sequence of disasters and disappointments' – there was absolutely no evidence of racist conduct on the part of police. As a member of one of the review teams remarked to the author:

> *'All this talk of racism really hacks me off. In my opinion, as someone who has spent over twenty years investigating serious crime, you can ascribe about 0.01% of the failure to get Stephen's killers to racism, and about 98% to downright inefficiency and professional incompetence. That doesn't make it right, but it does explain it better than some sort of witchcraft.'*[33]

Nonetheless there was broad agreement that the whole investigation was palpably flawed, and the Met subsequently acknowledged this to be the case. The review identified procedural weaknesses and omissions during the investigation which meant that as a result, subsequent attempts to solve the crime had been hampered. The report, in its entirety, was then handed to Sir William's Inquiry for consideration.

So hallowed is the name of Stephen Lawrence in the long history of race relations over the last half century, that even suggesting that the motives of those in positions of power were less than pure is tantamount to heresy. However, it is hard to avoid the conclusion that there were political (small 'p' and large 'P') considerations at play in the decision to set

---

33 Research interview by the author March 2009

up the Macpherson Inquiry. The government was anxious to establish its 'anti-racist' credentials and to show itself as wholly different from the recently defeated and unlamented Tory administration. All their special advisers were acutely aware of the growing significance of the ethnic minority vote in many Labour heartland constituencies and realised, cynical as it might seem, that using the Stephen Lawrence case as a stick to beat the police (whilst simultaneously standing up as the party of law and order) would play very well with their core supporters and those so recently drawn into the New Labour fold. Coupled with this was the broader strategic issue of Police Reform, which was to become a topic of major significance for the Home Office in the years after 2000. Here was an opportunity to seize the initiative, ostensibly on the grounds of social justice, and direct the course of policing over the first decade of the new century. It was clearly an opportunity not to be missed.

Lastly, there was the issue of the popular press and the fact that the 'Daily Mail' had taken up the Lawrence case following the coroner's finding of 'Unlawful Killing' and had named, and shown photographs of, the five principal suspects in a front-page article on 10th February 1997 under the banner headline, 'Murderers'. Effectively, the newspaper was throwing a figurative gauntlet down and challenging the government to take effective action.

The police service within London and at a national level was ill-prepared for what was to come. As the recruitment of black officers had accelerated throughout the 1980s, a new issue had arisen linked to their retention and advancement. There was increasing debate about the extent to which such individuals left the police early, allegedly under the pressure of a racist 'canteen culture' which undervalued the contribution they had to make, and the underrepresentation of black and ethnic minority officers at ranks above constable. Logically, the latter point should not have been of great significance because as the largest part of the new cohort of black officers had less than five years' service, they would, in any case, only then have been approaching the point where they were qualified for promotion. The same would apply to white officers of similar service and experience. Nonetheless, concerns were raised which in the climate of the times could not be ignored.

A number of focus groups involving black officers and police managers (the Bristol Seminars) were held during early 1994 whilst the Stephen Lawrence case was very much in the headlines. The Crown Prosecution Service had dropped charges against the principal suspects because of 'insufficient evidence' in July 1993, following which a private prosecution was launched by the Lawrence family in April 1994. A head of steam was building and the Met Commissioner, Sir Paul Condon, was powerless to stop it. In September 1994, after the Bristol seminars had ended inconclusively, a small number of black and Asian officers in the Met announced that they intended to form a 'Black Police Association', modelled on those that already existed in many big-city police forces in the United States. Condon could do little other than be seen to be supporting the initiative. At the launch, he said: 'I have made it clear where I stand. I see the formation of this Association as the only way forward', which was true to a certain extent but ignored the fact that by giving explicit permission for the BPA to operate within the Met, he was implicitly criticising the vast majority of white officers under his command and side-lining the legally constituted representative staff associations, most notably the Police Federation. By 1999 there were BPA branches in virtually every force in the UK and a national executive organisation was formed (the NBPA) in November of that year. The scene was set for confrontation, with a high profile and emotive denial of justice, a public inquiry, a Black and Asian police workforce with a new-found sense of militancy, and a Commissioner at Scotland Yard who was clearly in difficulties from a strategic point of view.

In exactly the same way that Lord Scarman was a stellar figure in English jurisprudence, so Sir William Macpherson of Cluny was very much a member of the judicial aristocracy of the legal establishment in Scotland. A recently retired High Court judge he was also a Scottish clan chieftain with an ancestral home at Newton Castle in Blairgowrie. He was assisted by three 'advisers', the selection of whom says much about the way events subsequently developed. They were a black Church of England bishop, Dr John Sentamu; Dr Richard Stone of the Jewish Council for Racial Equality, and a retired Deputy Chief Constable from West Yorkshire, Tom Cook. The inquiry, with closed and public sessions in which witnesses, including the principal suspects, were cross-examined by counsel, ran from March 1998 to the middle of November and was a media feast throughout. It has been variously described as 'a farce', a 'Stalinist show-trial', and 'an earnest attempt to seek the truth', depending upon the point of view of the commentator. The final report made seventy recommendations covering such diverse areas as police stop-and-search powers; guidelines for the handling of victims and witnesses; changes to the police disciplinary code, and even amendment of the National Curriculum in schools to 'better reflect the needs of a diverse society'. One recommendation played directly to the managerialist strand of government ministers, proposing the establishment of a Ministerial Priority for 'increasing the trust of ethnic minorities in the police', together with associated Performance Indicators. In other words, they were suggesting a government target for trust! In the fullness of time, all but a few of the recommendations would be implemented, but the Macpherson Report is not remembered for its recommendations. It is famous, some would say 'infamous', for coining and using one particular phrase – 'Institutional Racism'.

At a stroke, the entire police service in London and every officer from John 'o' Groats to Land's End was effectively branded as racist. The damage that that simple phrase did to policing in the United Kingdom still cannot be quantified. Macpherson was pilloried in the press, received death threats, and was credited with reducing national police morale to the lowest level it had ever been. The Police Federation were unable to contain their anger and openly criticised the learned knight. Writers and polemicists from every point on the political spectrum loaded their pens with pure venom and set to work on his findings. Michael Gove, now (in 2023) a government minister, writing in the 'Times' shortly after publication of the report, described it as having, 'tendentious reasoning and illiberal recommendations'[34]. For many, the phrase just cannot be justified.

---

34 Michael Gove, The Times (10 October 2000). 'Be politically astute, not politically correct'.

It is worth examining precisely what Macpherson said about 'Institutionalised Racism' (rather than 'Institutional Racism'). This might seem to be a fairly abstruse semantic point but the latter phrase, which has gained great currency, implies an attitude which is structural and built into the fabric of an organisation. 'Institutionalised Racism' is less definite and suggests something that has been tacitly accepted over time.

The Macpherson report said,

'The Inquiry was not of course an inquiry into the general relationship between police and minority ethnic communities, and detailed examination of other individual cases would have been misplaced. Inevitably the Inquiry has heard many sounds and echoes concerning, for example, stop and search and the wide perceptions of minority ethnic communities that their cases are improperly investigated and that racist crime and harassment are inadequately regarded and pursued.' (Macpherson Report para 2.16)

Macpherson then went on to say that the Inquiry had established that,

'Unwitting racism can arise because of lack of understanding, ignorance or mistaken beliefs. It can arise from well-intentioned but patronising words or actions. It can arise from unfamiliarity with the behaviour or cultural traditions of people or families from minority ethnic communities. It can arise from racist stereotyping of black people

as potential criminals or troublemakers. Often this arises out of uncritical self-understanding born out of an inflexible police ethos of the "traditional" way of doing things. Furthermore such attitudes can thrive in a tightly knit community, so that there can be a collective failure to detect and to outlaw this breed of racism. The police canteen can too easily be its breeding ground.' (Macpherson Report para 6.17)

Sir Paul Condon stated in evidence to the Inquiry his belief that:

'I recognise that individual officers can be, and are, overtly racist. I acknowledge that some officers stereotype, and differential outcomes occur for Londoners. Racism in the police is much more than "bad apples". Racism, as you have pointed out, can occur through a lack of care and lack of understanding. The debate about defining this evil, promoted by the Inquiry, is cathartic in leading us to recognise that it can occur almost unknowingly, as a matter of neglect, in an institution. I acknowledge the danger of institutionalisation of racism. However, labels can cause more problems than they solve.'

Sir Paul did not accept that there was institutional (or indeed institutionalised) racism within the Met, but by failing to challenge the intellectual flaws in Macpherson's argument, he surrendered the debate to the Inquiry team, which profoundly affected subsequent direction of racial politics within the police service.

The Inquiry Team admitted that they had great difficulty defining precisely what was meant by 'institutionalised racism' but eventually drafted a definition for use during the Inquiry. It is clear however that they did not believe that they had had the final say on the matter and cautioned against using their model as an authoritative statement (a warning that has been comprehensively ignored by the police, the press and academe ever since). The definition that Macpherson proposed is set out below.

> *'The collective failure of an organisation to provide an appropriate and professional service to people because of their colour, culture, or ethnic origin. It can be seen or detected in processes, attitudes and behaviour which amount to discrimination through unwitting prejudice, ignorance, thoughtlessness, and racist stereotyping which disadvantage minority ethnic people.' (Macpherson Report para 6.34)*

> *'It persists because of the failure of the organisation openly and adequately to recognise and address its existence and causes by policy, example, and leadership. Without recognition and action to eliminate such racism it can prevail as part of the ethos or culture of the organisation. It is a corrosive disease.' (Macpherson Report para 6.35)*

Perhaps as an acknowledgement that the Inquiry Team realised the damage that they were doing, Macpherson conceded that racism was not the sole prerogative of the police – a statement of the blindingly obvious – for he then made the following sweeping statement without ever having heard any evidence to support his contention,

> *'Racism, institutionalised or otherwise, is not the prerogative of the Police Service. It is clear that other agencies, including for example those dealing with housing and education, also suffer from the disease. If racism is to be eradicated there must be specific and co-ordinated action both within the agencies themselves and by society at large, particularly through the educational system, from pre-primary school upwards and onwards.' (Macpherson Report para 6.54)*

Macpherson thus nailed his colours to the mast, and the police service recoiled in horror. Few Chief Constables and senior policymakers in the police service, such as Her Majesty's Chief Inspector of Constabulary, were prepared to challenge the philosophical and logical flaws in Macpherson's argument. It is disappointing, but probably true, that many remained silent rather than show leadership because they saw the way that the wind was blowing in terms of Police Reform under a government with an unassailable parliamentary majority. Frankly, most did not want to be identified as part of the 'awkward squad'. Promotion and patronage are never to be found in that direction.

It is clear from Macpherson's drafting that there is much to challenge, had anyone taken the time and effort to do so. His hyperbolic use of the word 'disease' to describe racism says much about the line he intended to take. However, of greater concern is the fact that he pins his entire argument on actions that are committed, not within the stated policy of an organisation, but 'unwittingly' or by 'ignorance', 'lack of understanding', or even 'well intentioned words or actions', by individuals within that organisation.

To follow his line of argument, one has to accept that individuals within an organisation can do something without anyone being aware that they are doing it, aided and abetted by colleagues and managers who are acting unwittingly and possibly with the best of intentions. No intent, no motive, no '*mens rea*'; nothing even approaching something of substance that might be recognised by a court, or even a dispassionate observer. By branding every police officer in the UK, from the gale-blown Shetland Isles to the tip of Cornwall, as members of a racist organisation, Macpherson did immense damage to policing for years to come. Blame should be shared with a government pursuing a party-political agenda unrelated to the real needs of the public in terms of policing, and with a significant number of Chief Officers who failed to show the leadership that might properly have been expected of them.

David Lloyd George once commented, in relation to the responsibility of leadership in public life, 'The man at the top is there to make the "grey" decisions. They do not come along very often, but when they do, they are difficult, that's why he is at the top. Any fool can make the black and white decisions, they are easy'. Uncritical acceptance of Macpherson's recommendations by those responsible for the stewardship of the police service at the time required very little effort. The abject failure of these Chief Constables and Inspectors of Constabulary ensured that as they shuffled off into comfortable retirement, they passed a poisoned chalice on to their successors.

Thus, as the new millennium dawned, the police service was in a parlous state in terms of the way in which it confronted the multi-faceted subject of race. Critics on all sides offered Macpherson in aid whenever they pointed out failings of delivery or management. Morale at every level of the organisation was at rock bottom, with junior, and not so junior, officers being in constant fear that they might be denounced for some perceived racist remark or conduct and drummed out of their job.

The Race Relations Act 2000 extended the 1976 Act by specifically outlawing any form of discrimination by the police or other public bodies, introducing civil and criminal penalties for anyone breaching the law. This was further extended by the Equality Act 2010, which underlined corporate liability. The combined effect of the post-Macpherson atmosphere and the new legislation was that the police service turned in on itself. This new world of breast-beating 'mea culpa' extended to everything that was done, from the simplest operation, through all aspects of training, to selection for promotion, and on to high strategy. Race awareness consultants earned vast sums conducting 'audits' – which miraculously always concluded that there was an urgent need for training which they could provide – at a price. The Home Office set targets for each force to recruit a specific number of ethnic minority candidates so as to mirror the racial mix of the area they policed. Most of the targets were unachievable but were nonetheless scrupulously enforced by the Home Office through focussed inspection by HM Inspectorate. Chief

Officers vied to outdo each other with more and more ideologically driven and often 'barmy' schemes in a bid to better demonstrate their 'equality' credentials.

An example came to notice in September 2006, when the Gloucestershire Constabulary admitted breaking the law with a secret policy of 'deselecting' more than 100 potential recruits for no other reason than being white men[35]. Appearing before an Employment Tribunal a senior representative of the force said that they had been trying to 'advance diversity' when they rejected 108 men in favour of women and ethnic minority candidates. The Chief Constable, Timothy Brain, admitted that they had acted unlawfully and agreed to pay one of the claimants £2,500 in damages. The tribunal said the force had been 'at the very least disingenuous and at worst misleading'. The decision sparked a barrage of further claims, each of which had to be settled from police funds, i.e. by the local taxpayers. In its defence the force claimed that it was under pressure to meet a government target of ethnic minority recruits, set at seven per cent of force strength by 2009. At the time, they comprised only 1.6 per cent requiring them, so they claimed, to take desperate – and illegal – measures. Tim Brain, now retired, is a Visiting Professor at the University of Gloucestershire and regular media commentator on policing matters – *Plus ça change.*

As all things related to race and discrimination took centre-stage in the late 1990s and early 2000s the concept of 'diversity' and 'celebrating' diversity seized

---

35 'Police force admits discriminating against white recruits' – Daily Mail 22.9.2006

the imagination of lobbyists both within and outside the police service. Gender equality and gay rights suddenly became matters of consuming interest, with a minority of female and gay officers seeking to argue that they too suffered discrimination in the same way as Black and Asian officers. This was, of course, a gross exaggeration and gave the impression to many observers of a collective attempt to jump on a bandwagon. In no sense could the experiences of a tiny number of gay officers even be considered alongside the perfectly legitimate and evidenced claims of racial discrimination in society as a whole. To do so and try to claim 'We are victims like you!' was an insult to their Black and Asian colleagues. Female officers based their grievances on their claimed lack of visibility at senior levels in the police but it is significant that senior women officers, who have achieved much within a police service that they would say has always been against them, are those most likely to join associations which differentiate them from their more junior sisters, whilst simultaneously claiming that they have been disadvantaged and are part of an underclass. As the proportion of female to male recruits edges towards parity, there is value in asking why the British Association for Women in Policing (BAWP) feels that there was a need for what they grandly referred to as 'The Gender Agenda' which advocated sweeping, and patently illegal, proposals such as:

To achieve a representative service within 5–7 years we must adopt a twin track approach of:
  a) positive action, and
  b) affirmative action, i.e. time limited managed

> *disproportionate recruitment of capable people to redress the current imbalances.*
> *(Gender Agenda 2 (BAWP 2006))*

Indeed BAWP's definition of what it regarded as a 'representative service' is extremely ideological and might easily have been drafted by a political lobby group, rather than an 'ad hoc' police support organisation.

> *'To achieve a gender, ethnicity and sexual orientation balance across the rank and grade structure and specialisms, consistent with the proportion of women in the economically active population.'*
> *(Gender Agenda 2 – Executive Summary (BAWP 2006))*

So there you have it. The Holy Grail is equality at any cost; no mention of skills, differential ability, or the need to ensure that expertise is targeted to a particular specialism or role. No account is taken of the fact that, for example, the number of gay or black women might vary widely from one part of the country to another, or that skills might not be available in all or any of these sub-groups.

Interestingly the needs and wishes of the public do not appear to be of any concern amidst this utopian redefinition of the role of women in policing. One looks in vain through BAWP's glossy document for any indication of how their beautifully crafted vision and strategy adds any value to the day-to-day policing delivered across the land. The focus is unashamedly inward – the public at large do not even justify a mention.

As time has gone by, and a philosophy of victimhood has developed, so the number of Associations and support groups has proliferated. The world of 'equality' in the police service has become balkanised. Listed below are just a few of the current crop of police lobby groups claiming a place at the top table on behalf of their favoured minority, or 'disadvantaged group'.

The National Black Police Association (NBPA)
The Association of Muslim Police
Metropolitan Police Sikh Association (MPSA)
Metropolitan Police Hindu Association
The Chinese and Southeast Asian Staff Association
The Metropolitan Police Emerald Society (Irish Staff Association)
The Jewish Police Association
The Christian Police Association
The Catholic Police Guild of England and Wales
The British Association for Women in Policing (BAWP)
The Association of Senior Women Officers of the Metropolitan Police
The ACPO (now NPCC) Women's Forum
The National Disabled Police Association
The Gay Police Association (GPA)
The National Trans-Gender Police Association

Undoubtedly there will be more to come, increasingly marginal and exclusive, yet offered as tokens of the police service's unswerving commitment to anything which has the vaguest connection with diversity.

Constable Andy Pardy serves with the Hertfordshire Police, has over twenty years' service and is one of the 'Equality and Diversity Representatives' for the force. He is proud to call himself a 'pagan' who worships the Norse gods Odin and Freya. So committed is he to his beliefs that in 2009 he announced his intention to set up a national Pagan Police Association to 'provide support and guidance' to pagan police officers who want to fit their beliefs around their police work. '[Paganism] has been practised in this country since before the concept of God arrived here,' he stated to the press. 'It is all about dedication to nature. Most pagans practise some kind of conservation work as well, to give something back to the planet.' The environmentally conscious PC Pardy then went to his Chief Constable and asked to take eight pagan holidays each year, including the Summer Solstice and Halloween, on the grounds of religious observance.

Against all common sense and logic, but remaining staunchly true to his force Diversity Statement, which proclaims that Hertfordshire Police will '*promote diversity by recognising, valuing and respecting the different contributions and needs of our communities and staff*', the Chief Constable immediately granted PC Pardy's request, thereby ensuring that on eight days each year there will be one less officer to police the county and protect the good people of Hertfordshire.

The National Black Police Association, formed with the blessing of government and the then Commissioner of the Met, Sir Paul Condon, has had a somewhat chequered history which has done little to enhance its credibility or assist those it seeks to represent. From the outset the organisation was feted by policymakers who ensured that office accommodation and administrative support was provided (at no cost), at the Home Office. A budget of up to £180,000 per year was awarded from central funds, in addition to the agreement by a number of forces to 'carry' the salary costs of various officials of the organisation whilst seconded to the NBPA executive. Sadly, these funds were managed in a less than professional way, resulting in a full-scale criminal inquiry by the Independent Police Complaints Commission (IPCC) which started in 2007, and examined the conduct of senior members of the Executive between 2003 and 2005. The inquiry established beyond doubt that thousands of pounds of public money could not be accounted for, but worse still, that there had been little or no overview or supervision by the Home Office until too late in the day, when it was clear that the NBPA's accounts could not be trusted. It is of significance that very few senior black and Asian officers have allowed their names to become too closely associated with the NBPA. For example, Mike Fuller, formerly the Chief Constable of the large and busy Kent force, and the first black Chief Constable of any force in the UK, is a man of high principle and great ability – and whilst supportive of the BPA in Kent always seemed careful to keep the NBPA at a respectable distance.

Much of this has to do with the aura that surrounds the former President of, and Legal Adviser to, the Association, Iranian-born Commander Ali Dizaei who was suspended from duty in September 2008 over allegations of serious criminal misconduct. *Dr* Dizaei, as he prefers to be known, was promoted to his very senior rank having already appeared at the Old Bailey in 2003 where he was acquitted of serious criminal offences. Subsequently, in a classic piece of self-justification he published his story and his grievances in a controversial book entitled 'Not One of Us', and also received a large sum in compensation from the Met, after suing the force. It is thus unsurprising that the NBPA, subsequently, had great difficulty in finding anyone of senior rank and real status to take on executive positions.

Indeed it was only after Dizaei had been sentenced to four years imprisonment for perverting the course of justice in February 2010 that confirmation emerged of just how weak management resolve had become when confronted with any issue that touched upon race. Here was an officer, in respect of whom there was real concern about his lifestyle, associates, probity and honesty. Someone who had already admitted, during his first trial, breaches of discipline and outrageous behaviour towards a woman friend, that in previous times would have seen any other officer drummed out of the force. Yet Dizaei, seemingly because of his position of power within the NBPA, appeared to many to have 'carte blanche' to act with impunity, with the then Commissioner, Sir John (now Lord) Stevens, welcoming him back into the force from suspension in 2003 and publicly telling him that he did not have a blemish on his character. Within a matter of a few years, in a move that generated real anger amongst many in the force, Dizaei was promoted to Commander – one of the most senior and influential posts in policing in the capital.[36]

---

36 On 30th September 2011, Dizaei successfully appealed against his conviction on the grounds that one of the witnesses who gave evidence against him was 'unreliable'. He was reinstated to the force and then immediately suspended. In 2012 he faced a re-trial, was convicted, and sentenced to three years imprisonment. He is now

In the early years of the NBPA, however, things were not as bleak as they are today. When local branches of the Black Police Association were established in forces up and down the country, Chief Constables went to extraordinary, and frequently demeaning, lengths to show their supposed personal commitment to equality and diversity. The most excruciatingly embarrassing performance by any senior officer, one which has gone down in the annals of the 'diversity and equality' world, involved the Deputy Chief Constable of the North Wales Police. In March 2004 he was invited to the inaugural gathering of the North Wales BPA at the force headquarters. He had been asked to say a few words to mark the occasion, with everyone expecting that he would make a brief speech before sitting down and taking part in the business of the meeting. How wrong they were! To an audience that was reportedly slack-jawed with amazement, he launched into a 'rap' that he had composed.

On and on he went, for a full eleven stanzas, until the patience of his audience was exhausted. Not to recognise how deeply patronising he was being is one thing, but to fail to appreciate the total disconnect between his behaviour and the wider world requires a level of intellectual arrogance that is truly staggering. The chairman of the CRE, Trevor Phillips, said as much in a speech to black civil servants some weeks later when he commented upon the dangers of liberal Britain and the 'misguided' policies of ethnic minorities that were inherently racist. His comments pulled no punches.

(2023) the Managing Director of Covert Security, a private company providing international security advice to business.

'I mean, for example, the deputy chief constable of a police force going to the inaugural meeting of his force's black police association and, despite the fact that most of the members of the BPA are British-born or British-raised, and many of them of South Asian origin, addressing them in rap. Presumably this was an attempt to "get down" with their supposed culture. How wrong, how patronising! Can we imagine Sir John Stevens [then Metropolitan Police Commissioner] turning up to address the London Police Federation and starting off with a rousing chorus of "Maybe It's because I'm a Londoner" before discussing his policing strategy in Cockney rhyming slang?'

The years pass by and yet no-one at the helm of policing seems to understand how ridiculous they appear to the public at large, so intent are they on being able to show that they 'care' more than their neighbouring force about race and diversity. Early in 2009, as part of a scheme to improve 'community understanding' in Sheffield, two sergeants and a community support officer dressed in head-to-foot burqas and other traditional clothing and went out shopping. The move was part of a police initiative called 'In Your Shoes' organised by the South Yorkshire Police Diversity Unit and drew withering criticism from the public, the local council and various community groups[37]. However, the force chose to ignore all comments which did not match their view of the world, and refused to respond to the press, who had

---

37 'Police dress up in burkhas "to improve community relations".' Daily Telegraph (4.8.2009)

asked for a comment. All were referred to the force in-house magazine which printed the following masterpiece of spin:

'The exercise is just one of many activities South Yorkshire Police has planned with communities and ethnic minority leaders to secure strong relationships, celebrate diversity and encourage integration, working towards a safer, closer society.'

The perceived need to demonstrate full-blooded commitment to equality, whatever the cost, has created a 'topsy-turvy' world in which any attempt to argue against the process is interpreted as something akin to heresy. A Metropolitan Police Inspector of some fifteen years' service, a history graduate, attended a mandatory Race Awareness training-day at which he was part of a group of twenty or so police officers of all ranks and civilian support staff, black and white. A white 'diversity consultant' was facilitating the proceedings and started to talk about the 'guilt' that all white people should feel for the horrors of the European slave-trade in the eighteenth and nineteenth centuries. In a perfectly reasonable tone, the Inspector sought to widen the debate,

'I mentioned that it was well-documented that many of the slaves had actually been seized by raiding parties from other African tribes and traded to Europeans on the coast for weapons and other goods. That didn't excuse the Europeans, but it did widen the issue of "guilt" because there was joint responsibility. The Diversity Adviser looked as if she would like to

strangle me, and then said, 'Comments like that add nothing to what we are discussing – you clearly don't want to engage with the subject', and for the rest of the seminar ignored me. When I went back to my station the following day, I was called in to see my Chief Superintendent who told me that a complaint had been made that I was "negative and disruptive" at the seminar. My boss was sympathetic to me and said that he would "square it up" so that there would be no more trouble but said something that has stayed with me – "We all have to be so careful these days, you never know who's listening and any suggestion that you are not 'toeing the party line' will kill your career stone dead."[38]

Within police forces, nowhere is the subject of race and equality more divisive than around the important area of promotion and advancement. Logic and common sense would suggest that the promotion of any individual should be on the basis of their proven ability, their skills, and their potential to perform competently at the next rank or grade. The police, in common with many other areas of the public service, have pay-scales that are directly linked to rank, which means that an officer's salary will only increase substantially if he or she achieves promotion. For this reason, if for no other, promotion from constable to sergeant, sergeant to inspector, inspector to chief inspector, and so on up the ladder is much prized. A further factor is that the police service is one of the last remaining employers

---

38 Interview – Author's research April 2009

in the UK to offer an inflation-linked final-salary pension, which is tied directly to an officer's annual pay in his or her last year of service.

From the late 1990s the basis upon which decisions about promotion are made has been the subject of an almost constant barrage of civil actions and Employment Tribunal proceedings against the Commissioner of the Met and most Chief Constables up and down the country. The vast majority have been brought under legislation relating to racial and/or gender discrimination, indeed the volume is such that the Metropolitan Police has had to set up and staff an entire department at Scotland Yard to deal with the correspondence and pleadings. In the period of just one financial year, 2008/2009[39], this single unit in one force (albeit the largest force in the country) processed no less than 120 new Employment Tribunal cases comprising 52 cases of Race and/or Sexual discrimination made by serving Met police officers and a further 30 made by PCSOs and other non-police members of staff. The remaining 38 had not been categorised at the time of disclosure. In the same period, the Met disclosed that £69,858 was paid out by the Commissioner following court proceedings, whilst £179,825 was paid to claimants in 'out of court' settlements. A further, considerably larger, sum was paid out but was the subject of a 'special confidentiality agreement prohibiting disclosure'. It will be noted that most cases are settled 'out of court' in order to reduce the drain on the public purse, but the few that end up in court tend to be hideously expensive, not only in terms of legal expenses, counsel's fees etc, but

---

39 Freedom of Information request to MPS – July 2009

also as a result of the impact that they have on procedures and policy. In the ten years since, up to 2018/2019 (the most recent date for which there is available data), the through-put of civil actions has increased by around 50% despite management action to address perceived issues of discrimination.

By attrition, the police promotion system has now become a bureaucratic nightmare, as various checks and balances have been applied to 'equality-proof' the selection process. There are qualifying examinations, replete with competencies such as 'Community and Customer Focus' and 'Respect for Diversity'. Following success at the written examinations there are role-playing exercises which are claimed to test the officer's knowledge of how to apply the competency framework. Lastly there is a structured interview where assessors challenge the candidates on what they have done in their careers to advance Diversity, Customer Focus, and Openness to Change, etc etc, and how they might approach such matters in the future. From the earliest days of their career, officers are required to maintain a portfolio of what they have achieved so that they will be in a position to 'evidence' their claims when applying for promotion or a specialist post. Each achievement logged in a portfolio must have a witness, or the signature of a supervisor in order for it to be validated. An experienced Detective Sergeant, shaking his head wearily, remarked to me,

> *'It's like being at school and being told you must keep a diary with each page signed by your teacher. We have to do everything bar colour them in with crayons, and I suppose that'll come before long'.*

The pressure for forces to demonstrate that they have facilitated the promotion of able female, gay and ethnic minority officers has meant that some have been 'pushed through' before they were ready operationally, or experientially, solely on the basis of their gender, sexuality, or ethnicity. This outrageous tokenism, which has taken place at all ranks up to and including chief officers at NPCC level, has had precisely the opposite effect to that intended. Most police officers are not fools, and can quickly recognise when a new boss, white, black, brown, female, gay or heterosexual, is out of his or her depth. Their skin colour or what they do in the bedroom is not of any consequence – the only question is whether or not they can do the job. In those instances when 'minority' officers plainly cannot, they not only fail those that they have been appointed to lead, but more importantly they diminish the contribution of truly able 'minority' officers who have got where they are by virtue of real ability. This is a constant source of resentment amongst many white, black, gay, and female officers.

It would be no exaggeration to describe the police service in the United Kingdom in 2023 as simultaneously obsessed and transfixed by anything to do with race, equality, and diversity. Whether this is a function of sincere commitment to the philosophical principles, however, is rather more doubtful. All senior officers spend an inordinate amount of time looking over their shoulder to ensure that nothing that they do or say might attract denunciation in the Kafkaesque world in which they spend their working lives. They are driven by the need to avoid giving the slightest cause for their own staff to embark upon proceedings before employment tribunals and must be constantly on guard against making any statement that might be misconstrued as racist, or sexist, or any other '-ist'. This organisational paranoia cascades down, and the officers at shop-floor level respond in the way that is safest for them – they over-react and treat race and gender as if they were strategic issues of such importance that real policing is of second-order priority. Everyone spends time trying to convince each other that skin colour is of no relevance and therefore should not be mentioned. 'We must be colour blind' say the leaders of the service, without acknowledging that colour-blindness, in medical terms, describes deficient vision.

During the worst of the period in 2008 and 2009 and in the years since, when knife attacks by black gang-members on other black teenagers seemed to be claiming a life every day in London, the debate hardly ever touched upon the responsibility of the black community. Well over 70% of the victims and the assailants were black or mixed race, and yet the police and the media, together with many commentators, spoke only of 'young men' being involved without any reference to ethnicity. It is a problem, they chorused, of the alienation of 'our youth'. So it is, but no favours are done to anyone when the police close their minds to what is obvious, and for specious reasons of alleged sensitivity, refuse to acknowledge ethnicity as a feature of an event.

CHAPTER 4
THE POLICE WORKFORCE

THE SHOP FLOOR

Figures released by the Home Office in March 2009[40] (prior to the Comprehensive Spending Review of 2010/2011) indicated that there were 142,151 police officers in England and Wales, something like 16,000 more than there were in 1997. However, the years of austerity following the financial crash of 2008, in which funding for the police was savagely cut, resulted in a gross reduction in the headcount of more than 20,000 experienced officers. This was only reversed by recent attempts at mass recruitment, taking the total to 123,171 full-time police officers in 2019, still the lowest figure since the late 1990s.

The comparable figures for Scotland show that in the eight forces north of the border in 2009 there were 16,339 police officers serving, the highest level that the Scottish police strength had ever been. The devolved government in Scotland went to great pains to protect policing in the

---

40 Home Office statistics 2008/2009

wake of the 2008 financial crash, and during the period in which the national force was being created in 2013. Thus, the total headcount for Police Scotland has barely changed since amalgamation and stands at 16,644 (2019 total). The figures for Northern Ireland are difficult to interpret because of structural changes to the Police Service for Northern Ireland (PSNI) since the Good Friday Agreement and the role of the full-time Reserve but stand at around 7,500. The government has made no secret of the fact that it would like to see that figure drop to 6,000 or marginally less to meet the recommendations of Lord Patten, following his review of policing in the province some years ago.

The total cost to the public purse of policing in the United Kingdom is in the region of £20 billion per annum. Almost a fifth of that sum (around £4 billion) is swallowed up by the Met to police the capital, and to discharge national functions such as co-ordination of the counter-terrorism response, protection of the Royal Family, and planning for major state occasions (such as the funeral of HM Queen Elizabeth II, and the coronation in 2023).

Policing, by its very nature, is a manpower-intensive activity. People are required to discharge all its functions large and small. Uniform police officers at stations, detectives dealing with serious crime, specialists examining crime scenes, traffic officers dealing with motorway crashes, all must be recruited, trained, paid, and at the end of their career provided with a pension. Between 78% and 85% of the entire budget is spent on what are referred to as 'staff costs'. At the lowest estimate this means that at least £14.1 billion every year is spent on police salaries, overtime, and pensions nationally. In London, where there are currently just over 35,000 police officers, the budgeted figure for 2022/2023 staff costs is £3.62 billion. The vast majority of police officers, between 85% and 90% of the total establishment, are constables and sergeants who although paid significantly less than their senior officers, nonetheless consume most of the staff cost allocation (around £12 billion nationally, and £3.1 billion in London) by virtue of their greater numbers. These figures emphasise one fact above all others – that fully warranted, fully trained police officers are a very expensive commodity. You could build a lot of hospitals and buy a lot of helicopters for our troops with just a small proportion of what we spend on our boys and girls in blue. Indeed the police are more expensive now than they have ever been, and if the present economic downturn has a plus side, it may well be that it forces us to concentrate our minds on whether we are getting true value for money from the police service.

There is political consensus that we face a crisis which requires policymakers to 'think the unthinkable' and challenge much of the received wisdom about policing that has come down to us over the years. In looking at the workforce, junior and senior, there are three questions that we need to ask. Firstly, what do we expect from the police officers that consume so much of our national treasure? Secondly, is it necessary for us to have so many of them? Lastly is there a cheaper, but just as effective, way of policing our communities and protecting our nation? In order to answer all of these questions we need to look at these constables and sergeants, and those charged with leading them, in rather more detail.

We have already established that the model of street

policing that many people believe still exists, 'bobbies on the beat' etc, was comprehensively abandoned a number of years ago. People no longer know who polices their community (or even if it is policed at all in the accepted sense). There is little evidence of visible patrolling by trained officers and the police response to emergencies is derisory. So who, and where, are these people that we pay £14 billion each year?

From the establishment of the first police forces in the early nineteenth century, through to today, the vast majority of men (and now women) attracted to the job came, and continue to come, from a working-class or artisan background. They are people that in former times might well have gone into the armed forces and carved out successful careers as junior NCOs or worked in business or industry as trusted clerks. Sir Ranulph Bacon, who was head of the CID at Scotland Yard in the 1960s, once commented that the entire constable strength of the Metropolitan Police was formed from *'delivery van drivers, farmhands, and a selection of life's lance-corporals'*[41]. His comments could have been put more diplomatically but to a great extent he was correct. Pay levels, at least until the Edmund-Davis reforms of 1978 were on a par with the industrial average, and even middle-ranking officers at the level of Inspector and above could not expect anything approaching the salary that managers at a comparable level in commerce might receive. In the early post-war period, prior to 1949, a police constable in London earned less than a bus-conductor.

---

41 Quote from Alex Marnoch OBE QPM (died 1999) – Author's research

The attraction of a police career in those days was linked to three things. The generous pension, which was payable after 25 years, allowed an officer to retire in his mid-forties and take up another occupation. A further attraction was less easily quantifiable but was a function of the status within the community that being a policeman conferred, and the third was the fact that policing, certainly at ranks up to and including Superintendent, was effectively 'classless' and offered an almost unique opportunity for an ambitious young man to better himself and improve his station in life. This was particularly attractive to many ex-servicemen who had a clear understanding of the role of discipline and hierarchy in big organisations and saw promotion to Inspector as admission to an officer corps that would almost certainly have been denied to them in the military because of their social origins. A vast gap in rewards existed between constable, or even sergeant, and superintendent. For example, whereas a constable's pay at the end of the nineteenth century began at £1 and 5 shillings (£1.25p) per week and rose by annual increments of one shilling (5p) per week to a maximum of £1 and 13 shillings (£1.65p) per week, the annual wage of a superintendent was over £400 per annum (£8.00 per week).[42] Since no rank could be skipped, the longer an officer worked for the police the better were his chances of advancing significantly and reaching the more rewarding ranks. Persistence thus offered ordinary workers the rare opportunity to develop a career and cross the class boundary into the middle class

---

42 Stanley Savill, The Police Service of England and Wales (London: John Kempster, Police Review Office, 1901), pp. 273–74.

proper. Police officers were time and again promised that 'when ability as an officer is displayed it surely leads to notice and advancement.'[43]

In 1999, the Director of National Police Training, a post which no longer exists but was at the time responsible for national recruiting policy, described to the Parliamentary Home Affairs Committee the type of candidate the process was attempting to select.

> *'There are a number of things that forces will be looking for. They will, for example, be looking for somebody who is honest and has the right attitude in order to be a police officer. They will be looking for somebody who is physically capable of doing the job and, therefore, there will be some physical tests in place to see that they are actually capable of doing it. In terms of the police initial recruitment test, and any tests or assessment that will be put in place by individual forces, it is very much to examine whether the individuals are capable of undertaking the training that they will subsequently undergo— both, that is, at National Police Training Centres and within the police forces'.* [44]

In other words the basic educational requirement only extended to ensuring that the recruit could cope with

---

43 'Extracts from Reports by District and Divisional Superintendents', Annual Report of the Commissioner of the Metropolitan Police to the House of Commons, PP, 1884, vol. 42, p. 367.

44 'Police Training and Recruitment' – Parliamentary Home Affairs Committee, Minutes of Evidence and Appendices (pub. 8.7.1999)

the limited amount of classroom work during the formal training period early in his or her career. This is significant because even as little as a decade ago there was clearly no suggestion that recruits should be intellectual giants. They only needed to be honest, physically fit, possessed of the 'right attitude' (whatever that might be), and able to assimilate the training. It is also worth noting that officers recruited at that time and under that philosophical framework, now have twenty or more years' service and a large proportion are probably supervisors at sergeant, inspector, and superintendent rank, influencing the generation of recruits that is following them. Until 2002 the Home Office sponsored a Graduate Entry Scheme for the police which, from 1968, had attracted some excellent graduates from the best universities on the promise that if selected they would be rapidly promoted to Inspector after serving two years as a constable in a force of their choice. A significant number of these graduate entrants went on to become highly effective Chief Constables. This scheme will be discussed in more detail when we examine those at the helm of today's police service. These few 'high-flyers' aside, all other entrants to the police then and now come through the standard recruit selection process, which means that the overwhelming majority of the leaders of the service, certainly at the pivotal rank of Superintendent, have come up through the ranks and often bear the stamp of their origins. In addition, this also means that because of the lead-time involved in training and promoting officers, the senior cadre of the 2020s and 2030s has, in effect, already been selected.

The expansion of Further and Higher Education, which

started under the Tory government in the 1990s, when perfectly good Polytechnics and FE Colleges re-branded themselves as universities, was eagerly taken up by New Labour after 1997. The almost exponential increase in degree courses, where none existed before, has meant that a whole new generation of working-class youngsters have attended 'uni' (as they will insist on calling it!) and have begun to present themselves as 'graduates' to the police service. Amongst them are a small number of men and women from Oxbridge and the twenty or so Russell Group universities, but most come from the newer universities. On the face it, it might seem that the police service is spoiled for choice and that the reservoir of talent from which they can make their selection is now wider and deeper than it has ever been. That is certainly what successive Education Secretaries would have us believe, but those close to the selection process know differently. The head of Human Resources in a large provincial force commented to the author, under strict conditions of anonymity,

> *'We're not stupid. Just because someone comes to us as a "graduate" we don't necessarily have to give them any extra credit at all. You will never convince me that a First in Film Studies from the new University of Upper Mudshire should in any sense to be considered alongside a 2.1 in Politics Philosophy and Economics from Oxford. It's a no-brainer, it's like comparing lard with butter. No, we look at where they've studied and if it isn't a "real" university with a good academic track record we disregard their degree as any sort of plus factor in their selection. We might well accept*

them, but not on the basis that they are marked for stardom because they have a degree.[45]

This may be disappointing to the new cohort of applicants as they present themselves for selection over the next few years, but it is a statement of reality. There is a continuing debate about the extent to which the police should be a 'graduate only' career. However, with the inexorable increase in the number of applicants holding low-status degrees awarded by less than academically rigorous institutions, and the consequent devaluation of the status of 'graduates', the police in common with other sensible employers will have to find other ways of identifying their high-flyers. Most, like the individual quoted above, will seek the reassurance of a CV which lists a good independent school and a Russell Group university.

The increase in police numbers since 1997, coupled with the fact that there was a 'spike' in retirements of those baby-boomers who joined during the period from 1968 to 1978, and reached pensionable age after thirty years' service between 1998 and 2008, has radically altered the age structure of those occupying the ranks of constable and sergeant; they are on average some five years younger than a generation ago. In addition, the vastly increased rate of recruitment of women has altered the gender balance appreciably. Nationally, some 32% of all police officers are now female, but that figure is edging towards parity as the recruitment of women is seen by many forces as an equality issue. At the operational cutting edge, their presence is

---

45 Confidential interview 2009 – Author's research

much greater due to the fact that an enhanced bulge of younger recruits has filled the vacancies created by the large number of retirements of the past five years. Further, the 20,000-recruitment uplift introduced in July 2019, to ameliorate some of the damage caused by austerity after 2009, has added to this statistical bulge, but at some cost to standards.

In 2022 HM Inspectorate reported that the Metropolitan Police are recruiting officers who are 'functionally illiterate in English'. The report stated that whilst it was right that ambitious recruitment targets were being set, that should not be at the expense of standards. HM Inspector warned that the force is at risk of 'recruiting the wrong people' and noted that the new Commissioner Mark Rowley had made it clear he wants to 'dial down the requirement to meet those targets' to ensure the right people are recruited. In 2021, the then Commissioner Dame Cressida Dick announced plans to recruit 40 percent of the Met's officers from black and ethnic minority (BAME) groups by 2023, but the number of BAME officers in the capital remains at less than 17 per cent. In the drive to meet the diversity targets, HM Inspector found strong evidence that the Met consciously lowered standards. The Inspectorate report, whilst saying that it would be 'clearly wrong' for the force to be an 'overwhelmingly white police force' confirmed that there is clear evidence from the Met training school indicating that significant numbers of student officers cannot read or write English and are incapable of writing up crime reports or statements for evidential purposes.

So, what would the average group of operational police officers look like, if we could winkle them out of their stations and cars and manage to persuade exactly 100 of them to stand in serried ranks outside their police headquarters? It is fair to say that most people would be surprised by what they saw. At least 30 of the officers, perhaps even 32, would be women. Only 5 would be black or Asian (compared with just 2 ten years ago), and none of those would be female. The average age of the group would be about twenty-five, although the 12 ex-servicemen amongst them would have an average age of more than thirty-two. Ten of the officers would be university graduates, but only one would have graduated from a good Russell Group university, and he or she would probably be on some form of Accelerated Promotion Scheme. If the Gay Police Association is to be believed, at least 10 of the officers would be openly gay, lesbian, or bi-sexual, but the casual observer would have no way of knowing which. A significant proportion of the officers, male and female, would be of or slightly below average height. This is because height standards for police recruits were deemed to be racially discriminatory in the 1980s following the Scarman report[46]. If our group of a hundred were from an inner-city police station in London, or Manchester or Birmingham, it would be doubtful if more than one of them lived in the area that he or she policed; the other 99 would almost certainly live in the suburbs or outside the city altogether and would commute in to work. Significantly, almost all would probably have a scowl on their face as they surveyed the public before them, and

---

46 All height restrictions for police recruits in the UK were abandoned from 1990. Police Constable Robin Port who serves with the Devon and Cornwall Police, based at Tiverton, is just 4ft 11ins tall (2010) – 'This is Exeter' (14.1.2010)

probably would be standing with their left foot forward in what is termed the 'ready' position. This is because the public cannot be trusted and the personal safety of police officers, and that of their colleagues, is now the paramount factor in their working lives – beyond the concept of service, beyond commitment to the public, often beyond common sense.

OFFICER SAFETY AND ATTITUDE TO THE PUBLIC

When the history of the decline of British policing is written there will be a whole chapter on 'Health and Safety', and the corrosive effect it has had on attitudes, discipline, and the service ethos. The sorry saga began in the early 1990s when there was a spate of violent assaults with weapons on police officers in London. In 1991 Sergeant Alan King was stabbed to death by a suspect he had stopped on night-duty in Walthamstow. Later that same year Detective Constable James Morrison, who was off duty, attempted to arrest a thief in Convent Garden, who fatally stabbed him. Early in 1993 PC Patrick Dunne confronted 'Yardie' suspects in a suburban street in Clapham, who promptly shot him dead. Lastly, in 1994 Sergeant Derek Robertson was stabbed to death as he attempted to arrest armed robbers at New Addington near Croydon. Four conspicuously brave men, two of whom would be awarded posthumous gallantry medals by the Queen, they died within months of each other. Amongst 'rank and file' police officers throughout the UK there was an almost audible clamour for something to be done to protect officers on the street against such attacks. The call for protective equipment was, in the circumstances, absolutely justified and commanded the quite proper attention of the senior echelon at Scotland Yard (all the dead officers were from the Met) for over two years.

The problem as they saw it was how to equip all officers, male and female, with a ballistic and stab-proof vest which was light, easy to wear, and effective. Effectiveness was a real issue because despite contacting suppliers worldwide it proved impossible to source equipment that gave protection against bullets and knives, but at the same time remained unobtrusive enough to be worn under standard uniform. There was a desire to avoid the necessity, if at all possible, of kitting out officers in military 'flak-jackets' which would inevitably alter the image of the British police officer in the eyes of the public and quite possibly raise the fear of crime. Eventually an interim solution was found in the shape of the 'MetVest', a light stab-proof vest which also gave reasonable protection against low-calibre bullets. The vest, which had the advantage that it could be worn under existing clothing, was rushed into production and issued to all front-line officers in London. It was not an unqualified success, for whilst affording some protection it was uncomfortable to wear for extended periods of time, particularly for women, whose different body shape it had not been properly designed for. Officers were not, at that time (prior to 1998), compelled to wear the equipment and it soon became clear that many were voting with their feet and refusing to wear the MetVest, preferring instead to spend their own money and buy body armour advertised by specialist suppliers in this country and the United States.

The Met and other forces were at a loss to know what

to do next. Officers were demanding that they be properly equipped to face a perceived, although often over-hyped, operational landscape in which they claimed that they were in constant danger of being stabbed or shot. Various committees were established to examine options for this or that piece of kit, whilst ordinary constables and sergeants began to wear 'mix and match' uniforms of various sorts. It started to become clear to the leaders of the service that they were fighting a rear-guard action on an issue that they were not guaranteed to win. Eventually the then representative body for Chief Constables, ACPO, under pressure from several forces who had already made piecemeal changes, decided to opt for the overt wearing of a heavy-duty stab-proof and ballistic vest by all operational officers. It soon became abundantly clear however that the full implications of this move had not been thought through in enough detail.

As soon as the overt ballistic vests were issued, changes in the rest of the police uniform became inevitable. Officers could only wear it with a shirt or a jumper, so the police tunic, which had existed in one form or another for 150 years, had to go. As an aside, this also meant that police sergeants, who had their 'stripes' embroidered onto the sleeves of their tunics, could no longer be identified by constables or the public except by a small silver badge worn on the epaulette on their shoulder – a loss of status from which sergeants have never recovered. With the tunic consigned to the dustbin of history, it was found that officers no longer had any pockets in which to keep the ever-increasing number of forms and notebooks that they were required to carry, so a heavy 'equipment belt' was designed, replete with pouches in which everything could be stored, or on to which items could be attached, such as handcuffs and batons. Burdened by such equipment on what looked like a weightlifter's body belt, it was then found that officer's uniform trousers were not equal to the strain and were pushed down. So, trousers and skirts were replaced by heavy duty cargo-pants with added patch pockets. Raincoats were discarded in favour of short car-coats because long clothing impeded access to the equipment on the belt. When any headgear was worn at all (an increasingly rare occurrence), peaked caps or even baseball caps were favoured over the traditional helmet. Within less than five years the distinctive, reassuring and instantly recognisable appearance of the British police officer had changed forever. Most young officers gloried in the fact that they now looked more like patrolmen in Los Angeles, even though they might be patrolling the mean streets of a Shropshire village. With this shift to a faux-US appearance, attitudes amongst officers on the shop floor of policing began to change. 'Why', they asked, 'have we been given all this equipment? It must surely be because the public that we deal with on a daily basis are a danger to us'. Worse was to come.

On 1st July 1998, following much lobbying by the Police Federation, the body which represents all officers from Constable to Chief Inspector, the Police (Health and Safety) Act 1997 came into force, amending a 1974 piece of legislation which had been drafted to protect industrial workers from preventable injuries. The 1997 Act re-designated police officers as 'employees' for the purposes of Health and Safety legislation and introduced criminal sanctions against Chief Constables for failing to comply with the law by, for example, not conducting 'risk-assessments'. Thus, a twenty-year-old piece of legislation originally intended to apply to boilermakers and furnace-men was now to cover the myriad operational roles of police officers. Furthermore the guidance produced with the legislation made it abundantly clear that supervisors and managers who did not take the requirements of the new law seriously would be personally and corporately liable before the courts. Something akin to organisational panic swept through the police service, and literally thousands of man-hours were spent drafting desk manuals and training syllabuses in every force in the land. New policies complete with forms and checklists by the thousand were produced.

The current Metropolitan Police generic risk-assessment checklist (Form RA1) requires any officer, before conducting any sort of operational activity, to choose from a menu of 238 possible hazards, before submitting the document, with covering forms RA2 and RA3, for detailed assessment by a manager. That individual has then to consider what 'control measures' need to be applied, before submitting his recommendation (with form RA4) to his 'portfolio holder' for the risk assessment to be confirmed and signed off. This masterpiece of bureaucracy, worthy of the 'Office of Circumlocution' in *Little Dorrit*, would be bad enough in terms of the impact that it has on operational policing, but the effect of slavish adherence to bad law, coupled with the new concept of 'officer safety', has had an even more disastrous impact on the mindset of individual officers.

Indeed the concept of 'officer safety' has assumed a life of its own. Having started with the perfectly laudable aim of ensuring that individual officers were adequately protected from violent attacks, a combination of over-reaction to the requirements of legislation and poor leadership has fundamentally undermined the relationship between the police and the public at large. From 1997, in an effort to avoid any possibility of proceedings under the new Act against Chief Officers, every police force has adopted a 'belt and braces' approach to Health and Safety. The positive need to be 'risk averse' has now cascaded down to the most junior personnel and virtually imprinted itself on their DNA. They have no organisational memory of what went before, and so to them any refusal to place themselves at risk, no matter what the circumstances, seems perfectly normal.

One of the most compelling examples of this individual and organisational dereliction of duty occurred on June 6th, 2004, at the village of Highmoor Cross in Oxfordshire, which is within the Thames Valley Police area. Vicky Horgan, aged 27, and her sister Emma Walton, aged 25, were having a family barbecue in the garden of Vicky's home when her estranged husband Stuart, who was drunk and under a direction not to harass or intimidate his wife, suddenly appeared brandishing a .410 shotgun. Also at the barbecue was their mother, Jacqueline Bailey, who attempted to intervene to protect her daughters. Stuart Horgan shot and seriously injured Mrs Bailey before fatally shooting his wife and her sister. According to an internal review overseen by the IPCC, Thames Valley police received two 999 calls at 4.37pm, and armed officers were promptly dispatched to the scene, but waited outside the house for over an hour, on Health and Safety and officer safety grounds, despite the fact that they were told that Stuart Horgan had fled the scene and that there were gravely injured victims on the premises. The women were left in the house and had it not been for the bravery of a neighbour, Georgina Gibson, who did what the police officers were not prepared to do, there is little doubt that the mother of the sisters, Mrs Bailey, would have died of her wounds. As Mrs Gibson rendered first aid, her husband Roy, armed only with a piece of wood, stood over her and used a mobile telephone to give police outside a running commentary about what was happening. It was not until 6.04pm that the police brought an ambulance crew into the house, by which time the two sisters had been dead for some time and their mother was in a coma. In a weasel-worded statement, Thames Valley Police apologised for the 'over-cautious' response to pleas from Mrs Horgan's neighbours and added, '[We] regret very much the distress which the additional delay caused to victims and witnesses.' In earlier times, failures on this scale would have been regarded as shaming, and quite rightly so. They might even have been considered a resigning issue, but in 2004 the only comment from the IPCC was that 'no individual' should be held to account for a failure to render prompt assistance which left two women dead and a third gravely injured.[47]

Attitudinally the impact of 'officer safety' has been just as profound. The philosophy has moved from a reactive/defensive posture to proactive/aggressive one. Every borough operational command unit (BOCU) in the Met and every territorial division across the country now have a full-time 'Officer Safety Trainer' who works from a nationally agreed College of Policing manual. All officers

---

47 IPCC comment on TVP report on fatal shootings at Highmoor Cross (referred 9.6.2004) – nationalarchives.gov.uk

are trained to be *'continually on guard against attack'*, to *'regard every situation, no matter how seemingly benign, as a threat situation'*, to handcuff suspects *'even before the individual has actually offered violence'*. The lesson to be drawn is that the public are your enemy. Police officers, the majority quite young, have been trained to believe that they are continually under threat and must be continually on their guard. The public at large, and particularly crowds, are to be viewed with fear and suspicion.

Nowhere was this more apparent than in the hours of video footage of police dealing with protesters at the G20 demonstrations in the City of London in 2009. Officers routinely holding their steel batons aloft and advancing on peaceful protesters shouting, *'Get back! Get back!'* is a classic example of officer-safety training in action, where the personal safety of yourself or colleague is always at a premium and where the safety of the public is a lower order priority. It is clear that there is a significant minority of officers who see the public as their enemy and groups, larger than two or three individuals, as a potential hazard to be dealt with aggressively. A supervising officer with over ten years' service, who regularly performs duty at public order events and polices a busy division with an active night-time economy, commented upon the developing effect of 'officer safety' training on young officers,

> *'We are now taught an "interview stance" – A way of standing ready to pop into the "ready stance" should circumstances change. Always in pairs, one officer speaks to the suspect [or member of the public], whilst his partner stands with his hand on his baton saying*

nothing but watching the person's body language. At the slightest hint of aggression, say, a raised voice or **disagreement with the officer** *[author's emphasis], the partner will be ready to intervene. Needless to say, officers such as myself take this with the large pinch of salt it deserves. Younger officers, however, are completely reluctant to become directly involved with the public at a community level, something which perhaps should be made compulsory.'[48]*

Eminently sensible and mature officers such as this are becoming something of a rarity as their generation moves on and a harder-faced cohort replaces them. He also made a telling and wise comment, which does him much credit.

'We are not and should never be viewed as the masters. I see that in some colleagues and despise it. These officers are the few who fail us in full glare of the world's press.'[49]

This structural change in attitude has to be set alongside the simultaneous withdrawal from day-to-day street patrolling that has taken place in England and Wales (less so in Scotland), since the turn of the century and the introduction of PCSOs. Where once all young officers would spend their first two, three, or more years getting to know local communities and local people by patrolling designated beats, tightly supervised with disciplinary

---

48 Confidential interview 2010 – Authors research
49 Ibid

sanctions by their sergeants and Inspectors, all that has now been abandoned. New recruits, fresh from training which emphasises the primacy of their own safety over that of the public, now learn from those senior to them, who also know no better, that their job is to respond in groups of never less than two (for officer safety reasons) to emergency calls. When they arrive at the scene of an incident, discretion and common sense are too often abandoned. Most seem to see their role as confined to arresting as many suspects as possible, for any offence, to feed the ever-open maw of government crime performance targets.

Section 110 of the Serious Organised Crime and Police Act 2005 was enacted to replace Section 24 of the Police and Criminal Evidence Act (Arrest without Warrant: Constables), and for the first time since 1829 has empowered any constable to arrest and detain any person without warrant for any offence, no matter how trivial. The police may now arrest for offences which do not attract a sanction of imprisonment and are merely summary in nature, such as minor traffic offences and bye-law offences. In all cases they may use reasonable force, may detain with handcuffs, and may require a DNA sample to be taken. Prior to 2005 powers of arrest were linked to the seriousness of offences, and in particular, whether or not the offence attracted a lengthy term of imprisonment. To arrest someone – to take away their liberty and detain them in a cell – is a matter of constitutional and legal significance and should never be entered into lightly. It is for this reason that officers used to be required to learn 'powers of arrest' under various statutes by rote. To make a false arrest was a serious matter which placed an officer in real danger of losing his job. The large number of summary offences which did not allow for the arrest of the offender (such as breaches of traffic law) would be dealt with by reporting the person for service of a summons, or latterly by issue of a fixed penalty ticket. Since 2005 all those checks and balances have been removed. People can, and have been, arrested for not wearing a seatbelt, for building a snowman on the pavement and refusing to knock it over, for allegedly 'over-feeding' birds in their garden, and even for climbing a tree in one of the Royal Parks. One must ask why such an illiberal power was tacked on to a piece of legislation which supposedly had the primary purpose of setting up the Serious and Organised Crime Agency (SOCA). Those closely associated with the policy-making that went on behind the scenes as the legislation was drafted offer two possible explanations, each one as disturbing as the other.

The first theory relates to violent crime statistics. There are three levels of assault recognised under the law, each becoming progressively more serious. A 'Common Assault' is any minor assault such as a slap or a push which does not lead to injury; the majority of all reported assaults fall into this category. More serious is 'Actual Bodily Harm' which can involve bruising, a minor abrasion or a slight cut. The most serious, as the name implies, is 'Grievous Bodily Harm', which is defined as any assault with or without a weapon leading to serious injury, such as deep lacerations or broken bones. Prior to the passing of Section 110, there was no power of arrest for Common Assault. Victims were usually referred to their 'civil remedy', i.e. advised to take out a private prosecution in the civil courts, or if the offender was known, police would occasionally summons the individual before a magistrate's court.

From 1997, with the police service increasingly driven by the need to meet performance targets for all crime, common assaults were rolled up in the grand total for 'violent crime' but were not being cleared up at the same rate as more serious offences because the police largely dealt with them, as indicated above, outside the criminal justice system. Immediately the Section 110 power was introduced, arrests for trivial common assaults skyrocketed. This was a classic case of lazy policing allowing officers to exercise powers of arrest (which they enjoy), whilst simultaneously boosting the clear-up figures for violent crime (which satisfied the government). The fact that the vast majority of these arrests never lead to the appearance of an offender before a court is, frankly, of absolutely no consequence to the bean-counters in police forces and at the Home Office. A crime can be recorded as 'cleared up' on the delegated authority of a senior officer when someone, usually relatively junior, decides that it has effectively been solved. In many cases this is when an individual who has been arrested accepts a police caution in lieu of appearance before a court. There will be greater discussion of the burgeoning scandal linked to cautions in due course, but in the context of the behaviour of constables at street level, it is easy to see the performance advantages to forces that flow from giving their most junior personnel the widest possible powers of arrest.

The second theory is more sinister. Despite intensive lobbying by ACPO (and its successor body, the NPCC), and their supporters in the Home Office, the police service has not been granted permission to establish a compulsory DNA database for all citizens in the UK. Indeed the coalition government came into office in 2010 with a commitment to curb police excesses in this area. DNA samples are currently taken, by force if necessary, from anyone detained at a police station who has been arrested for an 'arrestable offence'. The individual does not have to be convicted, cautioned, or even charged with the offence; the mere fact that they have been arrested is sufficient to justify the taking of a sample, which is then placed on the DNA database. Whilst not a stated policy (how could it be?), it is claimed that police forces are more than happy for the maximum number of people to pass through police station custody suites, whether or not they are subsequently charged, in order to boost the DNA database. Despite a landmark ruling in the European Court of Human Rights in 2008, that police should not retain the profiles of innocent individuals on the national DNA database, by September 2009 more than 90,000 unconvicted persons had been added since the date of the hearing – the equivalent of 1,480 a day. The Home Office estimate that 20.8% of people on the database are innocent out of a current total of 4.8 million as at 2021. It thus seems likely that the DNA profiles of more than one million innocent people are being retained.

It would be fair to ask how, in a relatively liberal and well-informed western democracy, we have arrived at a position where the youngest, least experienced and most impressionable officers have been invested with such sweeping powers, virtually without any senior supervision. How is it that these same officers are being trained to develop an antipathetic mindset towards the very citizens that they are supposed to be serving and protecting? The answer is in the crisis of leadership that exists in today's police service.

Shortly after being appointed in June 2009, the new Met Commissioner Sir Paul Stephenson spoke to a gathering of all his borough commanders in London. These were his most senior officers at an operational level; all experienced Chief Superintendents, each with responsibility for a workforce of up to 900 personnel. In a surprisingly frank statement which was not meant to be reported, he admitted that he was aware that many Met officers had never patrolled alone in their entire service; that walking the streets in pairs (when they were on the streets at all) had become routine over the past twenty years because no-one had questioned the practice. In a comment that was in effect an admission of weakness, he said that a drive to get uniformed officers out and about on their own had met strong resistance because many simply preferred to have someone to chat to, and managers had been unwilling to intervene. He added,

> *'Cops do like company, just like anybody else, and without intrusive supervision they may slip back into patrolling together. There is no doubt one officer will engage with the public in a different way than two officers gossiping about the latest football results. There are some police officers who joined the Met who have not known much else'.*[50]

During the meeting one borough commander joked that an officer may only need one pair of shoes for his entire career because of the lack of patrolling. When the Chief

---

50 'Bobbies to walk the beat alone, says Met Commissioner' Daily Telegraph (16.3.2009)

Officer of a force of over 33,000 admits that his workforce will not do what he wants, largely because they would prefer to do something else that suits them better, one has to ask why he is being paid £234,000 per annum.

The abandonment of preventive patrols by the police has opened up the market for spurious privatisation of enforcement and has provided some strange bedfellows for our local constabularies. It is absolutely vital in the interests of good governance that powers of enforcement conferred by statute are only vested in individuals who have been rigorously trained, are legally accountable for their actions and understand the need to respect individual rights. Current policy does nothing to support the view that such thinking is anywhere near the centre of police thinking. Since October 2017, nightclub bouncers in Norwich's Prince of Wales Road area, which is where the majority of the city's 'night-time economy' is centred, have been given the power to issue on-the-spot fines on their own authority without consultation with the police. The Norfolk Constabulary, who dreamed up this initiative as part of their strategy to embrace and include their own 'wider police family', have sought to reassure the public by pointing out that they will train and accredit selected bouncers (now referred to by the neutral and bland title 'door-staff') before they are given powers to issue fixed penalty tickets for disorder and drunkenness, more usually issued by police officers. However, it is disturbing to note, but perhaps symptomatic of prevailing attitudes, that local magistrates were neither consulted nor informed about the scheme, and only discovered by chance some eight months after the first bouncer had been accredited. It goes without saying that the public have never been officially informed of this fundamental change in enforcement powers[51]. Sixty miles south of Norwich, in Cambridge, the local police have 'accredited' security guards at the Addenbrookes Hospital site. Using powers under the little-known Police Reform Act 2002, they have now been given authority to demand names and addresses and to issue fixed penalty tickets of £80 for a variety of offences that used to be the exclusive preserve of police such as disorder, insulting or threatening behaviour, and drunkenness[52]. Yet again, in what seems to be a pattern of behaviour, there was absolutely no consultation or discussion prior to the introduction of the scheme; even the Police and Crime Commissioner for Cambridgeshire was kept in the dark until the fact was reported in the press.

There is thus compelling evidence that the average police constable dislikes, with a vengeance, any suggestion that he should walk a beat or work on his own, and actively chooses not to do so. It is also clear that this average police constable regards the public as something between a threat and a nuisance. Most people would take the view that patrolling the streets and looking after the interests of the public were actually the two key elements of his job description, so if our average police constable is not doing either, just what are he and his colleagues doing all day?

The short answer is – not very much at all. The limited number of officers posted to 'response duties' dash hither and thither answering 999 calls which are seldom if ever

---

51 'Magistrate protest as bouncers get power to give on-the-spot fines' The Times (25.7.2009)
52 Ibid

graded in terms of seriousness and importance in the way that they are supposed to be. When arrests are made the response team are immediately 'off the road' as they deal with the mind-numbing bureaucracy of the custody suite. The time-wasting that follows an arrest is not of their making – it is a function of slavish adherence to procedure and the desire of government to monitor targets – but time-wasting there is which means even longer absence from the streets. Those employed on Neighbourhood Policing are few and leave the limited amount of active patrolling that is still done to their PCSOs. The remainder are engaged on a myriad of other duties, all of which are claimed to be worthwhile and focussed on criminality and intelligence-gathering, but which in reality add to an ever-growing list of functions which suck uniform officers away from what should be their core activity – patrolling the streets.

It is worth asking whether these officers, who are supposed to be patrolling our streets, care that more and more of their core activity is being hived off to unaccountable jobsworths, security guards and bouncers? Do they realise that every time they fail to deliver what the public want, they bring the day nearer when the public will wake up to the fact that they are not so special after all, and that perhaps the jobsworths are more effective and cheaper? Every security officer who is given enforcement powers; every PCSO who wanders aimlessly around chatting to his 'partner'; every club bouncer who is held in the embrace of the fictional 'wider police family', all further diminish the role and status of the ordinary constable. Each becomes proof-positive that uniform policing is a low-skill low-status activity that anyone can do after a few weeks' training.

ARMED TO THE TEETH

Only a fool would suggest that the police do not require access to protective equipment and weaponry. On all too many occasions, lives depend on how quickly an individual officer can lay his hands upon a weapon to defend himself or someone else. Such occasions are not rare, so there is a strong argument for such equipment being in the possession of as many trained officers as possible, but it is a fine line between 'needing' the equipment and 'wanting' it.

The police have always had access to firearms. As Michael J Waldren points out in his excellent book *'Armed Police: The Police Use of Firearms Since 1945'*, pistols had been available to officers working on protection duty for many years and for other emergency situations. After the Second World War, the War Office agreed to keep 4,000 rifles and 8,000 revolvers at 14 depots around the country and would make them available to the police on receipt of the memorable, if somewhat bizarre, code words, *'Polwin Section Two Scat Homeffen Collect'*. Twenty-five tons of these weapons were held at Mill Hill in North-West London, close to the Metropolitan Police Training Centre at Hendon.' For over one hundred and fifty years the only weapon that the ordinary police officer was authorised to possess was an 18-inch hardwood truncheon, kept concealed in a pocket in his uniform. There is little doubt that over that time a fair number of officers died or sustained serious injury because they did not have recourse to anything better, but until the mid-1990s there was no groundswell of support for equipping officers with anything more effective. However, the perceived increased risks faced by street-duty officers that have already been described, and the very real increase in the criminal use of firearms from 1990 onwards, changed all that. Specialist armed response units and more frequent deployment of overtly armed personnel at airports and public buildings ensured that the public became more used to seeing 'bobbies' with side-arms or carrying a Heckler and Koch sub-machine gun. The presence of these highly trained and highly effective units also reassured ordinary officers that 'in extremis' they would be able to call for back-up that would be more than equal to the task of protecting them. On pre-planned operations against violent professional criminals, firearms teams are indispensable and justify their existence every time that they are deployed – they are worth every penny that is spent on them. What is often overlooked however is that the sort of policing that they are involved in is not the norm, despite all the hype from the press and media who would have us believe that the streets of our cities and towns swarm with criminals armed to the teeth with guns and knives.

As the 'officer safety' debate developed during the late 1990s, the twin issues of protection of ordinary street-duty officers and the need to have a professional response to determined armed criminality became conflated. The naive assumption was made that every time a constable stepped out of his police station, be it in tough Brixton or picturesque Stratford-upon-Avon, he was placing himself at risk of death and injury. This is nothing short of ridiculous. Most officers, in most places, will serve many years before they suffer the slightest injury. In the twenty-two years between 1985 and 2007, in England, Scotland and Wales, 38 police officers died as the result of criminal assaults. Interestingly

12 (33%) were killed as the result of being run-down by a vehicle. Of the remainder, 12 were shot, 11 stabbed and three died after being beaten. Whilst this is 38 too many deaths, the figure puts the risk to individual officers into some sort of perspective – it means that the chance that an officer will die as the result of a criminal assault in any given year is about 99,000 to 1 – considerably better odds than an infantryman fighting in Afghanistan or Iraq whilst serving on the real 'front line', in those recent conflicts.

Nonetheless, under the dual pressure of Health and Safety legislation and highly effective lobbying from the Police Federation, officer-safety equipment became ever more sophisticated and obtrusive. Old-style truncheons were replaced, first with long acrylic side-handle batons imported from the United States, and then with the murderously lethal ASP, a heavy steel extendable baton which could be worn on the new equipment belt. During the early 1990s Kwik-cuffs were issued to all officers to replace the old pre-war style handcuffs. They are not as benign as the name might suggest because although primarily manufactured to allow for rapid application on a struggling suspect, the two wrist loops are joined by a rigid bar which can be twisted by the arresting officer to inflict great pain in order to subdue the prisoner. From around 1996 the 'protective weapon' of choice became CS spray, which although used in various forms by the majority of police departments in the United States, was and continues to be the subject of heated debate about its effectiveness, safety, and long-term impact on health. Nonetheless in March 1996 ACPO authorised a pilot scheme in which officers in sixteen forces were allowed to use CS spray operationally when subduing violent prisoners. A training officer in the Northamptonshire Police, described by the 'Independent' as 'one of the country's leading police self-defence experts', Inspector Peter Boatman, was barred by his Chief Constable from taking part in the pilot because of legal liability over what was regarded as a dangerous weapon. We shall meet Inspector Boatman again. Nonetheless, after evaluation of the pilots and continuing pressure from rank-and-file officers, CS spray canisters were added to the equipment carried on the belts of all officers.

By the beginning of the new millennium the transformation of the British police officer was almost complete. In less than six years, at a cost of hundreds of millions of pounds, and without any public debate whatsoever, his uniform, attitude and individual kit and equipment had changed beyond recognition. The service ethos, so long prized as the distinguishing feature of British policing, was now honoured in the breach, with officers being actively encouraged to take no risks on behalf of the public which might in any sense prejudice their own personal safety. Gone were the days when officers would leap into the Thames to rescue someone or cover their faces with a wet towel before entering a smoke-filled room to find an unconscious child. These are now jobs for 'properly equipped and trained professionals', such as the Marine Police or the Fire Brigade, and even if the person in the river is swept away or the child in the room dies, the prudent officer must await the arrival of others and not take action which might hazard his safety. His job is done once he has made the call. However, despite all that had been done and all that had changed to the perceived benefit of rank-and-file officers, the clamour for more, and yet more sophisticated, protective equipment continued unabated.

Tom Swift is the hero of a series of early science-fiction novels published in the United States from 1910, and throughout the twentieth century. Aimed at young readers the stories describe how Tom, who is a brilliant inventor, designs and makes all manner of technological marvels for the benefit of mankind. The books are tremendously popular in the United States, have never been out of print, and even today are written by a series of ghost-writers. In the mid nineteen-seventies Jack Cover, an astro-scientist who worked at NASA, invented and patented the very first stun gun which used high voltage electricity to overload the subject's nervous system. Because it fired a projectile and because he was a life-long fan of the Tom Swift novels, he named his invention the 'Thomas A. Swift Electric Rifle', now more commonly known by the acronym TASER.

In the early 1990s an entrepreneur named Rick Smith contacted Cover with a proposition to develop the Taser as a self-defence weapon and widen the market coverage so that it could be sold to private individuals, law enforcement agencies and the military. Having found an investor to provide funding, they formed 'Air Taser Inc.' which would later become 'Taser International Inc.' The company commissioned technical research and as a result re-engineered the gun to work with a nitrogen propellant rather than gunpowder which meant that it was no longer categorised as a firearm under US law (although technically it is still illegal in the UK and classed as a prohibited weapon). Initially only the Los Angeles County Sheriff's Department adopted Tasers – sales to other law enforcement agencies were poor. In 1998, the company embarked on a new development programme, named 'Project Stealth', with the aim of streamlining the design so that it could deliver a sufficiently high voltage to stop 'extremely combative, violent individuals,' especially those who were resistant or immune to non-lethal chemicals such as Mace. As a result of this development work the Advanced Taser was brought to the market in 2000.

The company were supported by a number of retired and serving senior officers from the military and law enforcement worlds who all vouchsafed that the Taser was efficient and safe. The Taser parent company became a regular exhibitor at law-enforcement and other specialist conferences and tradeshows in the USA and Europe, offering their product as a non-lethal alternative for the police market. Following a period of intensive marketing in the US in 1999 and 2000, the Advanced Taser became a runaway success. By the following year, around 750 American law enforcement agencies had either tested or deployed the weapon. By 2010 more than nine thousand police, prison and military bodies in over forty countries were using the full range of available Taser weaponry. By any definition, 'Taser International' is a big business. They have sold nearly two hundred thousand separate units to police forces in the USA alone and a further one hundred thousand to private individuals in the forty-three American states where it is legal to do so. As of 2021, according to one study, over 15,000 law enforcement and military agencies around the world used Tasers as part of their use of force strategy. On average, Tasers are used 904 times per day worldwide, or about once every two minutes. The company are aggressive in defending the reputation of their product and do not hesitate to use the courts to challenge any suggestion that the weapon is unsafe or causes death, despite the fact that there are real concerns in many quarters about just how safe it is for anyone to be felled with a 50,000 volt charge.

It is at this point that we meet Inspector Peter Boatman again. Prior to his retirement from the Northamptonshire Police in 2002 he was the head of operational training for the force and as such had been entrusted by his Chief Constable with the responsibility of researching the viability of 'less lethal weapons' for Northamptonshire and for ACPO. His Chief Constable at the time was Chris Fox, who by 2006 had been knighted and was highly influential, making national policing policy as the President of ACPO. Boatman, who already had a reputation as a very visible proponent of the use of CS spray by police, had apparently first encountered the Taser at an exhibition held in Germany in 1999. The following year, Boatman developed the first Taser training programme in Britain, which was adopted and further developed by ACPO. By 2001 he was described as 'a national and international expert' on Tasers and apparently advised Home Office scientists who were at that time carrying out research into 'less lethal' weapons.

In a well-researched but little read article published in 'The Times' in October 2005, two experienced investigative journalists, Ali Hussain and Gareth Walsh, set out the intriguing background to the relationship between Boatman, 'Taser International Inc.' and the subsequent roll-out of the Taser to police officers in the UK. Their research disclosed that Boatman had a 50% share in a company that sold Tasers, 'Pro-Tect Systems'. Simultaneously, in his senior operational role as a serving police officer in Northamptonshire, he was devising Britain's first police training programme for the use of such weapons and was in charge of assessing the merits of Taser as an 'impartial' expert on the weapon. In the three years after he retired in April 2002, his firm provided 1,500 Tasers worth about £1million to twenty British police forces. By 2009 'Pro-Tect Systems' could proudly proclaim on their website that they were the sole UK distributor for all 'Taser International' products. As Hussain and Walsh showed, disclosure of the apparent conflict of interest came after Taser International, the US manufacturer, was accused in the US courts of providing American police officers with share options potentially worth $1 millon. Companies House records seen by the journalists showed that Boatman had taken a 50% stake in a start-up company, Pro-Tect Systems, in December 2000. He became a director of the firm on December 5 and resigned three weeks later, on December 27, but continued to hold his stake in the company. In February 2001, Pro-Tect received the Taser exclusivity contract for the UK. Within two months Boatman was acting as an adviser to the Home Office on whether to issue Tasers to British officers. In December 2001, three months after the Home Office approved trial imports, Boatman publicly rebutted claims by Police Federation officers that Tasers could be dangerous. He wrote 'with sadness' to the widely read Police Review magazine that *'this technology is very effective — more than any other technique, device or equipment for establishing control over violent and dangerous subjects'*. Boatman retired from the Northamptonshire police on April 16, 2002. Two days later he was installed as chairman of Pro-Tect Systems. His fellow founding director and friend, Kevin Coles, had been running the firm in the meantime.

Boatman was challenged by Hussain and Walsh on the detail of their investigation, yet despite the records at Companies House he insisted he had had no connection with Pro-Tect Systems before retiring from the police and had never been paid by Taser to do anything on their behalf. 'Taser International Inc' said it was not aware that Boatman had a share in Pro-Tect Systems whilst still a serving police officer. In November 2004 Boatman put on a public demonstration of his confidence in the safety of Tasers by firing one at his wife, Stephanie (who was a senior account manager with the firm). The demonstration marked the high point of a five-year campaign by Boatman and his company to convince the Home Office and ACPO that the Taser should be accepted as a standard piece of police equipment. In April 2003 the Home Office approved trials of the Taser in five police forces after it beat rival bidders in subduing violent offenders without killing them. It was cleared for national use in September 2004 by the Home Secretary and ACPO, and in October 2005 ACPO agreed that it should no longer be confined to the kind of threatening incidents where a normal firearm could be used. This decision opened the floodgates for issue and deployment of the Taser to officers as personal issue equipment because it cleared the way for ordinary-duty personnel, not just trained firearms officers, to be allowed access to the weapon. Despite serious concerns about the independence of the process of selection and endorsement of the Taser, concerns about the role that Boatman might have had in influencing the decision, and the apparent official disregard of data relating to safety, the Home Office remained adamant that it had reached its decision on the basis of independent research. Indeed, the love affair that the Home Office had with the Taser had grown stronger and deeper as the years passed by, almost certainly as a means of keeping the loyalty of the police during the 'War on Terror' by giving them more and better toys. In November 2008, the then Home Secretary Jacqui Smith announced that she would make £8 million available in order to buy around ten thousand extra Tasers for the police in England and Wales, with additional funding for the training of 30,000 officers. She took the decision in the face of stark opposition from the Metropolitan Police Authority who refused to equip non-firearms trained officers with the equipment[53], and Amnesty International who claimed that Tasers had been responsible for at least 320 deaths in the United States alone.[54]

The transformation of the Dixonesque 'bobby' is still a work in progress but it is unlikely that the trend can be stopped or even reversed, so deep are the attitudinal changes of those now serving. In a relatively short period of time the operational model for policing in the UK has changed from

---

53 Public Service Review – Home Affairs, Issue 19 (3.4.2009)

54 A tragic footnote to the subject of Tasers and their use by the police service came in October 2010, when the Home Office withdrew Pro-Tect's licence following suggestions that the company had provided equipment to Northumbria Police in breach of its licence during the Raoul Moat manhunt. On 2nd October it was reported in the media that Boatman had taken his own life as a result. An inquest in 2011 returned an open verdict.

policing by consent, to policing by compulsion, and the role of those at the top of the organisation, the 'bosses', has been absolutely pivotal in terms of what they have, and have not, done to meet the challenge of change.

THE BOSSES

Towards the end of 1944, the Permanent Secretary at the Ministry of Aircraft Production, a career civil servant by the name of Mr (later Sir) Harold Scott, was busily engaged seven days a week on behalf of his Secretary of State, Sir Stafford Cripps. All the problems associated with manufacturing, supplying, and maintaining the thousands of aircraft that the Royal Air Force needed to fight a war in Europe and the Far East landed on Scott's desk. In no small measure, the success of the air war against Germany had been due as much to the diligence of this anonymous civil servant as it had to the bravery and sacrifice of the aircrews. He was firmly of the view that he had a job to do that would take him beyond the end of the war and into peacetime, as the role of the RAF changed with the introduction of jet aircraft, and the new military challenges that the nation would face in a post-war world. Scott was therefore extremely surprised one morning to receive a telephone call from the private secretary to Herbert Morrison, the Home Secretary, asking him to 'pop along Whitehall' to see the minister.

Scott had absolutely no idea why he was being summoned to see such an august figure as Morrison. He had joined the civil service in 1911 after coming down from Cambridge and for a short period in those days before the First World War had worked in the Home Office police policy department, before moving to the Prisons Commission, and thence to other Whitehall departments. He knew Morrison from their time together in the early years of the war when they had both served at the Ministry of Home Security and assumed that the Home Secretary wanted to discuss some aspect of civil defence planning. In his autobiography published in 1954, Scott describes their meeting,

> *'Mr Morrison, who has a sense of humour, may have been aware of what was in my mind and wished to take me by surprise, for one of his first questions to me was, "Can you ride a horse?" Somewhat disconcerted, I replied that I had never been much of a horseman and had not ridden for many years; but I said I had no doubt I could ride well enough not to disgrace myself. The Home Secretary then invited me to accept after the war the position of Commissioner of Police of the Metropolis.'[55]*

Such was the way that senior appointments were made in those far distant days. No advertising of the vacancy in the Sunday broadsheets, no recruitment consultants, no long list or shortlist, not even an interview; just, 'Can you ride a horse?' and an immediate offer of the most important job in policing.

Sir Harold Scott served with distinction as

---

55 Page 11 'Scotland Yard' Sir Harold Scott (pub. Andre Deutsch (1954))

Commissioner of the Met from 1945 until 1953 and was held in the highest regard by everyone in the force, from the newest constable up to and including his senior team at Scotland Yard. He remains the only civilian with no previous police background to hold the post since the Second World War, and one of just fifteen individuals to serve as head of the Met in that time. For a variety of reasons, Scott stands out as someone who really made a difference, along with only one or two others in the half century since he retired. He steered the Met from war to peace and crushed the petty corruption that existed in the police in austerity Britain. Because of his background in government ministries where scientific innovation had been the impetus for beneficial development, he introduced technological change and promoted individuals who showed an aptitude for intellectual enquiry – something that was almost unheard of in the late 1940s. His greatest contribution however was in terms of the status of policing and the 'behind the scenes' lobbying that he did to improve conditions of service and pay. His legacy was a stronger, more effective, and more self-confident Met that acted as an exemplar to other forces throughout the nineteen-fifties and beyond. Scott's commissionership gives the lie to those who would claim that only senior officers who have spent their entire career in the police can be entrusted with the top jobs and that such individuals must have operated as police officers before they can truly understand the business of policing. In fact, Scott provides the perfect example of someone who already had an established track-record of excellence in an unrelated field, with transferable skills that could be applied to something new and different. It is tempting to suggest that if the concept worked with an individual drawn from the civil service, why should it not work with a similarly skilled man or woman from business or industry?

Sadly, most of the other Commissioners who followed Scott came and went barely leaving a ripple on the surface of public life or any lasting impression on the Metropolitan Police. Who now remembers Sir John Nott-Bower in the mid nineteen-fifties, or Sir David McNee in the seventies? A few were brought low by allowing unmerited confidence in their own ability to cloud their better judgement when confronted with operational challenges. At least one was simply not up to the job. Interestingly, there is a consensus amongst those who have some knowledge of the subject that there has been just one other Commissioner in the seven decades since 1945 who can be compared with Scott as someone who truly shaped the future of the force and left an enduring impression on policing in the UK.

Sir Robert Mark, who was Commissioner from 1972 to 1977, was in many ways an 'outsider'. Cerebral, principled, and not afraid to operate as a minority of one when he knew that he was right, he had spent his entire police career in the provinces, eventually being appointed as one of the first Chief Constables to have worked his way up from constable, serving in every rank on the way. His skill, unusual in those days, of being able to define and implement his vision for policing, together with his reputation for unimpeachable integrity, brought him to the notice of the Home Office very early on. In 1968 Sir Joseph Simpson, who had been Commissioner for ten years, unexpectedly died in office and was replaced by his somewhat lack-lustre deputy, Sir John Waldron. To the surprise of many, and the chagrin of a number of corrupt CID officers at Scotland Yard, Mark was plucked from the relative obscurity of Leicester where he was serving as Chief Constable and prevailed upon to take up the vacant post of Deputy Commissioner of the Met. Undoubtedly, he was the right man for the job at the right time. It was an open secret in Fleet Street and amongst those in the know at the Home Office that systemic corruption amongst the CID in the Met was effectively out of control. The Obscene Publications Branch at the Yard was literally in the pocket of West End criminals, largely nightclub owners who ran this lucrative trade by intimidation and the bribery of senior police officers in Soho and Scotland Yard. From the day that he arrived in London, despite lacking the support of Waldron who clearly did not want him, Mark was ruthless with any officer found to be corrupt and during his four years as Deputy Commissioner and five as Commissioner (1972 to 1977), over 90 such officers were sacked, more than a dozen imprisoned, including a Commander, and over 200 driven out of the force under the threat of suspension and disciplinary proceedings. Until he took over at the Yard, the CID in London was, to quote a famous comment attributed to a very corrupt and very senior detective, 'A firm within a firm!' A flavour of the time can be gained from the following anecdote related by an officer who served in the Obscene Publications Branch in the early seventies, but who returned to uniform duties at his own request when he realised the extent of the corruption around him.

> *'I was a Detective Constable in COC1 from about 1970. I really thought that I had "arrived" being part of a top squad at the Yard, but I soon saw the way*

things operated. You were tested early on, and if you didn't take your share then you were immediately "sent to Coventry" and excluded from any of the really good operations. You were just given rubbish jobs to keep you out of the way. I didn't want any part of it and decided that the way out for me was to take promotion and return to uniform as a Sergeant, so I studied hard and in 19-- passed the competitive exam coming in the first hundred. In those days that meant that you automatically got an interview at the Police Staff College at Bramshill for the Special Course [Accelerated Promotion Scheme] which would fast-track you to Inspector. I really wanted to get on the course, so I worked bloody hard, went down for the interview and waited. A couple of weeks later, on a Friday evening, my D.I. (who was a spectacularly corrupt guy) called me into his office to tell me that he had received a memo saying that I had failed the interview. I was pretty choked and must have shown it because [Detective Inspector] got a bottle of Scotch out of his desk, poured me a drink and tried to cheer me up. He smiled, patted me on the shoulder and then said something that I have never forgotten, which tells you all that you need to know about the CID in those days, "Never mind L-----, you haven't missed anything. They may teach you to be a senior officer down at Bramshill, but they don't teach you how to count £500 in fivers in the dark and hide it in your underpants!'[56]

---

56 Confidential interview (2009) – Author's research

Divisional detectives across the capital did not see themselves as in any sense answerable to their local uniform Superintendents at police stations, only to their own senior officers in the CID. Officers on elite units such as the Obscene Publications Branch or the Drugs Squad barely considered themselves to be part of the Metropolitan Police at all, and regarded Mark's efforts to clean them up as an unwarranted intrusion by someone they dismissed as a provincial hick. There were active attempts to undermine and discredit him whilst he was Commissioner and Deputy Commissioner, with contacts in the press being used to plant false stories that Mark had psychiatric problems and had had a nervous breakdown because of the pressures of the job. Junior and some senior detectives indulged in wholesale destruction of documents, concealment of evidence and obstruction of investigations by outside forces into the activities of the Met CID (notably by the Dorset Police during 'Operation Countryman' in the mid-seventies). The fight for the soul of policing in London went on for all of the time that Mark held office, but as he retired in 1977 it was clear that he had changed the culture of the organisation forever. His changes saw the end of what was sometimes referred to as 'noble cause' corruption, where criminals were effectively framed when detectives knew them to be guilty but just did not have the evidence. He completely overhauled and professionalised the investigation of complaints and corruption in the Met and, most importantly of all, placed all detectives firmly under the command of senior uniform officers on divisions and elsewhere. It is no exaggeration to say that Mark broke the back of police corruption in London and whilst there will always be the occasional example of criminal behaviour by a few senior and junior officers, these are now the exception, and the days of systemic wrongdoing are long gone.

As with the Metropolitan Police, so it is with every other force in the country. The strength and resilience of any organisation is a function of the ability and skills of the people at the top. There are examples galore in the private and public sectors of organisations which have failed because they have paid insufficient attention to the recruitment, selection, training and mentoring of their next generation of leaders. Continuity is the key in this process, because without an organisational memory there is the ever-present danger of repeating past errors and wasting the time of highly paid senior people on initiatives aimed at re-inventing the wheel. In big organisations such as the police, the problem is compounded by the fact that the numbers required are enormous (there are some 4,000 posts across the UK above the rank of Inspector), and the national pool of talent of those with the necessary character and intellect is limited. Thus, if the police service is to be managed effectively, with a self-replacing cadre of senior people who have been brought up in the culture of the organisation, there needs to be an aggressive strategy to recruit the best available talent.

In a thoughtful article[57], published in the early 1990s but still relevant today, the former Director General of Army

---

57 'Leadership' – Lt General Sir Robin Carnegie (Senior non-Service Member of the Home Office Accelerated Promotion Scheme for the Police, Prison and Fire Services) (1992)

Training, Lieutenant General Sir Robin Carnegie, made the point that a 'direct entry' officer stream, whilst it meets the needs of the military admirably, would not suit the police service because the role of 'officers' is very different. He also noted that fashions change; that throughout the seventies and the eighties the received wisdom was that people with the necessary leadership skills could only be found in the limited pool of university graduates. That was a far too doctrinaire view to take, because even with the widening of further and higher education then just starting, there were still many reasons why intelligent men did not go to university, '...*some do not wish to delay their entry into the police service; others are late developers. There must always be a route to the top for them*'. Carnegie came down firmly in favour of the Accelerated Promotion Scheme for Graduates (APSG) (formerly known as the Graduate Entry Scheme), which would seek to recruit the best candidates from the best universities and fast-track them through the ranks of constable and sergeant so that they reached Inspector with about four years' service and Superintendent in under ten years. The scheme would also be open to applicants from within the service who were already constables, but who might or might not be graduates; just the sort of late developers referred to by Carnegie. On the face of it, such a scheme would meet the needs of the service, but there were and are unintended consequences in designating such individuals as the future high-flyers of the organisation.

The first problem has to do with unfulfilled expectations. Not everyone will have a Chief Constable's baton in his knapsack, indeed some will plateau at lower ranks, and some may not take off at all. This led to a very high drop-out rate from the scheme with good recruits leaving the service entirely, because of a perception that it had not delivered what was promised. Another difficulty relates to the constant need for those at the helm of the service to continually demonstrate their commitment to 'equality' in the broadest sense of the term. In 1999 and 2000 Her Majesty's Inspectorate of Constabulary conducted research into the APSG. Amongst other things the findings demonstrated that nationally as few as 13 graduates were offered places on the APSG in some years and that only 1 ethnic minority graduate had won a place in the previous four years. Analysis showed that this disproportionality was largely due to the fact that the APSG 'milk round' each year was confined to those universities where previous good quality applicants had been found, which tended to be Oxford, Cambridge, and the well-established Russell Group institutions. Almost by definition these were not places where large numbers of ethnic minority students tended to study. There was a great deal of 'angst' about these findings at the time which resulted in the APSG liaison officers being directed to visit more 'new' universities and ex-Polytechnics which had a more diverse student body.

The re-direction of resources made absolutely no difference whatsoever, and at a Home Office conference on 'Ethnic Minority Recruitment' in April 1999, Her Majesty's Chief Inspector of Constabulary, Sir David O'Dowd, told those assembled,

> *'The message that the service sends to ethnic minority communities about the fast-track promotion scheme*

is depressingly clear. If you are a white university graduate your chances of reaching the final stage of selection, as a potential leader of the service, is about one in 20. If you are from an ethnic minority you will have to settle for odds of 1 in a hundred or worse.'

Putting aside the fact that his comments were obviously based upon a flawed understanding of statistics; in common with so many leading figures of the time O'Dowd was adopting the mantra that simple proportionality was the ultimate aim, irrespective of the quality of the applicant.

The pressing need to find police leaders has been a source of animated debate for decades within the service. The 1929 Royal Commission on the Police challenged one of the basic principles that had been set out by Sir Robert Peel in 1829, which had stated, *'It would be inimical to the police interests to limit appointments to the higher posts to those who had entered the police as Constables. Such posts should be filled by the best men available irrespective of the source from whence they are drawn.'* As a result, in 1930 the Dixon report[58] recommended the establishment of a National Police College to be jointly funded by the Home Office and all other local police authorities. It was intended that the college would provide, *'higher training for officers for their work as instructors, detectives, Staff Officers and Chief Officers together with the creation of facilities for higher instruction in a variety of subjects and provide for the development of senior officers. It [would] cater for young*

---

58 National Archives – HMSO (1930) Sir Arthur Lewis Dixon

officers of potential and senior officers who needed to develop their careers.' The proposal was accepted by the Home Office but was vehemently resisted by the Police Federation who interpreted the scheme as introduction of an officer class by stealth. In the event they need not have worried because the Depression and a decline in public finances ensured that the National Police College never saw the light of day in the inter-war period.

In 1931, Lord Trenchard was appointed Commissioner of the Metropolitan Police. As the man who had transformed the Royal Flying Corps into the Royal Air Force, he was used to dealing with the complexities of big organisations and his military background, which included threatening to shoot 5,000 mutinying soldiers in Southampton in 1919, was thought to equip him for the role. A martinet with scant regard for 'the lower ranks', on taking up his post at Scotland Yard he soon decided that all the many problems that plagued the Met in the inter-war period were the result of poor leadership and the lack of an officer cadre. Sir Arthur Dixon, who had written the report which proposed the National Police College in 1930, had lunch with Trenchard at Brooks Club in the West End late in 1931 and suggested to him that the Met was large enough on its own to justify such a college. Trenchard jumped at the idea, and the Hendon Police College was created as a direct-entry officer system for the force. The first course in 1932 had 32 students, all of whom were destined to become Inspectors at the end of their training. Twenty-two of them had been selected from within the force, whilst the remaining 10, aged between twenty and twenty-six, were direct entrants with an examination pass at school certificate level, or were exempt because they held some higher educational qualification.

Their reception into such a conservative organisation as the Metropolitan Police in the nineteen-thirties was far from straightforward. These young Inspectors, sometimes more than twenty years younger than the other Inspectors at their stations and clearly marked for stardom, were the cause of bitterness, jealousy, and resentment. However, subsequent research[59] has shown that the impact of the Hendon-trained 'Trenchard Scheme' men can be exaggerated. Of the 197 students selected for the scheme, 92 (48%) never progressed from Inspector to Superintendent. It is suggested that this may have been due to prejudice within the force and poor selection at the initial recruitment stage. Undoubtedly there was an element of both, but in the long term it did not matter; Trenchard was replaced by Sir Philip Game in 1935 after the scheme had been running for a mere three years. Game had no enthusiasm for a direct entry 'officer corps', disliked Trenchard intensely, and shortly after his appointment he changed the entry rules for Hendon and insisted upon a compulsory length of qualifying police service for direct entrants. One unintended consequence of the Trenchard scheme was the fact that it produced a large cohort of comparatively young Inspectors and Superintendents, who then competed with officers who were not Hendon graduates, thereby causing a blockage in the promotion system denying advancement to many able men. A few

---

59 National Police Improvement Agency (NPIA) (2009) – Bramshill Police College Library

of the Trenchard scheme graduates went on to have distinguished careers, ending up as Chief Constables of various forces up and down the country, but overall there was settled agreement that Trenchard had very nearly ruined the Metropolitan Police by effectively closing many avenues of promotion to the non-college man. By 1935 morale was on the floor and had Trenchard not left when he did, he might well have had another mutiny on his hands, rivalling anything that he had faced in 1919.

After the war, there was another attempt to put Dixon's 1930 proposal into effect with the opening in 1948 of the new Police College at Ryton-on-Dunsmore near Coventry which had the stated aim of providing higher training for police, as opposed to developing a direct entry officer class. However the following year the Oaksey Committee reported that it was not convinced that the enduring problem of finding future leaders of the police service had been adequately addressed and appeared to be less than impressed by what was planned at Ryton. Throughout the nineteen-fifties there was growing concern that the police service was 'sleepwalking' to a position where in subsequent decades, because of a failure to take immediate action, there would be insufficient men of experience and ability to lead the police service in the 1970s and beyond. Yet another Royal Commission on Policing was established under the chairmanship of Sir Henry Willink, which reported in 1962. He laid out the problem in graphic detail and stated,

> *'It is therefore important, if the Service is to produce enough leaders of the right calibre, that training of*

the right sort should be made available to those who have demonstrated that they are suitable for higher rank'[60]

The search for those future leaders, together with the structured career development of more senior officers started in 1962 with the new Special Course. Intended for young constables who had passed their sergeants examination and had been identified at an extended interview as having exceptional potential, they were taken away from their force for a year at the Staff College. There they received a whole raft of specialist and academic training before returning to their forces as Inspectors, ready for promotion to the highest ranks. Competition was fierce, with only 4% of applicants managing to get on to the course. The first course was launched amid much publicity with the Daily Telegraph reporting, 'Thirty-six constables have been selected for the pilot course of a new scheme to offer accelerated promotion and to give special training to potential leaders of Britain's police forces'. Ever conscious of the disastrous consequences of the Trenchard scheme and the need to keep the Police Federation on board, it was made abundantly clear to all concerned that the course was only open to officers who were already serving as constables in the police. The trick was in identifying them at an early stage and monitoring their development.

By 1967 the Special Course was well established, with around 40 students per year; however, in that year a Home Office working party was set up to review the extent to

---

60 Final Report of the Royal Commission on the Police (Chairman: Sir Henry Willink MC QC), Cmnd 1728, May 1962

which applicants with higher educational qualifications were being attracted to the police and came up with disturbing findings. Analysis showed that in the twenty years between 1945 and 1965 of the half million people who graduated from all the universities in England and Wales, only 25 joined the police service. In 1965 five graduates were recruited; in 1966 the number rose to 16, but as the total recruit intake in that year was 6,800, graduates represented a mere 0.2%. Hardly reassuring for the service as a whole because the 1966 cohort would not retire until 1996 and would therefore have to provide a large proportion of the 'top teams' for all 43 police forces in the 1980s and 1990s.

It was at this point that the Home Office and senior policymakers encountered a strategic problem about what to do with graduates, should the police service be able to attract them in greater numbers. Although it had never been stated explicitly, the assumption held by the few graduate entrants already in the service, and by those managing them, was that possession of a degree automatically meant that the individual would achieve Chief Officer rank (i.e. Assistant Chief Constable, or Met Commander, or above). From the late 1960s, with the nature of policing changing to keep pace with a rapidly changing society, the Home Office began to think seriously about what sort of police service the country needed in terms of the personnel it employed. As was pointed out in a confidential Met report,

> *'Police work has always carried unique powers and responsibilities. It requires high qualities of judgement*

in balancing the needs arising from the fight against crime, against the need to avoid infringing individual liberties. It has been apparent that the police service has no less need of well-educated personnel than industry or other public services. The need is not confined to the highest ranks in the service. There is a need for a general improvement in the educational level of the service. The Home Office consider it reasonable to aim at a wide distribution of recruits with higher educational qualifications throughout a broad range of ranks. It would be unrealistic to expect a graduate to join the police with the expectation of remaining a constable throughout his service, but the Home Office does not accept that only the very top jobs are suitable for graduates or that only graduates should fill them."[61]

The 1967 Home Office working party considered the evidence before it and proposed the establishment of a Graduate Entry Scheme (GES), which came into existence in 1968. Professionally advertised and marketed the scheme was aimed at undergraduates in their third year and offered them the chance to be selected for the Special Course, ahead of actually joining the Police service. After a slow start (only 1 successful applicant in 1970), it reached its peak in the mid to late eighties with over 30 successful applicants per year. As was the case with internal applicants for the Special Course, competition for places on the GES was fiercely competitive

---

[61] Confidential submission to Assistant Commissioner 'D' Dept, Metropolitan Police, December 1967 – Author's research (NPIA) Bramshill Police College Library

with anything from 1,500 to 1,800 undergraduates applying each year. This allowed the assessors to be highly selective and the proportion of successful applicants offered places seldom rose above 5% and on occasions was as low as 1%. Within a few years the nature of the Special Course changed as increasing numbers of successful GES officers took places on the scheme, together with 'internal' applicants who had not joined via the GES but nonetheless held degrees. By the late 1970s and early 1980s, almost by default and without there being any stated policy, the Special Course was almost exclusively a 'graduate only' course. Between 1971 and 1988 the number of graduates in the police service rose from 267 to 6,625 and has continued to grow in the thirty years since. As already discussed, real concerns about the value of some of the degrees now offered by the 'new' universities has, to a certain extent, devalued the currency but the fact remains that there is now an effective bar on the advancement of any officer even to middle management roles unless he or she possesses a university degree. Indeed the possession of an MBA or a doctorate in addition to a first degree is almost '*de rigueur*' for senior posts. Whilst the number of applicants tended to rise and fall with the availability of good graduate employment elsewhere (in the professions, the City, etc), the police service had, by the late nineteen-nineties, established itself as a graduate employer of choice and many of the concerns about the availability of the next generation of leaders seemed to have been solved.

As the police service entered the new millennium, however, short-termism once again became the order of the day. The HMIC review of the Accelerated Promotion Scheme for Graduates (APSG) damned the concept with faint praise, and offered no real philosophical or strategic approach to a problem that had bedevilled the service since the 1920s. From the Inspectorate, who had oversight of the scheme on behalf of the forces in England and Wales, there was a deafening silence – so intent were they on ensuring that everything they did was 'equality and diversity' compliant. In 2002 the APSG was scrapped – branded as 'elitist and discriminatory' but the challenge of identifying leaders for the 2030s, 2040s and beyond has not gone away.

In March 2009, Peter Neyroud, former Chief Constable of Thames Valley, Winchester old boy, Oxford graduate, and at the time Chief Executive of the National Policing Improvement Agency (NPIA) which oversaw all recruiting, training, and career development of police officers in England and Wales, made some pretty robust comments to the 'Times'[62] when asked about the position of graduates in the modern police service. His views were radical and did not necessarily represent mainstream thinking in the police establishment, but Neyroud was influential and had the rare skill of being able to think strategically and speak incisively. Interviewed at a careers fair at his old school he was scathing about the Home Office's decision to scrap the GES, describing it as one of the 'most foolish' decisions of the past decade. As head of the NPIA he decided to revive the scheme and said that it was time for the service to end what he referred to as inverted snobbery. He did not believe that there is a shortage of young graduates wishing to join the police, but said that the service must do much more to offer a professional career.

---

62 'Police seek to recruit university graduates', The Times (20.3.2009)

'If we are going to attract the people we need, we have to offer people from middle-class backgrounds, whose children now have an expectation of a university education, the challenge of a profession that meets a graduate's expectations. [At this career fair] the amount of information on medicine and law was about three inches thick; the folder relating to the police was only a couple of brochures – it says it all. What I inherited was a structure that decided that [being at careers fairs or good universities] was not the right place to be. It was completely and absolutely barking mad. You have to go out and recruit at the best universities. If you take the top twenty Russell group of universities, the police service was not routinely and regularly at their career's fairs.'

The successor body to the NPIA, the College of Policing (established in 2012), far from reintroducing the Graduate Entry Scheme opted instead for a policy which simultaneously balkanised and privatised the entire process. It is acknowledged by participants and practitioners to be a disaster and barely 'fit for purpose'.

From April 2023 it will no longer be possible for any applicant to join the police service unless enrolled under a complex raft of schemes defined by an alphabet soup of acronyms. There is the Police Constable Degree Apprenticeship (PCDA) intended for non-graduates in which they will study part-time whilst serving, for 3 years, for a 'police degree'. The Degree Holder Entry Programme (DHEP) is a two-year work-based route for established graduates in any discipline ending up with a graduate diploma in Professional Policing Practice awarded by the College. A more intensive route than the DHEP is the Detective Degree Holder Entry Programme (DDHEP), a two-year work-based degree programme biased towards applicants seeking direct entry posts as investigators. The Professional Policing Degree Holder (PPDH) route is intended for applicants who have completed a specialist degree in policing, currently offered by a number of low-status 'new' universities and former colleges of Further Education. Graduation with such a degree does not, however, guarantee selection for a post in a force. Lastly, there is the National Leadership Development Programme (NLDP) overseen by 'Police Now', a private company contracted by the Home Office with a somewhat confused remit to oversee recruitment, campaign against anti-social behaviour, and raise the status of policing with the public. No-one has ownership of the strategic policy for graduate recruitment, and no-one has ever defined precisely what the police service is looking for. There is no hint of 'joined up thinking' on the subject.

None of this goes anywhere near Neyroud's original vision, which was that graduate 'high achievers' with identified potential would be accepted for appointment to a force, and after two years' initial training as a constable, provided the young entrant passes the necessary promotion examination, would be accelerated through the middle ranks to Superintendent level. Neyroud's vision is clear and unambiguous:

'A 20 or 21-year-old wants to know clearly what we offer and that is what the private sector provides.

Two years of training and then rapid promotion, provided you have made the grade. We [also] need to encourage forces to accept that a percentage of jobs need to be advertised externally. After all, those that do not do it will quickly become very insular.[63]

Most importantly, for the first time in the police service, there would also be private sector style discipline for those failing to make the grade – a door marked 'Exit'.

The debate about graduate entrants has forced policymakers to consider the extent to which senior officers actually need higher level qualifications to do their job more effectively. As we have seen, forty years ago the Home Office was firmly of the view that graduates could and should be in evidence at all points in the organisation, not just at Chief Constable level. That in turn raises the question – who are the 'bosses' in today's police service, apart from the Chief Officers at the top tier? In terms of span of command and budgetary responsibility, the answer is simple. Any officer of the rank of Superintendent or Chief Superintendent must be regarded as a 'boss'. In London for example all borough commanders are Chief Superintendents, and most are responsible for anything up to 900 personnel and a total resource budget of millions of pounds. In the provinces the situation is similar.

Bedfordshire Police are typical. A small force, at the time of writing it has just two territorial divisions each commanded by a Chief Superintendent – Luton Division, a large and challenging conurbation, and Bedfordshire

---

63 Ibid

County Division (now named 'Local Policing'), which as the name implies covers everywhere else in the county. Apart from Vauxhall Motors and the NHS, the constabulary is the largest employer in the county and between them the two Chief Superintendents run the majority of the operational policing in Bedfordshire and have direct responsibility for all divisional personnel. Indeed, it would be interesting to know what the Chief Constable, Deputy Chief Constable, Assistant Chief Constable, Head of People and Workforce Development, and Director of Corporate Services at headquarters find to do all day.

Less than fifty years ago most of the police command units in England and Wales which are now run by Superintendents or Chief Superintendents were separate police forces under the command of a Chief Constable. The development of the Cambridgeshire force is a case in point and is typical of most forces outside London. The original Cambridgeshire Constabulary was formed in 1851 to police the then small rural county around, but not including, the city of Cambridge itself. In 1965, the county force fully amalgamated with Cambridge City Police, together with the quaintly named Isle-of-Ely Constabulary, Huntingdonshire Constabulary, and the Peterborough Combined Police – five separate forces which each had their own Chief Constable. The amalgamated force was named Cambridgeshire Constabulary in 1974, when the new non-metropolitan county of Cambridgeshire was created under local government boundary changes. Five forces, five Chief Constables, yet just a few decades later half of the new county of Cambridgeshire and the whole of the city of Cambridge is under the command of just one Superintendent as is the other half of Cambridgeshire plus the whole of the county of Huntingdonshire. Lastly, in the north of the force area, the whole of the city of Peterborough, formerly a force on its own, is likewise run by a Superintendent.

Investigation of major crime is a core priority for all forces and is usually placed under the command and control of a senior and experienced detective at Detective Chief Superintendent level, as the head of the force Major Crime Unit. Whilst run-of-the-mill crime is investigated at local level by divisional detectives under the command of the uniform Chief Superintendent, serious and series crimes such as Murder, Rape, Kidnapping, Terrorism and complex or unusual crimes are the responsibility of the senior detective at force headquarters. In every sense he (or increasingly 'she' these days) must be regarded as one of the bosses of the organisation. There are around 250 Divisional and Borough Command Units (BCUs) in England and Wales, some of them very large incorporating significant towns and parts of major cities as well as whole counties. In addition there are 32 Borough Operational Command Units in London (BOCUs). Add to this the 40 plus heads of CID across the country, and even if Chief Officers of ACC/ Met Commander are not included in the total, it will be readily seen that the leadership tier of UK Policing PLC rivals anything in business or industry. Indeed the status and importance of those Chief Superintendents who run BCUs and BOCUs or head Major Crime Investigation Units raises real issues about the extent to which policing is any longer delivered by Chief Constables. When spans of command were much narrower and Chief Constables had much more focussed responsibilities, they spent a large part of their time micro-managing the work of their subordinates, who in any event were responsible for much smaller areas. In these days of government performance targets imposed from 'on high', the role of force headquarters, and the Chief Officers who serve there, has so diminished that little more than support activity is undertaken. All Chief Constables claim to be demonstrating leadership and adding value at every stage of the process but are in fact not doing very much more than acting as points of contact to facilitate the allocation of funds and personnel.

Precious little strategic policy is made by headquarters, as the real power and influence is vested in those Chief Superintendents at the cutting edge. Activity is driven as a response from below, not leadership from above. Most people do not have the faintest idea who their Chief Constable is, although they are likely to read the name of their local BCU or BOCU Chief Superintendent in their local paper on a regular basis, because he or she is the person who actually runs the policing of their town or county and is therefore more relevant to them. The need to re-focus and redefine the role of Chief Officers in the twenty-first century is something that we will return to.

The only in-depth study of Chief Constables as a 'type' was conducted by Robert Reiner at the London School of Economics and published in his book 'Chief Constables' in 1991. Using a methodology which employed anonymous interviews with practically every such officer in the country, he examined their social origins, attitude to their job, occupational and political ideologies and the extent to which they represented an atypical group within the public sector. The individuals who were the focus of his study had all joined in the late 1950s to late 1960s and were exclusively a product of the recruits drawn into the service at the time. Only a few of the youngest were graduates (mainly products of the GES), many were ex-servicemen who had held commissions, and all but a few held extremely 'right of centre' political views, often barely hidden. As a group they were almost completely socially unrepresentative, being exclusively male, white, middle-aged and middle-brow. Had Reiner been writing his book today he would find that the landscape is markedly different. Currently (as at January 2023) there are 19 female Chief Constables of the 49 posts nationally. There has only ever been one black Chief Constable, Mike Fuller, who retired as head of Kent Police in 2010, and no British Asian has ever reached Chief Constable level. Although there is a dozen or more women and ethnic minority officers at Deputy and Assistant Chief Constable level, waiting in the wings. Without exception all are graduates, with a significant proportion also holding master's degrees and Doctorates. Politics is a tricky subject and I suspect that few of today's Chiefs would openly admit an allegiance or even a preference for any political party, but philosophically and culturally most would regard themselves as quintessential 'establishment' figures. Governments may come and go but the establishment has remained reasonably immutable over many decades and is consistently conservative (with a small 'c'). So it is with twenty-first century Chief Constables.

Reiner conducted his research in the early 1990s when Chief Constables viewed themselves as if they were a subset of the senior civil service. Whilst not actually an arm of government, many took the view that their role was to interpret government policy through strict adherence to the word and spirit of legislation. The oft-quoted description of their position was that they were 'apolitical', and therefore utterly neutral. In actual fact they never were, and in most respects were no different from the generations of Chief Constables that had preceded them. One has only to look at the strategic response of the police service to the Miners' Strike in 1984, when pre-existing legislation was interpreted in a way that was clearly intended to preclude lawful movement around the country, to see that little had changed in the seventy years since the police had acted as strike-breakers for the government during the Tonypandy 'riots' in 1910. Indeed attitudinally the senior officers of today still see their role as guardians of the status quo. During a TV interview following the less than successful police operation for the 2009 G20 conference in London, the officer in overall charge, Commander Robert Broadhurst, frankly admitted that he had difficulty reconciling a right of lawful protest with any activity which was technically illegal, such as obstruction of the highway. His view, which would undoubtedly be shared by the vast majority of today's chief police officers, was that there is equivalence between rights of assembly and technical breaches of minor legislation, but the latter cancels out the former!

From the late 1990s, in a process that accelerated after Labour came to power in 1997, there was a further important change in the landscape that Reiner could not have foreseen. In 1992, when the then Tory Home Secretary Kenneth Clarke appointed Sir Patrick Sheehy, the Chairman of British

American Tobacco, to inquire into the efficiency of the police service, the report that he eventually received was precisely what Clarke and the Home Office had expected. Sheehy's proposals were intended to introduce a 'business' model into policing by forcing senior personnel to operate in the same way as senior managers who ran the best businesses in the private sector. This was a naive and intrinsically unachievable ambition unless private sector financial incentives for senior officers were linked to a business model of accountability, i.e. hire and fire, and there was no appetite at any level of policing or indeed the government for that. By the time that legislation was drafted, John Major's administration was in its dogdays and much of Sheehy's change package was lost in the Labour landslide of 1997.

A few elements were retained however and some of the philosophical drivers have never gone away, but were viewed as too contentious to implement because of vehement resistance by the Police Federation. Sheehy and Clarke had wanted to see the whole police pay system based on skills and performance with regional pay variations reflecting the average wage in different parts of the country, rather than a nationally applicable pay structure. The so-called 'jobs for life' culture of junior as well as senior ranks was roundly condemned, and its removal was the centrepiece of a wide ranging and radical package of changes. Fixed term contracts for all officers; the abolition of three ranks (Chief Inspector, Chief Superintendent and Deputy Chief Constable) to create a slimmer management structure, and tighter restrictions on medical retirements were the key proposals. The main mechanism by which Chief Constables were to be converted into 'captains of industry' was by the provision of performance bonuses of up to 30% for high-achieving Chief Constables who met or exceeded testing operational targets. Clarke made no secret of the fact that he thought that the police management structure was 'top heavy' with overlapping responsibilities and that variations between forces sometimes gave responsibility to low-ranking officers and denied it to those in higher-ranked posts. Personnel systems were 'ineffective and inefficient' and there were 'serious weaknesses' in performance management arrangements. In the end, all that remained of Sheehy and Clarke's brave new world was five- and seven-year Fixed Term Appointments (FTAs) for all Chief Constables and Assistant Chief Constables, and performance bonuses for Chief Constables who hit their crime performance targets. Most, but not all, Chief Constables have taken on the mantle of business Chief Executive with alacrity and have been more than happy to accept the odd £6,000 to £10,000 on top of their salary each year if their force has done well. To their credit, one or two have refused to accept any such payments on the grounds so ably set out by the eminent economist W E Deming many years ago that 'individuals achieve nothing – only teams achieve, and it is they who should be rewarded'[64].

The bonus culture in policing can be very corrosive. In 2007, in the wake of the shooting of Jean Charles de Menezes, Ian Blair faced a revolt from his most senior colleagues at Scotland Yard after he indicated that he was prepared to accept a £25,000 performance bonus whilst

---

64 Deming, W. Edwards (1986). *Out of the Crisis*. MIT Press. ISBN 0-911379-01-0. OCLC 13126265

the force was embroiled in criminal proceedings over the death. The Commissioner, whose annual salary at the time was £228,000, wrote a furious hand-written letter to his deputy, Paul Stephenson (who subsequently succeeded him in the post), effectively accusing him of disloyalty after discovering that he had formally waived his own bonus. Stephenson's decision to turn down the bonus, in a formal approach to the Metropolitan Police Authority, was widely supported by all his senior colleagues, who believed that accepting a bonus would be viewed as insensitive, inappropriate and would almost certainly have been a PR disaster[65]. The gradual acceptance of business ethics and the impact that it has had upon the present generation of Chiefs would have given Reiner another solid chapter for his book and is 'work in progress' insofar as the extent to which it will further alter the relationship that they have with the post they hold, the people they lead, and the public they are supposed to serve.

In terms of police 'bosses' as a group, much could be written about the role and purpose of the Association of Chief Police Officers (ACPO), now the National Police Chiefs' Council (NPCC), which progressed, over a period of three decades, from being little more than an occasional dining club for Chief Constables, to an influential policy-making body which sits at the top table with ministers and officials. Established on 1 April 2015, the NPCC replaced the former body, following a government commissioned review into the management and functions of ACPO by General

---

65 'Yard chief faces no-confidence vote over claims he wanted to take £25,000 bonus' Daily Mail (22.10.2007)

Sir Nick Parker, the recently retired Commander-in-Chief UK Land Forces. In 2010, the Cameron government, in the wake of the 2008 financial crisis, announced a series of police reforms which ostensibly had the purpose of 'widening local accountability' through the introduction of locally elected 'police and crime commissioners (PCCs)' for each force, the creation of the National Crime Agency (referred to in the tabloid press as 'Britain's FBI'), and the College of Policing. Following the Parker review a group of Chief Constables and newly elected PCCs began working together to implement Parker's recommendations and develop terms of reference for the NPCC as a national body. From the outset it was abundantly clear that far from heralding a new dawn for policing, the Cameron-led initiatives amounted to little more than an exercise in deckchair movement on the Titanic. The key problem, identified by most commentators at the time, was that policing was expensive and the government had run out of money. It was politically unacceptable for the Conservative Party, as the party of law and order, to take the blame for what was to be a massive dis-investment in policing. The logical, albeit cynical, solution was to transfer the blame to the elected PCCs, who, according to the legislation establishing them, could hire and fire individual Chief Constables, had the legal responsibility to provide 'effective and efficient policing' in their area, and the power to raise a local tax precept to pay for it. It should be noted that this responsibility does not extend to any involvement in operational matters, that is something exclusively reserved to the Chief Constable. At a stroke, the Tory administration could step back and claim that local policing was a matter for local people, who if they wanted improvements would merely need to pay for it through local taxation raised by their democratically elected PCC. This neatly avoided the fact that all the PCCs had been elected on a party-political ticket, and in true-blue shire counties stuck to the Tory party line and did nothing to rock the government's boat. In the urban heartlands, including London, Liverpool, Manchester and elsewhere, where crime and social problems were at their worst, Labour mayors, councils, and PCCs were largely frozen-out of central debate for Home Office funding and told that policing was a local issue for them to sort out.

To say that there is a democratic deficit in terms of the legitimacy of PCCs to claim a mandate is a gross understatement. In the first PCC elections in 2012, despite widespread publicity, voter turnout across the UK hovered around 10%. Even by 2016, the last elections held before the global pandemic, the turnout had barely risen to 20%. Nonetheless PCCs and the NPCC claim joint stewardship, under the hand of the Home Office, for the direction of policing in England and Wales.

Speaking, as it does, for and on behalf of all officers of Assistant Chief Constable (Met Commander) and above, the NPCC also assumes the right to speak for the police service as a whole on matters of strategic importance and has a committee structure covering all areas of significance from Air Support to the Protection of Endangered Species, and back again via Traffic Policing and Criminal Justice Policy. Reiner barely touched upon ACPO in his book, but had he done so he would probably have commented upon how little real policy is generated from a body whose 'raison d'être' was the discussion of live issues and formulation of strategic responses. Sadly, it must be assumed, that in terms of the NPCC this is because of the 'comfortable' relationship it has developed with the Home Office and senior officials in recent years. Increasingly the NPCC treads very lightly when issues cross the boundaries of government departments and particularly when they impinge upon taxation. A classic example of how they fail to confront matters that go to the heart of public concern is in relation to binge drinking, the policing of which consumes vast amounts of police time and effort on virtually every night of the year across the land.

Until 2008, Steve Green was the Chief Constable of the Nottinghamshire Police and for a number of years prior to his retirement was very visible on the subject of alcohol abuse and the damage that so-called binge drinking was doing to civil society in many of our towns and cities, including his own Nottingham. He scrupulously followed the then official ACPO line that the problem was an enforcement issue, and dutifully conflated the problem with underage drinking. This suited the Home Office, because they knew very well that under-18s were not the main group despoiling our town centres with vomit, urine, and disorder. It was much more convenient to blame everything on the evil owners of off-licences and corner shops selling cider and alco-pops to teenagers and was an effective way of diverting attention from the real culprits.

Because everyone close to the issue knew that the owners and operators of the myriad bars, pubs, and nightclubs which had sprung up following the introduction of light-touch regulation of liquor licensing had a high degree of culpability that they barely acknowledged. Steve Green is an honourable and intelligent man and during 2006 and 2007 he began to go 'off message', pointing out the damage that licensees were doing with their 'two for one' promotions and 'happy hours'. He argued against changes in the law which had curtailed the extent to which police could object to the grant of public house licenses or challenge their renewal. This did not please Whitehall policymakers. Green knew very well, but was constrained from saying, that any effective challenge to binge drinking is only partially to do with enforcement, but is almost wholly to do with taxation, planning policy, local authority rates, and the collapse of the manufacturing economy in the UK.

The sad truth, obvious to government ministers, most serious academics, and presumably obvious to the policymakers in the NPCC 'cabinet', is that with the withdrawal of manufacturing, the collapse of the mining and motor vehicle construction industries, the export of textile production, and the impact of Brexit, hundreds of thousands of 'real' jobs have disappeared, with many towns across the country becoming economic wastelands. Local authorities have been placed in an untenable position. They retain the legal obligation to provide all manner of services, from refuse collection to social housing, but how is this to be done as economic activity haemorrhages from towns with the consequent decline in income from rates and retail expenditure?

The answer, since 1997, has been the promotion of that wonderfully euphemistic concept – the 'late night economy' – a strategy for filling our town centres with so-called entertainment and leisure-based businesses that provide the opportunity for feckless louts from a thirty-mile radius to drink themselves into oblivion during the hours of darkness, whilst simultaneously providing a rates income for the local council. In urban centres from Newcastle to Penzance, where nothing is made anymore and the only employment is in call-centres, or out-of-town logistics warehouses, the late-night economy has replaced the real economy as the only way of generating a local tax base for local services. One would have hoped that on an issue such as this, senior officers, and certainly senior police policymakers, would have joined up the dots and adopted a wide strategic approach. Instead they have merely accepted the 'late night economy' at face value, with any response being linked to maintenance of the status quo under the over-used umbrella of 'partnership' with the licensed trade. This is the same licensed trade that Green pointed out is the starting point for the £20 billion per annum cost to the economy of alcohol abuse. An example of the way in which ACPO (and now the NPCC) always seemed to take the line of least resistance on controversial topics, be it 42 days detention, policing lawful protest, or as in this case, binge drinking, can be drawn from the following extract from an interview with Scotland Yard Assistant Commissioner Chris Allison in 2007.

> *'Planning needs to involve partnership consultation between the trade, police, local stakeholders, and authorities, and should provide all partners with a clear view of what the city centre should look like, and how it should attract a variety of ages and social types. We also have to extend the use of cumulative*

*impact policies to ensure pleasant, easily policed streets, as well as **improving trading conditions for licensed businesses** [Author's emphasis].*⁶⁶

It has been commented upon elsewhere, that the top tier of policing seldom seems to 'grasp the nettle' when contentious issues arise. Many of their pronouncements possess something that is difficult to define but easy to see – an all embracing 'blandness'. With a few notable exceptions, many of those at the top of policing today give the impression of being clones of one another. As if cast from an identical mould, they speak in the same way, write in the same way, respond to criticism in the same way, and have the same unerring confidence in whatever happens to be the current management vogue. Cumulative Impact Policies, Policing Pledges, Charter Marks, Safer Neighbourhood Strategies, all are meat and drink to such individuals who never display an atom of doubt that each new initiative will change the world as we know it. It has been suggested that this is a function of the process of selection; that GES and APSG assessors who are themselves products of the various accelerated promotion schemes that have been in operation over the years consciously or unconsciously select in their own image. The following extract, taken from an ACPO response to a government green paper on policing and signed by Sir Ken Jones, the President of ACPO in 2008, contains a 102-word sentence and was submitted for the 'Golden Bull Award' of the

---

66 Extract from interview in 'Night – 24 Hour Business People' (February 2007) Leo Batchelor

Plain English Campaign. Sadly, there is no guarantee that our current body of Chief Constables would see anything wrong with it.

> *'The promise of reform which the Green Paper heralds holds much for the public and Service alike; local policing, customized to local need with authentic answerability, strengthened accountabilities at force level through reforms to police authorities and HMIC, performance management at the service of localities with targets and plans tailored to local needs, the end of centrally engineered one size fits all initiatives, an intelligent approach to cutting red tape through redesign of processes and cultures, a renewed emphasis on strategic development so as to better equip our service to meet the amorphous challenges of managing cross force harms, risks and opportunities.'*

It is undoubtedly the case, particularly since 1997, that any Chief Police Officer (or for that matter BCU or BOCU commander) who tried to break the mould and gingerly distance him or herself from the sort of nonsense set out above would be quickly stamped upon by Home Office officials and Ministers, who value conformity above individuality. Nonetheless it would be refreshing, indeed healthy, for the police service to nurture a few iconoclasts – men and women who might occasionally display a sense of humour, an interest in art, literature, history, or civil liberties, with imagination that extends beyond the best way to present performance management data on an Excel spreadsheet.

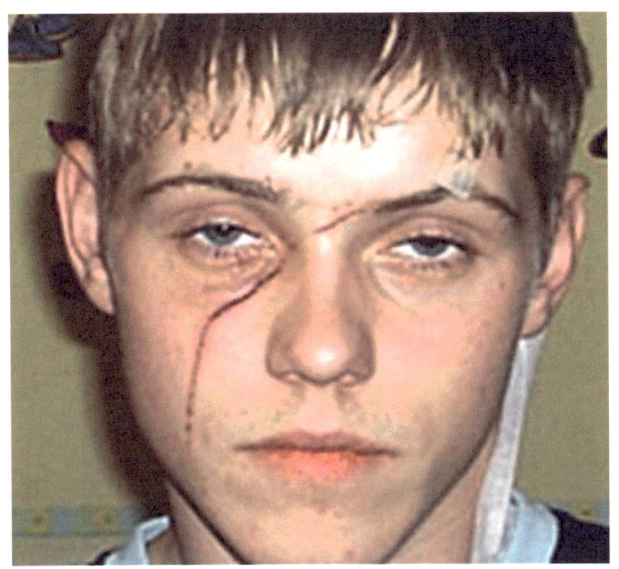

Peter Woodhams, following the assault upon him in January 2006 which was so disgracefully investigated by the Metropolitan Police. (Reproduced by kind permission of Peter's partner, Jane)

*Peter, with his son, in happier times.
(Reproduced by kind permission of Peter's partner, Jane)*

*Jack Warner as Constable George Dixon of Dock Green;
everyone's idea of what a 'real' copper should be.
(Copyright BBC © acknowledged)*

*Police officers 'protecting civil liberties' at the G20
demonstration in the City of London in 2009.
(Copyright 'The Guardian' © acknowledged)*

Hugh Montague Trenchard, the 1st Viscount Trenchard GCB, OM, GCVO, DSO, Commissioner of the Metropolitan Police (1931–1935) who almost destroyed the morale of the force with the introduction of an 'officer class'.
(Copyright MilitaryImages.Net © acknowledged)

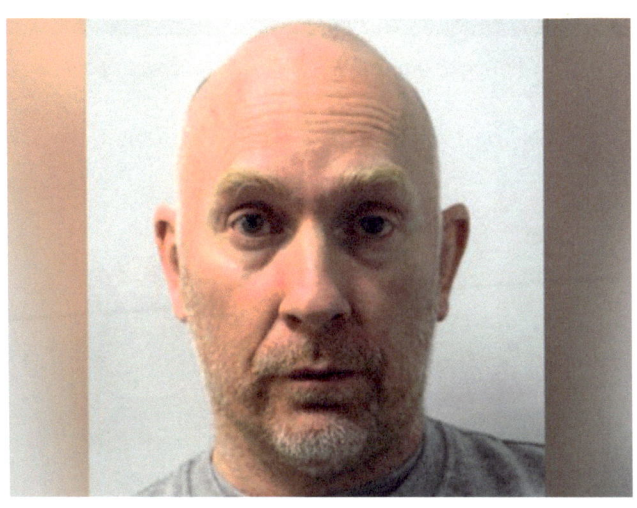

PC Wayne Couzens. Murderer, Rapist, and Metropolitan Police Officer.
(Copyright 'Metropolitan Police Service' acknowledged)

*PC David Carrick. Rapist, Sex Offender, and Metropolitan Police Officer.
(Copyright 'Hertfordshire Police' acknowledged)*

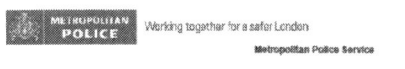

Metropolitan Police Risk Assessment form (RA1) – First page of three which must be completed in relation of every operational activity no matter how large or small.

CHAPTER 5
CRIME, TERRORISM AND CIVIL LIBERTIES – A MATTER FOR THE POLICE?

CRIME AND CRIMINALS

> *'Let's have fewer terrorism acts, fewer laws attacking our right to speak frankly and freely. Let's stop filling our prisons with junkies, inadequates and the mentally deranged. How apposite in 2009 to have, instead, a few more laws to confront the clever people who have done their best to steal our economy'.*
>
> Sir Ken McDonald,
> Director of Public Prosecutions 2003–2008

During a speech at the Lord Mayor's annual dinner for judges at the Mansion House in July 2009, the Lord Chief Justice, Sir Igor Judge (*did anyone ever have a more appropriate name?*), made a plea to the government to pass less legislation. He pointed out that in the previous decade parliament had introduced no less than 27 criminal justice bills and created over 3,600 new criminal offences. Of these

1,036 are punishable with imprisonment, equivalent to a new custodial offence being added to the statute books every four days. Whenever the press or media report a scandal, or identify a compelling social issue, the default position for ministers and those that advise them is to set up a review to recommend 'new laws'. Without enforcement, however, legislation is nothing more than a hymn of praise to the good intentions of government, and to quote Friedrich Engels, *'An ounce of action is worth a ton of theory'*.

Ask the average man in the street, 'who enforces the law and investigates crime?' and the reply, almost certainly, will be that it is the responsibility of the police. To a certain extent our man in the street would be correct but it is not the whole picture. Large areas of the criminal law are not touched by police forces, often because they claim to have 'insufficient resources' but more often because other prosecuting authorities have a prior claim. Fraud is a case in point. Until the City of London Police was given national 'lead force' responsibility for the investigation of fraud in 2007, vast amounts of financial crime went unreported and was seldom investigated. Even today (2022) it is a mixed picture with the police deferring to the Benefits Agency and local authorities in relation to the investigation and prosecution of benefit fraud (more than 56,000 cases in England and Wales in 2017/2018), and the investigation of 'insider dealing', which is the responsibility of the Financial Services Authority (2 successful cases in the twenty-five years since the FSA was established in 1997!). Police forces seldom, if ever, deal with environmental crime, public sector corruption (unless specifically invited to do so), or specialist offences relating to cruelty to animals, trading standards, adulteration of pharmaceutical products, health and safety etc, all of which are dealt with by specialists with their own powers of prosecution.

Thus, the definition of crime is wide and does not lend itself to easy definition in ten-second sound-bites. However, the level of crime is of crucial importance to us all and is of enduring importance to politicians because their very survival in office may depend on whether the trend line on a graph is angled up or down. To have even a cursory understanding of the issues involved it is necessary to ask some fairly basic questions. Unfortunately the answers often generate even greater confusion.

But let us make a start. How much crime is there?

To answer that simple question it is necessary, first of all, to remember that Scotland is a foreign country, has a different legal system, and therefore counts her crime separately. Northern Ireland also maintains a separate register of criminal offences, so when the media talks about crime levels in this country they are almost certainly referring only to England and Wales. Because such data are so contentious and inherently political, crime figures have been 'massaged' over many years, much in the way that unemployment figures were counted in different ways throughout the 1980s and 1990s to conceal the true number of people without jobs. A whole raft of tactics has been employed to ensure that police forces look good, many of which teeter on the edge of downright malpractice.

For example, from Hadrian's Wall to Penzance, police forces regularly record criminal damage as accidental damage, and therefore not a crime. They record burglaries in multi-occupancy dwellings in which a number of self-contained flats are entered as a single crime on the spurious grounds that the offender has broken into a single building and merely entered a few rooms. By 2002 the system had lost all credibility and ACPO were forced to introduce the National Crime Recording Standard (NCRS) which all forces in England and Wales were obliged to adhere to. One of its key elements was that the police were no longer able to claim 'professional judgement' as an excuse for failing to record an offence. If a victim alleged that his wallet had been stolen from his pocket in a restaurant, the allegation had to be recorded as a crime, no 'ifs' or 'buts'. Whereas formerly the police officer, to keep crime figures down, might have been tempted to disregard the victim and record the matter as lost property, he could no longer do so and the NCRS had the immediate effect of inflating crime figures in the years immediately after its introduction, but in the years since there is compelling evidence to show that 'old habits die hard' and the NCRS is seldom enforced with rigour.

In 2001, the year prior to the introduction of the NCRS, the Home Office had taken a radical step to compare, and contrast, recorded crime data with the experience of people living in communities across the land by presenting recorded crime statistics alongside data from the British Crime Survey (BCS) (*now referred to as the Crime Survey for England and Wales (CSEW)).* This is a systematic victim study, currently carried out by the highly respected polling organisation. British Market Research Bureau Limited, on behalf of the Home Office. The CSEW seeks to measure the amount of crime in England and Wales by asking at least 50,000 people aged 16 and over, living in private households, about the crimes they have personally experienced in the last year. The survey is comparable to the National Crime Victimization Survey conducted in the United States. The British Crime Survey was first carried out in 1982 and further surveys were carried out in 1984, and then bi-annually until 2000. Since April 2001, BCS interviews have been carried out on a continuous basis and detailed results from that point are now reported by financial years. Initially the survey covered England, Wales and Scotland but the survey is now restricted to England and Wales. The Scottish Executive has commissioned a similar survey of victimisation in Scotland called the Scottish Crime and Victimisation Survey (SCVS). Since 1994 there has been a separate Northern Ireland Crime Survey, on a bi-annual basis from 2001, and continuously from January 2005. It is produced by the Statistics and Research Branch of the Northern Ireland Office.

The value of the CSEW is that it can provide a better reflection of the true level of crime than police statistics since it includes crimes that have not been reported to, or even recorded by, the police. The CSEW estimates that only around half of all crime it measures is captured as police-recorded crime, largely due to the fact that people do not bother to report crimes because they think the crime was too trivial or the police couldn't do much about it. The CSEW also provides a better measure of trends over time since it has adopted a consistent methodology and is unaffected by changes in police and Home Office reporting or recording practices.

The difference between police recorded crime statistics and BCS data is stark. The figures for 2020/2021 demonstrate the difference between the experience of victims, as exposed by the survey results, and the 'official' figures which the police rely upon to inform policy decisions about objectives and policing strategy. Overall, crime as measured by the CSEW indicated no change compared with the 2019/2020 survey results in most crime types. Crimes recorded by the police however showed a five per cent decrease compared with 2019/2020 with decreases in most crime types. When the data was published the NPCC issued a press release welcoming these 'encouraging' figures, only briefly referring to the disparity with the BCS.

Perusal of the data also indicates a great deal about crime, fear of crime, and the way that police seek to enforce the law, often very selectively. Thus, whilst a total of 4.85 million crimes in a single year (*not including 919,000 allegations of fraud and computer misuse*) may seem to be an inordinately large amount and immensely worrying to the average person, it must not be forgotten that aggregated crime data conceals the fact that not all offences are equal in terms of impact on the victim.

The Home Office data for 2008/2009 provides the best opportunity to examine the detail of crime recording policy because that was the last year that comparative data was comprehensively and independently audited. Thereafter, between 2010 and 2018 there were changes in reporting and recording protocols year-on-year, together with the failure of a large urban force to submit data, which skewed the figures. Totals for 2019 to 2022 do not lend themselves to comparative analysis because of the impact of the global pandemic.

Before embarking on any review of this complex subject, it should be remembered that there is no standard measure of equality in recorded crime. The theft of a bottle of milk from someone's doorstep counts as one crime for the purposes of statistics, but so does the theft of a diamond ring from an open display in a Bond Street jewellers' shop. Just over one million of the nearly five million crimes were relatively minor thefts of property with no suggestion of violence or injury to the victim, and in many cases no knowledge until later that the offence had even occurred. A quarter of a million crimes were drug offences, which by definition can only be recorded as crimes after an individual has been arrested; the crimes do not exist in the absence of an offender (*except in rare conspiracies to import or distribute drugs*). A category recorded as 'Violence against the Person – without injury' accounts for almost half a million of all the crimes recorded in 2008/2009 and includes 31,000 cases of possessing offensive weapons which, again, are offences that do not exist in the absence of an arrested offender. 197,000 crimes are shown as 'assaults without injury', common assaults involving a slap or a push, or even a shouted insult. In the grand scheme of things, whilst always a tragedy for those directly involved, really serious crime is nowhere near as prevalent in a country of 60 million people as the media, and a few senior police officers, would have us believe.

In 2008/2009 there were just 648 homicides in the entire country, the majority 'domestic murders' where the victim and the offender were known to each other (*the total for 2022 was 663*). During the same period there were 16,204 murders in the United States, over 9,000 by the use of firearms[67] (*the US total for 2021 was 22,900*). Serious

---

67 'Crime in the United States by Volume and Rate per 100,000

assaults, such as attempted murder, grievous bodily harm, actual bodily harm, robbery etc, and violent crimes such as rape and indecent assault amount to a total of just over half a million crimes (11.5%), far too many, but there is no reason to believe that BCS data would be significantly different, because these are exactly the sorts of crimes that would almost always come to the notice of police and therefore appear in the official statistics.

So far so good, but it is at this point that a process known as 'attrition' starts to affect the way in which crime is recorded and dealt with. Every avid reader of detective fiction knows what happens when a crime is reported. A world-weary sleuth immediately adds the investigation to his caseload and starts the process of diligently looking for clues to solve the crime and detect the offender. This is comforting but is nothing more than fiction. In the real world of twenty-first century policing vast amounts of recorded crime are not investigated at all. A large and growing proportion of reported crime is 'screened out' as soon as it is entered on the computer record system, with many allegations defined as 'No Crime' before any sort of investigation has taken place. Research by HM Inspectorate in 2009, and commented upon by independent researchers[68], demonstrated that across England and Wales around a third of all cases were classified as incapable of being solved within hours of an allegation being made. Under the screening system, crimes are logged in official figures, but no serious effort is made

---

Inhabitants, 1989–2009'. *Crime in the United States 2009*. Department of Justice — Federal Bureau of Investigation (USA). 2009.

68 'Force or Farce? – Police Recorded Crime 2009' Planet Police (4.12.2009)

to investigate, and victims are merely issued with reference numbers for insurance purposes.

The Metropolitan Police screens out almost half of all the crimes reported in London. Of the 844,938 allegations of crime recorded by the Met in 2008/2009, 404,609 (48% of the total) were screened out and not investigated. Amongst eighteen English, Welsh and Scottish forces which operate official screening policies, 697,000 offences were deemed unsuitable for investigation during the same period out of 2.2 million reported crimes (32% of the total). When the data is aggregated across the country it indicates that at least 1.7 million reported crimes per year remain on the books but are not subjected to any form of investigation. In defence of the system, senior officers cite the old excuse 'we don't have enough resources' and argue that 'screening out' allows them to concentrate their effort upon the most serious and the most solvable crimes, which are not necessarily the same thing. Police managers also insist that all offences are 'investigated' to some degree, although this might only amount to a phone call to the complainant, which hardly places it up there with the efforts of Hercule Poirot.

Murder, wounding and rape are always investigated, as one would expect and demand. Cases are also 'screened in' where there is a named suspect or forensic evidence. However, there is absolutely no consistency amongst forces in the way that they approach the issue, for example, Cambridgeshire has one of the highest 'screening out' rates in the country at 43% yet shares a common boundary with Essex where the rate is 3%. In parts of the country, an average of 75% of theft and handling offences are screened out. That figure is as high as 70% for criminal damage and 55% for burglary. More than 200,000 burglaries – almost 600 a day – went unsolved by police in England and Wales last year, disclosed in Home Office data published in April 2023, which details that 209,424 domestic burglaries, or 574 a day, were screened out and not investigated.

So, our original 4.85 million recorded crimes are rapidly converted into around 2.5 million 'viable allegations' after the screening process is applied. These are the offences that will receive some sort of investigation by the police, but it should not be assumed that the level of expertise applied is very high in the case of most crimes. For some considerable time there has been a shortage of trained detectives, largely due to lack of training facilities and 'policy drift' in terms of personnel policy where officers' careers were not managed effectively, and they were moved in and out of key specialist posts with no consideration of who might be available to replace them. This is particularly the case in London and the big cities, where as a result, junior officers who have not had any detective training are drafted onto teams dealing with serious crime that is often way beyond their abilities. Major difficulties have occurred when such officers, who through no fault of their own lack experience and expertise, are put in charge of sensitive enquiries into child abuse and rape. In terms of run-of-the-mill volume crime such as thefts from motor vehicles and domestic burglary, the investigators are hardly ever trained and qualified detectives; they are more likely to be uniform constables posted to plain-clothes duties for a few months 'to help out'. Hardly what the long-suffering public expects or deserves.

Most crime is never solved. Detection rates vary from

force to force and between different offence groups, but overall no more than about 25% of crime is ever solved, and even that low average is pushed up by 'easy to solve offences' such as drug possession which have an almost 100% detection rate for reasons we have already seen. The clear-up rate for volume crime is often scandalously low. In London and Nottingham which are property crime 'hotspots', the clear-up rate for domestic burglary is between 12% and 13%. All of this means that our initial total of 4.85 million recorded crimes, which became 2.5 million after screening, falls yet further to around 1.3 million detected offences in the average year.

Not unreasonably it is generally believed that once a crime is solved and the criminal identified, then as night follows day, the offender will be charged and placed before a court. The layman quite properly assumes that the definition of what is or is not a detected crime should be relatively straightforward. However because of the statistical 'Counting Rules' imposed by the Home Office, the precise definition of a detected offence is something that is of byzantine complexity. There are currently two forms of detection; the first, a 'sanction' detection, is logical, the second, a 'non-sanction' detection, is less so.

A detected crime is one where an offender has been identified and dealt with. A sanction detection might involve an offender being charged, cautioned, reported for summons, reprimanded (if they are aged seventeen or under), or issued with a fixed penalty notice, it may also include a warning for possessing cannabis. An offence which is TiC'd (Taken into Consideration) is also a type of sanction detection and is where other crimes are taken into consideration when sentencing an offender in court for an unrelated crime.

A 'non-sanction' detection, as the name implies, is where the offender has been identified but for a variety of reasons has not been made the subject of any form of proceedings. Non-sanction detection figures were first separately collated in 1985, and since that time the Home Office has made various revisions to the circumstances where such a detection can be claimed. In 1991 there were nine categories, which were reduced to eight in 1999. The most significant reductions came in 2007 when the figure was reduced to two. Some forces have in recent years made local policy decisions to restrict their use of non-sanction detections, because they are often viewed as ethically questionable. There is also the fact that since 2007 non-sanction detections can only be claimed for serious offences which would ordinarily be tried before a jury at a Crown Court and must be 'signed off' by a Crown Prosecutor who certifies that there is sufficient evidence to take the offender to court but has decided not to proceed with the case. Most forces take the view that the effort in securing such evidence is disproportionate to the result, so most do not bother, and the number of non-sanction detections has therefore dropped appreciably.

So, of the 4.85 million recorded offences we started with, we are left by a process of attrition with just 1.3 million *detected* offences, but even this reduced total will not lead to every offender appearing before a court as most victims hope and expect. Only around 50% of the offenders (some 650,000 per year) are dealt with by way of charge or summons – the remainder being disposed of through Fixed

Penalty tickets (130,000), Cannabis warnings (105,000), TICs (107,000), and Cautions (358,000).

CAUTIONS - 'A SCANDAL WAITING TO HAPPEN'

'Simple' Cautions were introduced in the 1980s to deal with minor offences – such as shoplifting – with the aim of reducing legal expenses and leaving courts free to deal with the most serious crimes. From the police point of view, part of the attraction of cautioning is that it saves a tremendous amount of 'back office' administrative work in terms of file preparation and collation of evidence etc. This, it is claimed, frees officers to 'get back on the beat', although precisely what beats they are returning to is somewhat debatable since the abandonment of preventive patrolling in the 1990s.

The reasoning behind administering a caution is that it is a 'last chance'. The offender admits his guilt and has the opportunity to mend his ways. Repeated cautions are therefore illogical (because you should only get one 'last chance') and it was always the stated intention of the scheme that having once been cautioned, a repeat offender would automatically be charged and appear before a court on the very next occasion that he came to notice. Crown Prosecutors have had powers since 2005 to impose 'Conditional Cautions', which are extra-judicial and have some of the same effect of a suspended sentence in that they can include the imposition of hours of community service. In the four years after they were introduced nearly 20,000 were applied against offenders without either party going anywhere near a court. In the period 2008 to 2009 the rate increased dramatically with between 600 and 700 a month (8,000 a year) being ordered. The police, as we have seen, have been able to impose cautions for over 30 years and now do so at an increasing rate. Indeed the majority of all arrested offenders are cautioned at police stations or served with fixed penalty notices, usually £80 fines, which government ministers were keen to extend to an even wider list of offences than at present.

Any pretence of standing by the original philosophy that a caution represents a 'last chance' was abandoned long ago in the interests of expediency. There are legion examples of offenders being cautioned twice, three, or four times in succession before they were charged. Simple and Conditional Cautions were imposed on more than 2.2 million people between 2010 and 2018. Of those, 550,000 offenders had received two or more cautions, and more than 51,000 had been cautioned on four or more occasions. The range of offences for which offenders are cautioned is no longer restricted to minor offences, as originally intended. Figures produced by the Magistrates Association in 2009[69], to support their growing concern about the use of cautions as an alternative to criminal proceedings, showed that between 30,000 and 40,000 serious assaults were dealt with by way of caution in a single year, including around 700 that were so serious that the offender should properly have been charged with grievous bodily harm. There are numerous examples of gross malpractice linked to cautioning, such as an offender with a lengthy and active criminal record

---

69 Reported in 'The Times' (9.11.2009)

being cautioned by police for possessing drugs with intent to supply, and a 15-year-old youth who was cautioned for the rape by penetration of a younger boy.

As has been pointed out by various commentators, from the offender's point of view there are real advantages in accepting a caution, because he avoids a trial and gets off with a fixed penalty or a recordable caution, rather than a heavier penalty or even a custodial sentence. But is it justice? Many in the legal system, including judges, magistrates, and even a previous Director of Public Prosecutions (now Sir) Kier Starmer, have become increasingly alarmed that not just trivial but increasingly serious and violent offences are being diverted from the courts. There are also real issues about the effectiveness of such a process, as research indicates that more than half of all fixed penalty fines levied as an alternative to proceedings remain unpaid, and the offenders end up being arrested on warrant and placed before the court anyway – so there is no financial saving[70].

These critics also raise concerns of principle. Is it right, ask judges and magistrates, that the police or prosecutors should decide the sentence in serious violent cases, away from any sort of public scrutiny? There is the constant risk, confirmed by statements made to investigators in a number of serious allegations against the police, that an offender will feel under pressure to accept a caution, which requires an admission of guilt, unaware that this will remain on his record. Courts are also deprived of the opportunity to order appropriate treatment, for a drug addiction,

---

[70] 'Courts owed £1.3 billion in unpaid fines' National Audit Office report to the Ministry of Justice (6.7.2010)

alcohol dependency or some sort of psychiatric problem. Most importantly of all, and of crucial importance in a democratic society, justice is not seen to be done – by the victim or by the public at large. With current financial restraints, the pressure on police and prosecutors to use out-of-court penalties will undoubtedly rise. Lord Justice Leveson, the Senior Presiding Judge for England and Wales between 2007 and 2009 and Lord Justice of Appeal until 2013, trenchantly commented in relation to the excessive use of cautions, 'It should not be at the discretion of police or prosecuting authorities to be judge and jury and impose sentence.'[71] Indeed the overuse of police cautions for the most spurious reasons has not improved in the decade since Lord Leveson made his comments and in the view of many practitioners at the Criminal Bar, is a 'scandal waiting to happen'.

THE WAR ON TERROR

When the Soviet Empire collapsed in 1989, there was a rather poor joke that circulated amongst those working in the Security Services at the time. It went something like this. Two senior spooks are enjoying a postprandial drink in a Pall Mall club when one says to the other, *'The Berlin Wall has just been knocked down; do you want to hear the good news or the bad news?'* His companion looks over the rim of his glass and replies, *'Oh I think I'd like the good news',* to which he receives the response, *'We've won the Cold War'.*

---

71 'But is it Justice?' Reported in the Sunday Times (8.11.2009)

Brief pause, much sipping of drinks before the listener says, '*... and the bad news?*' Another pause before the questioner responds, '*Yes, bit of a problem I'm afraid. We're all out of a job now!*' With the Bear dead, or at least out of commission until the Russian annexation of Crimea in 2014, the security services in the shape of MI5, MI6 and Police Special Branch units were forced to re-invent themselves if they were to keep any part of their operational budgets and retain their influence in Whitehall. The Thatcher government was intent on keeping the 'peace dividend' as a windfall that could be applied to the public sector, Health, and Education, which since 1979 had lacked real investment and were beginning to show signs of wear and tear. There was always Ireland of course, where the security services were actively engaged, but as the 1990s dawned it started to become abundantly clear that a judicious blend of war-weariness and pragmatism on the part of the PIRA and the government was leading inexorably towards some sort of settlement. The Good Friday Agreement of 1998 effectively marked the beginning of the end for MI5 in the province and meant that the domestic Special Branches of mainland police forces needed to find something new to do.

MI5 were first off the starting blocks. After a period of intensive lobbying across Whitehall, during which those at the head of MI5 and the intelligence community unashamedly pointed out the failings of the police in relation to serious, organised, and international crime, the Security Service were given the task of countering serious crime in 1996. This was a constitutionally unprecedented move but was the opportunity that most senior MI5 personnel had been praying for. It ensured that they could retain all their human assets, surveillance capability and technical equipment whilst deploying their full range of skills and resources, formerly used against terrorist and espionage targets, to combat the threat from serious crime. Virtually overnight MI5 became involved in the investigation of the international drugs trade, and large-scale organised crime. Work in this area was suspended in April 2006, following the launch of the Serious Organised Crime Agency (SOCA) – headed by a former Director General of the Security Service, Sir Stephen Lander – and the need to redeploy Service resources to combat the increased threat to the UK from international terrorism. During the intervening period, however, MI5 would claim that they were successfully involved in a number of complex and significant law enforcement investigations. In contrast with their national security work, they did not act independently in the investigation of serious crime, but theoretically only became involved when tasked by law enforcement agencies such as the Police or Customs. In fact, in order to justify their continued existence, the Security Service was much more proactive than they now care to admit. MI5 desk officers often saw themselves as the senior partners in joint investigations but their lack of understanding of the niceties of criminal law and the judicial and legal process led to more than one major enquiry being compromised from an evidential point of view.

The mainland Special Branch, its PIRA work diminishing and no longer confronted by the possibility that the country was in imminent danger of attack by Spetsnaz troops or KGB agents, looked around for new enemies and found the Far Right and the environmental lobby. Throughout the 1990s the police focus changed to intelligence-gathering around groups such as the British National Party, Animal Rights Activists, Hunt Saboteurs, and environmentalists protesting against road-widening schemes, by-passes, and GM crops. In the long run this was to have a profound impact on the police approach to civil liberties, as a wider and yet wider section of the public was categorised as 'suspect', justifying the use of sophisticated and intrusive surveillance techniques which previously had only been used in respect of real threats from real terrorists.

Interestingly, no-one in the intelligence and security community seems to have been very good at looking over the horizon to see what new threat might have been creeping towards us during the 1990s. Research papers by the thousand, academic seminars in the UK and abroad, and off-the-record briefings from political refugees from all points of the compass, were unanimous in identifying militant Islam as the next major challenge, yet little appears to have been done to meet that challenge prior to 2001. As early as 1995 the French government, through their highly effective security service, the DGSE *(Direction Générale de la Sécurité Extérieure),* were warning the UK government of the danger posed by the Algerian GIA (Armed Islamic Group) and even identified activists who had either been given asylum in Britain or were part of a growing body of French Algerian 'students' at British universities and colleges. Very little seems to have been done beyond the opening of various files, and this should be a matter of concern to us all. Britain has been a multi-ethnic community for a number of decades, with a large proportion of our citizens having familial roots that link them directly to Pakistan, the Indian sub-continent, Somalia and other areas where there is or has recently been religious and political conflict. It would not be too much to expect that amongst the army of highly qualified analysts and policymakers in the Security Service, at least one could have 'joined up the dots' and worked out the strategic threat for Britain that was emerging around the world as the millennium came to an end.

It would be insulting to suggest that those at the helm of the security services and Special Branch breathed a sigh of relief on September 11th, 2001, but it is nonetheless the case that the world really did change for them immediately after. In the wake of the terrorist attacks on the World Trade Centre and the Pentagon, MI5, the Secret Intelligence Service (SIS) and the police were now back in their comfort zone, dealing with a determined enemy that required deployment of all the techniques that had been so useful during the Cold War and the 'Troubles' in Ireland. Electronic intelligence-gathering through GCHQ at Cheltenham; development of Covert Human Intelligence Sources (undercover agents), sophisticated surveillance and practically limitless funding were once again the order of the day. Between 2001 and 2008, four separate pieces of legislation were passed by Parliament dealing with terrorism and the powers of police. In the fevered atmosphere immediately following 9/11, and then again during the aftermath of the London bombings in July 2005, the police and security services had powers conferred upon them that were unprecedented in peacetime.

Particularly contentious was the application of powers under Section 43 and 44 of the Terrorism Act 2000, a piece of pre-9/11 legislation that had originally been enacted to deal with dissident Irish Republican terrorism. Under Section 43 of the Act any police officer, whether he is in uniform or not, can stop and search any person providing that they reasonably suspect that the person is a terrorist – a test of reasonableness that is difficult to define and even harder to challenge. The person can even be detained and taken to a police station in order to be searched to discover whether or not they have in their possession anything which may constitute evidence that they are a terrorist. The powers, as interpreted by Home Office guidance, are incredibly wide ranging. Coupled with Section 44 of the Act the power of search almost became arbitrary. Under Section 44 the Home Secretary gives delegated authority to police chief officers to designate any area for an allotted period as a place where Section 43 searches can be conducted, but without the necessity for any 'reasonable suspicion'. In various parts of the country, but particularly in London, there was compelling evidence that the power was roundly abused. For example, every London borough was designated under Section 44 on a rolling authority that was renewed immediately it expired – effectively removing the need to have any reasonable suspicion to justify searches. Between January 2003 and February 2008, no less than 191,478 people were stopped and searched under Section 44 across the capital. Of these, 2,108 (1.1%) were arrested, but not one of the arrests was for a terrorist-related offence. The definition of what constitutes terrorist-related behaviour had been unilaterally widened by the police service to such an extent that lawful protest and even photography were deemed to be reasons for police action.

Problematic use of Section 44 powers was not restricted

to political protesters. There were numerous well-evidenced accounts of journalists, lawyers, amateur and professional photographers, train spotters, politicians and even children being subjected to stop and search on suspicion of being involved in terrorist activities whilst engaged in perfectly lawful acts such as sketching or photography. The taking of photographs in public spaces is permitted under legislation that goes back to 1988 dealing with a concept known as 'freedom of panorama'[72]. The Terrorism Acts do not prohibit such activity although certain restrictions on photography were introduced with the Counter-Terrorism Act 2008, against a background of genuine concern by civil liberties campaigners and others who saw the move as disproportionate and having little to do with the threat of terrorism *per se*.

With no good reason police officers assumed, and built into operational procedures, that it was an arrestable offence to photograph any police officer when on duty under any circumstances, or any public building, on the spurious grounds that such photographs could identify individuals or locations and thereby be of use to terrorists. Tourists and innocent members of the public were detained and had their cameras seized; digital memory cards were removed, and the content erased, all done without any legal authority whatsoever. Uniform officers in the most out of the way places, mimicking their colleagues in more 'target rich' areas, indulged in this institutional paranoia in the belief that they were all front-line combatants in the War on Terror. One is reminded of the 'Spy Fever' during the

---

[72] Section 62, Copyright Designs and Patents Act 1988

opening months of the First World War, when anyone with a bushy moustache, a foreign accent, and a sketchpad, was assumed to be a German spy in daily contact with the Kaiser. In October 2008 police stopped a 15-year-old schoolboy in south London who was taking photographs of Wimbledon railway station for his school geography project[73]. He was questioned under suspicion of being a terrorist and despite the fact that his parents raised concerns that his personal data could be held on the police intelligence database for up to six years, their complaints were disregarded. Andrew Pelling, the Conservative MP for Central Croydon, was stopped by police and closely questioned after being seen by officers photographing roadworks near a railway station[74]. Trainspotters were frequently subjected to stop and search. In August 2009 a rail enthusiast was pursued by Dyfed-Powys Police to his home in Lincolnshire for photographing a locomotive at a Murco oil-refinery in Milford Haven[75]. Indeed, between 2000 and 2009, the British Transport Police used powers under the Act to detain and search over 62,000 people at railway stations. In November 2009, a BBC photographer was searched and questioned by police outside the Tate Modern art gallery in London for photographing the sunset over St Paul's Cathedral, under suspicion of preparing for a terrorist act.[76]

---

73 'Schoolboy stopped under Terrorism Act for doing Geography fieldwork' Daily Telegraph (31.10.2008)
74 'Andrew Pelling MP stopped by cops for taking pictures of cycle path' Croydon Guardian (7.1.2009)
75 'Innocent trainspotter suspected of being terrorist' Daily Mail (25.8.2009)
76 'BBC man in photo terror stop' Amateur Photographer (30.11.2009)

This madness could not be allowed to continue and following a successful appeal to the European Court of Human Rights (ECHR) in January 2010, searches under Section 44 of the Terrorism Act were ruled unlawful as they breached Article 8 of the European Convention on Human Rights.

Beyond doubt, Britain currently faces a terrorist threat that is real, sustained, and complex. Whether it is a result of a misguided foreign policy or a failure to establish community cohesion in our cities, or a combination of both, is something that political pundits and academics will debate for years to come. The fact remains however that a significant minority of our own citizens, born, bred, and educated here, do not see themselves as contributing and valued members of British society and are vulnerable to the blandishments of more sinister individuals who have their own agenda of violent extremism. We have a problem, but we are not a country at war. Despite the horror stories pedalled in the tabloids, which would have us believe that evil bearded men are sitting in caves plotting our downfall through a network of ISIS and Al-Qaeda sleeper agents, the vast majority of our problems are 'home grown'. Outside help, such as it is, comes in the form of encouragement on open-source websites and the ravings of bizarre clerics who inhabit the fundamentalist outer-reaches of Islam and are rejected by 99.9% of British Muslims. It is for these reasons that all police activity which plays upon stereotypes is, by definition, counter-productive and achieves more for the committed terrorist than any of their own half-baked schemes or badly managed conspiracies. Police involvement in combating terrorism needs sophisticated and intelligent leadership; it needs a finely nuanced and developing strategy which is fed by high quality and validated intelligence from covert sources. Investigations need to be focussed, using the very latest technical resources, and employing the most accomplished personnel from whatever discipline can add value, be that the police, the security services, the military, the universities or even the private sector. All involved, from the newest surveillance team member to the Director of Operations, need to have a clear understanding of where he or she features in the broad strategy. Individuals may come and go but the core aim, to disrupt or prevent terrorist activity and to remove violent extremists from the scene by whatever legal means possible, should be enduring.

All of this must operate in parallel with community-based initiatives aimed at de-radicalising those members of our population who are at risk of being drawn into violent extremism, and building bridges to those teetering on the edge so that they see greater value in becoming fully paid-up members of British civil society, rather than the criminal alternative. Since 2008 both Tory and Labour governments have seemed to understand the need for a unified strategic approach, and the PREVENT Strategy which was introduced in 2008 is an intelligent piece of work which seeks to address the problems in many of our communities that few policymakers have been willing to acknowledge. Coupled with the CONTEST Counter Terrorism Strategy, which is enforcement based, the UK may well have a workable model for the future, despite ill-informed criticism from the right-wing press.

What is missing however is recognition of the fact that there is no place in this for the amateur, and that in terms of policing, the vast majority of shop-floor operational police officers are rank amateurs. In an effort to justify the new ward-based (and largely cosmetic) policing model, senior officers blithely claim that neighbourhood policing, delivered largely by PCSOs and the occasional police officer, creates trust and generates 'community intelligence' which aids the struggle against violent extremism. Those on the operational end of counter-terrorism know this to be what Winston Churchill once described as *'terminological inexactitude'*. Ordinary police officers, despite the fact that they would like to be seen in the front rank of the fight against terrorism, are actually on the periphery and for obvious reasons of security must remain there. They do not and cannot know the 'big picture'; they are not privy to confidential information, and yet they are allowed, indeed encouraged by their managers, to disrupt communities by using and misusing stop and search powers and indulging in obvious stereotyping. In truth, it is difficult to envisage an open-ended counter-terrorism intelligence-gathering role for ordinary duty local police officers, and definitely not for auxiliaries such as PCSOs, no matter how much senior officers might wish it to be so in the interests of inclusiveness and bolstering their sense of self-worth.

The comment below from a young officer stationed in a London suburb in 2019 is probably more representative of the 'shop floor' view than we would wish. It confirms a mindset which is almost completely at odds with what is needed and plays right into the hands of putative terrorists looking for confirmation that British society is their enemy.

'On my borough we've got one of the largest

populations of Pakistanis anywhere in the country, so that really puts us on the spot. There's no doubt in my mind that a good 50% of the youngsters would be happy to blow me and mine to smithereens given half a chance, so I see it as our job (and so do the rest of my team) to get out there and pick up as much intel as possible to feed into the system. That way we might stop another London Bridge attack happening, and if that means stopping and turning over twenty young Moslems a day, and pissing them off into the bargain, then so be it, it's a price worth paying. This isn't a race thing, or an anti-Moslem thing, it's about letting them know that we are watching them and keeping innocent people safe.[77]

Heaven help us all if this attitude is replicated elsewhere, because without the 'buy-in' of British-Asian communities in our urban centres, we have absolutely no chance of building confidence and preventing the radicalisation of young Moslem men and women. 7/7 and the subsequent attempted bombings on 21/7 were failures of community confidence in the police on a grand scale. Likewise the shooting of Jean Charles de Menezes at Stockwell which contributed to the premature end of Sir Ian Blair's career, and the bungled operation at Forest Gate in 2006 which cost £2.2 million and did much the same for the career of Assistant Commissioner Andy Hayman. The Manchester Arena bombing in 2017, and the London Bridge attack in the same year, underlined this fact with even greater emphasis.

---

77 Confidential research interview 2019

All are examples of what happens when community intelligence is not forthcoming because of a lack of trust in the police brought about by stereotyping and heavy-handed policing.

CIVIL LIBERTIES?

Basically, policing protesters is a relatively simple concept and easy to understand. It is not a science; it is not mysteriously imbued with rite and ritual known only to 'Scotland Yard Bosses' or 'Hero Cops on the Front Line', as tabloid newspapers would have us believe. However, public-order policing at practitioner and leadership level requires a highly developed skill set, which, although trainable, is very much dependent upon gaining 'hands-on' experience over many years. Every public-order event, whether spontaneous or pre-planned, will invariably follow the same pattern from initiation to resolution, and the College of Policing, which with the relevant NPCC committee oversees such matters, has logically defined the model in a core document, a manual of guidance entitled, *'Keeping the Peace'*, developed from an earlier ACPO document. As with any structured system, however, difficulties can and do arise because of the human element. It is the role, indeed the duty of senior officers to maintain a constant grip on affairs, to develop and oversee checks, balances, and controls, and most importantly, to ensure that junior officers rigidly adhere to instructions. There can be no equivocation on this point because any failure in a public-order operation that arises from a breakdown in tactics, or from misconduct or misunderstanding by junior personnel, is ultimately and unambiguously the responsibility of the senior officers involved. They cannot shift the blame onto anyone else.

For decades it has been an established principle of British policing, reinforced by training and enshrined in law, practice and policy, that the operational policing of legitimate public protest is so important that it must always be the subject of oversight and scrutiny by experienced senior officers. It must be managed professionally and should always be a judicious blend of maintenance of the right of protest, and facilitation of that right (so long as it does not adversely impinge upon the rights of others). In addition, there is an obligation to maintain public safety in its broadest sense and specifically to ensure the safety and well-being of protesters to the same degree as everyone else. Lastly there is the duty to maintain the law and prevent and detect offences.

An obvious additional factor is proportionality, which in recent years has increasingly been honoured in the breach. No matter what the circumstances, police action must always be proportionate to the threat. For example, it would be disproportionate to use firearms against a peaceful gathering (as happens elsewhere in the world), or to baton protesters who have shown no violence towards the police. In addition, there are operational considerations which relate specifically to the way in which officers discharge their duties and the way in which they are managed. These have been acknowledged throughout the police service for many years and are set out in written guidance and directions, notably *'Keeping the Peace'* and the Police (Conduct) Regulations 2020, which govern the behaviour of police officers. There are four themes which go to the heart of the obligation placed on the police to preserve civil liberties and the right of lawful protest.

i) *Visible and Accountable Leadership.*
ii) *Integrity.* Not only in terms of conduct and behaviour on the ground, but also in relation to the way in which senior officers plan operations and give directions.
iii) *Communication.* Common sense dictates that there is a real need to 'manage' crowds carefully. Large gatherings of agitated people need expert and careful handling and communication is at a premium. Not only does this apply to communication between the protesters and police (and vice versa), but also in terms of briefing and re-briefing junior officers who are actually face-to-face with protesters.
iv) *Intelligence.* Accurate and well-sourced intelligence is vital to all successful policing operations. Without it any operation is doomed to failure.

Leadership skills are not exclusive to those in recognised leadership positions. In the police, constables are regularly called upon to act as leaders in all sorts of operational settings and in their dealings with the public. Likewise Sergeants and Inspectors are also expected to display leadership, but the obligation upon them is much greater due to their rank and supposed experience. They are expected to brief, control, and closely supervise the Constables under their command. Particularly when dealing with public protest, this should be an ongoing and dynamic responsibility. Policing style, attitude to the public, and obedience to orders will all flow from the extent to which Constables are properly supervised. As has been amply demonstrated at various gatherings in recent years which have degenerated into violence and disorder, such as May Day 2001 in London, the Countryside Alliance lobby of Parliament in 2004, the G20 in 2009 and latterly at the student demonstrations in London in 2010, failure by Sergeants and Inspectors to enforce pre-existing instructions has led to all sorts of excesses. Most notable were those relating to the display of identifying numerals, or failures to intervene when Constables exceeded their duty and began assaulting members of the public. Indeed in recent years the concept of 'supervision' seems to have disappeared from the lexicon of police management – regarded as a confrontational and militaristic term. The role of Sergeants and Inspectors has morphed into that of friend and colleague to Constables. The *'We are all mates together!'* school of management has prevailed.

The tiered supervision structure, albeit that it was based upon a military model, worked, and served all sides well for many years. However, confusion in training policy and lax operational attitudes since the mid-1990s has wrought a fundamental change. Supervisors no longer supervise. Sergeants are openly referred to by their teams as 'PCs with stripes' and addressed by their Christian names. Inspectors rarely if ever patrol and in public-order situations seem to take the line of least resistance and too readily identify with their personnel. Inspectors seem not to 'inspect' anyone, as standards of appearance and behaviour across the police service confirm. By ignoring their fundamental supervisory responsibilities, Sergeants and Inspectors are in breach of their duty to their own senior officers, but more importantly, they are in breach of the duty of care that they owe to the public that they serve. Thus it is that public order operations are so often surrendered to young, poorly managed, Constables.

In their own defence, a number of Sergeants and Inspectors have argued forcefully to me that in far too many circumstances, both in relation to public order and the wider policing environment, even if they choose to intervene, they receive little or no support from their own Superintendents and other senior managers. Too often, it is claimed, the threat of career-stopping grievance procedures for 'bullying in the workplace' or 'discrimination' is enough to ensure that senior managers take the line of least resistance and fail to support their supervisory personnel. If true, and there seems to be strong anecdotal evidence in support of the claim, this is managerial cowardice of the worst sort.

In the same way that many Sergeants and Inspectors have failed to deliver what is required of them, so it is that more senior personnel have failed to meet the high standards that are rightly expected of them. Chief Inspectors, Superintendents, Chief Superintendents, and even Chief police officers (in appropriate circumstances) need to be visible in public order situations. It is they who must set the tone; adjust the policing style as conditions require, and rigidly enforce the operational strategy and underpinning philosophy. The average young constable may not know or care much about the inter-relationship between the European Convention on Human Rights and domestic 'rights of protest', but it is he who will be faced with angry protesters, with the obligation to preserve such rights. Junior officers have a right to expect that the orders that they receive from their senior officers are clear, precise, and unambiguous. They should also expect that such senior officers are visible and readily available for advice and support throughout an operation, particularly at times of stress.

Integrity, in the broadest sense of the term, is absolutely non-negotiable. Police officers are quite rightly held to a much higher standard of behaviour than the general public because they possess extraordinary powers by virtue of their office. All police officers, irrespective of their length of service, experience, or rank need to be acutely aware that if their integrity is shown to be flawed, their continued employment must be in grave doubt. None of this should be regarded as new thinking; the Police (Conduct) Regulations 2020 leave no room for doubt. The Standards set out in the legislation (see below)[78] are strictly binding on all police officers and it would be disingenuous for anyone to claim that they were unaware of what was expected.

Standards of Professional Behaviour
Honesty and Integrity
Police officers are honest, act with integrity and do not compromise or abuse their position.

---

78 Schedule 2 to The Police (Conduct) Regulations 2020 (HMSO)

Authority, Respect and Courtesy
Police officers act with self-control and tolerance, treating members of the public and colleagues with respect and courtesy. Police officers do not abuse their powers or authority and respect the rights of all individuals.

Equality and Diversity
Police officers act with fairness and impartiality. They do not discriminate unlawfully or unfairly.

Use of Force
Police officers only use force to the extent that it is necessary, proportionate, and reasonable in all the circumstances.

Orders and Instructions
Police officers only give and carry out lawful orders and instructions. Police officers abide by police regulations, force policies and lawful orders.

Duties and Responsibilities
Police officers are diligent in the exercise of their duties and responsibilities.

Confidentiality
Police officers treat information with respect and access or disclose it only in the proper course of police duties.

Fitness for Duty
Police officers when on duty or presenting themselves for duty are fit to carry out their responsibilities.

Discreditable Conduct

Police officers behave in a manner which does not discredit the police service or undermine public confidence in it, whether on or off duty. Police officers report any action taken against them for a criminal offence, any conditions imposed on them by a court or the receipt of any penalty notice.

Challenging and Reporting Improper Conduct

Police officers report, challenge or take action against the conduct of colleagues which has fallen below the Standards of Professional Behaviour.

Where officers are deployed in close-knit units, particularly when policing demonstrators, a direct audit trail can always be drawn between misconduct and breaches of the Regulations. The key responsibility to 'Challenge and Report Improper Conduct' seems to be almost totally ignored by the majority of today's young officers, for much is witnessed but little reported. In circumstances that are sadly reminiscent of the Blair Peach case in 1979, it must be assumed that misplaced loyalty within pseudo-elite groups such as the Territorial Support Group (TSG) has a bearing on the way they behave. But failure to act is a stinging indictment of the integrity and professionalism of the 'on the ground' supervisors at all ranks, up to and including the most senior officers.

All experienced senior officers know that the key to professional management of crowds is effective, real-time, communication, not only between the police and the protesters but also between police officers and their supervisors. One of the major critical success factors in any policing operation is the briefing and re-briefing of personnel as the operation develops. This is particularly important on those occasions when officers are deployed for extended tours of duty on containment cordons, where the mood of the protesters is angry, or the issue is an emotive one such as climate change or an international conflict such as Gaza or the War in Ukraine. In most public order operations only Inspectors and senior officers attend core briefings (which in the Met are usually held at New Scotland Yard). Junior personnel are briefed at their home stations by their Inspector when parading for duty on the day of the event. Thus, information is cascaded and, as a result, often becomes diluted. The following is a verbatim comment from a Met constable of twelve years' service, describing his experience of parading for the G20 operation in 2009 at an outer London police station and receiving a monumentally unsatisfactory briefing.

> 'Our personnel carrier was late arriving and our skipper [Sergeant] only had a couple of minutes to talk to our serial Inspector, who was from another station on the borough. As a result, our briefing was done in the vehicle, en route to central London and lasted about one minute. No intelligence, no explanation of the grand plan, nothing. It was a joke.'[79]

Equally important, however, in view of the urgent need to 'factor in' real-time intelligence about individual

---

79 Confidential interview (2009) – Author's research

protesters and groups of protesters as the operation progresses, is the need to re-brief and update junior officers about matters that concern them directly. The attitudes that officers adopt towards protesters is 'coloured' by rumour and the peer-group pressure of 'elite' units. If officers believe themselves to be isolated and under siege, the way in which they deal with protesters will often change for the worse. It is therefore vital that senior officers build into their strategy and tactics a system to ensure that constables 'on the ground' are regularly updated and made aware of changes in deployments, intelligence, and event management. Sadly, this is seldom if ever done, despite being the norm in Northern Ireland where the police have wide experience of dealing with disturbances that are much more challenging than anything seen on the mainland. A Sergeant with over fifteen years' service and much experience in the field of public order intelligence made the following comment:

> *'Briefings are the key in all this. I have occasionally been able to go to the main Scotland Yard briefing and I am grateful for the excellent and thorough briefing on the day of such events. A sergeant on a serial however will get a 20 second verbal input from the serial Inspector if they are lucky. Senior officers should ensure that all their officers know the tactical plan, and their role within it. This is not currently done. The tactical plan is kept secret, but you are told "Not to undertake activity which may seriously affect the tactical plan."[80]*

---

80 Ibid

Police officers, especially those officers in leadership positions, need to re-learn the skill of talking to people. During the 1980s and 1990s it was usual for Inspectors and Sergeants to be deployed on public order operations with hand-held loudhailers so that they could address crowds when necessary. It is virtually impossible for any protester, beyond the first line flanking a police cordon, to understand why movement of police lines has started (for instance, in order to clear a street). As a result, there is crushing and congestion, which leads to panic, anger, and retaliation. It is far better that a loudhailer announcement be made, in even tones, explaining why police action is about to take place. It also used to be standard practice, at static points and protected locations, to use high-visibility matrix notice boards on which were displayed requests to the crowd, announcements and other information. Emerging technology such as multi-texting allows for more imaginative and sophisticated ways of communicating with protesters in a non-confrontational way.

Lastly, the constables deployed on cordons and barriers need to understand that protesters are not criminals, or from some violent underclass. They have an inalienable right of protest, and it is the duty of the officers to preserve and maintain that right. Training, supervision, and briefing must be remodelled to ensure that the face of British policing that the world sees is not the granite-faced, sneering visage displayed at some recent protests, but a display of tolerance and intelligence.

Indeed there is real urgency about the need to confront these police-cultural issues. The image of just one scowling, gratuitously violent, police officer behaving inappropriately will be around the world in minutes on 'YouTube' and will do the reputation of the United Kingdom untold damage. It will be utterly pointless for the Commissioner or the Home Secretary to wring their hands, announce a review, and to claim meekly that the vast majority of officers 'are doing a great job' when people will be able to see what actually happened from the comfort of their own homes. The police blog *'Night Jack – An English Detective'*, which was awarded the Orwell Prize before the author, a Lancashire Detective Constable, was 'outed' by the 'The Times' and had to close down under threat of disciplinary action by his force, summed up the situation with the wry comment:

> *'Having gone from truncheons to tasers in a generation, I have to wonder what purpose the current police service has been built for... we are mostly approachable and pleasant people, it's just that we dress like Imperial Stormtroopers.'*

The Metropolitan Police Directorate of Media and Communication, and the media departments of other police forces, seldom acquit themselves well when dealing with issues of public protest and civil liberties. Most unbiased observers are left with the impression that their principal role is to act as spin-doctors for their employers. This cannot and should not be allowed to happen. It diminishes the reputation of the police service in the eyes of the public and leads to news and media outlets withdrawing their trust. The *'We are up for it!'* comment attributed to an 'unnamed' senior officer in the days before the extreme disorder at the G20 in 2009 was issued by the Met's media team as part of a press briefing. It was wholly counter-productive and undeniably had an adverse impact on the way that rank-and-file officers viewed the event on which they were about to be deployed – they thought that their bosses were telling them that they were there for a fight! There are only two possible explanations for the release of this comment – both equally disturbing. Either a senior officer did make the comment and authorised its release to the press, which must throw his (or her) professional judgement into serious doubt. Alternatively, and more disturbingly, the comment may have been devised by the media 'so-called' professionals at the Yard and released to the press in the mistaken belief that senior planners for the operation would have authorised the comment. Misleading, and downright wrong, information was likewise given in relation to the violent clearing of the Bishopsgate Climate Camp at the G20 in 2009, and the number of officers injured.

This latter point is of some significance and does not show the service up in a good light when post-event analysis is conducted. Simon Hart, the then Chief Executive of Countryside Alliance, has pointed out that just prior to the commencement of the IPCC inquiry into the disorder in Parliament Square in September 2004, the Met media department issued a press release, which claimed that 60 officers had been injured, yet enquiry showed that none of the local receiving hospitals had any record of treating any officers.[81] It might be argued by some that Hart has an 'anti-police' bias, but he is also on record as saying that just one

---

81 'Protests and the Hunting Act' Simon Hart (C.A. Website downloaded 17.4.2009)

week after 20,000 Countryside Alliance supporters were involved in confrontations with Met officers at the lobby of Parliament, another 20,000 supporters went to demonstrate at the Labour Party Conference in Brighton. Hart says,

'Tensions were high, this time with real anger added to the mix. Sussex Police handled the event to perfection. It was controlled and peaceful; there were no arrests and no injuries'.[82]

It is incumbent on senior officers to ensure that their press and media advisers act within ethical boundaries. They should not be given tacit or explicit authority to 'spin' or manipulate information that is of genuine public interest.

There is a world of difference between 'evidence' and 'intelligence'. The former will meet the standard required by a court; in many cases it will be corroborated. It will usually be direct and part of an audit trail linking an offender with the commission of an offence. Evidence will either involve the direct observation of a witness or the production of a document or exhibit. 'Intelligence' is seldom so precise, but all too often the two are conflated in descriptions of what might occur during major public order events.

As was shown during High Court proceedings in 2005 relating to the May Day 2001 containment of demonstrators at Oxford Circus in central London, and has been the case at other public protests since, it is clear that much operational planning by the police has been severely hampered by poor quality, or non-existent, intelligence.

---

82   Ibid

In essence, apart from open-source data gleaned from the internet and minor information from police information reports, there is little intelligence of real value coming from the welter of data recorded in police intelligence databases. A retired middle-ranking former Special Branch officer, with wide experience of public order planning, interviewed during the research for this book, has commented that most 'intelligence' was of low quality, being little more than surmise, unsubstantiated gossip, or shrewd guesswork on the part of police officers. He pointed out that very little of the material that he saw was truly 'actionable' from an operational point of view and usually involved little more than reported meetings between well-known organisers, coupled with vainglorious comments culled from websites and leaflets. His professional view was that it was wasteful of resources and often self-defeating for public-order planners to rely too heavily upon such data.

All large public order events will have an intelligence-gathering phase that commences weeks, or even months, before the proposed date of the demonstration or protest. Logic, and good practice, dictates that where *evidence* of planned offences by identified individuals is detected, action should be taken to arrest and prosecute those involved or, at the very least, disrupt their activities well in advance of the event itself. Garnering such evidence requires sophisticated surveillance and specialist detective skills. The former Special Branch officer referred to above is firmly of the view that the capacity of the Met to deliver such evidence, or even to elicit worthwhile intelligence, has been severely hampered by organisational changes following the formation of the Counterterrorism (CT) Command at Scotland Yard in

October 2006. He claims that for no good operational reason, the Metropolitan Police Special Branch was disbanded, and a small rump of its personnel subsumed into the new unit. The entire focus of the CT Command in the wake of the 7/7 bombings was the pursuit of international and domestic terrorists, usually with a militant Islamic background. The quiet and persistent surveillance of other groups deemed to be less of an immediate threat, which had been conducted by Special Branch for many years, became a low order priority. He commented,

'The only measure of success for the CT Command is, "how many Islamic terrorists can we arrest and convict?" Any intelligence that isn't sourced back to the Security Service isn't seen as having any value. The branch [i.e. Special Branch] people were not seen as players. As a result, most of our skills in knowing about the extreme left, or extreme right or environmental or animal groups was either disregarded or has been lost altogether as skilled officers retire or move on. It's a real shame because we used to have a really close relationship with CO11 [MPS Public Order Branch] and the FIT [Forward Intelligence] Teams and I don't think that exists anymore.'

In the context of long-running protests and other major demonstrations such as those linked to Extinction Rebellion and 'Just Stop Oil', the senior officers who have the responsibility of planning for the police response are required to work to directions and principles set out in College of Policing, NPCC, and force policy statements and manuals of guidance. The most important of these is the body of guidance and training material that the College maintains online, which was developed from the original 'ACPO Manual of Guidance on Keeping the Peace'. The manual was first produced in 2000 having replaced an earlier document – the 'ACPO Guide to Public Order Policing' – and is generally acknowledged to be much more authoritative. Whilst technically not prescriptive, the guidance nonetheless places an obligation on all forces in England, Wales, and Northern Ireland to incorporate it into their training and policy. Indeed, there has never been a single occasion when a police force has refused to implement guidance contained in an ACPO manual or College of Policing guidance. In the wake of profound criticism of the police handling of the G20 demonstrations in 2009, ACPO re-vamped the entire document in 2010 in order to ensure that it was compliant with the European Convention on Human Rights and domestic Human Rights legislation.

The manual marked a new approach to the development of police policy in the contentious area of civil liberties and public-order policing. For the first time it examined the nexus between crime and disorder, and public order; the nature of tensions and conflict resolution; conflict management; crowd dynamics, and the vital role of intelligence. Principles of policing were established and defined with particular reference to Human Rights and police commanders were reminded, in trenchant terms, of their duty, viz:

ECHR (Article 11) – Freedom of Assembly and Association
The starting point for policing public protest is

the presumption in favour of facilitating peaceful assembly. There is no basis in domestic law for describing a public protest as inherently unlawful. As a lawful activity, the majority of peaceful protests may not require police attendance.[83]

The guidance contained is specifically directed towards senior officers and those responsible for planning the management of public protests. Thus it is of crucial importance in advising and informing the policing of legitimate democratic protest and how it should be made an integral part of the briefing for all involved, from the officer in charge, down to the most junior recruit. Even without the explicit direction of published guidance, the police are under a legal, moral, and ethical duty to ensure that all relevant provisions of the European Convention on Human Rights (ECHR) and domestic Human Rights legislation are rigidly adhered to. Indeed, the guidance makes it clear that police are on notice that any failure to protect the ECHR rights of lawful protest is itself a breach of their duty. There are few things more vital to the health of democratic society than the active protection of civil liberties, yet it is debatable whether more than a tiny minority of serving officers of all ranks are aware of the real obligations placed upon them.

The ignorance of some very senior officers about their ECHR obligations is depressing. In research for this book, as recently as 2022, whilst interviewing an officer of Deputy Chief Constable rank in a large urban force in the north of

---

83 'Keeping the Peace' (2010 edition) Para 2.10 (published by the NPIA for ACPO)

England, I was confidently told that the ECHR no longer applied, '...*as, since Brexit, the UK is no longer bound by the court's decisions...*' This is, of course, complete nonsense. The ECHR stands separate from the institutions of the EU and our relationship with the court was unaffected by Brexit.

All tactical options used by police in dealing with protesters are on a continuum. The overall strategy and associated tactical plan should always be dynamic and capable of change or adjustment when circumstances change. It would be a truly unimaginative commander who decided, at all costs, to slavishly follow a pre-ordained decision to use one particular tactical option to the exclusion of all others. However, this is precisely what seems to have happened at the G20 in 2009, and subsequent student demonstrations (following a model devised for the May Day 2001 protests in London). Senior officers clearly decided that the containment tactic (inappropriately referred to by the slang term 'kettling') was going to be used, no matter what the circumstances demanded.

There is abundant evidence to show that irrespective of the mood of the protesters on the day, the decision to contain them had been made long in advance. From the point of view of a lazy police commander looking for a 'quick win', it can be seen that the police gain much from dealing with an isolated group of *violent* troublemakers in this way. There are obvious operational advantages, and it is much easier to deal with an isolated group 'en bloc' rather than in scattered groups or as individuals. However, use of the tactic raises real issues about how to identify 'violent demonstrators' and 'those intent on criminality', because they are the only two categories of protesters who legally justify such intrusive police attention. The courts have confirmed that it was, and remains, wholly improper to include innocent bystanders and legitimate peaceful protesters in such action. This in turn raises important issues about real-time intelligence and how intelligence flow should be managed, in order to identify protesters who might be 'violent' or 'criminal'.

It is for all the above reasons that the operational use of 'kettling' is hedged around with caveats and exclusions. Whilst technically available as a tactical option in public order policing generally, it is nonetheless restricted by the wider and deeper civil liberties issues discussed in the College of Policing guidance and the ECHR. Police tactics and training in relation to crowd management were greatly influenced by Lord Justice Scarman's Inquiry into the disorder that took place on 15th June 1974 at Red Lion Square, Holborn, when a Warwick University student, Kevin Gately, was killed during a political demonstration. Police action had been criticised, and in his report, Lord Scarman commented,

> *'...it is important for the officer in charge to ensure, wherever possible, that a crowd has sufficient means of moving away before taking action to disperse or disrupt it. Similarly, policemen behind a crowd should bear in mind that their action may be of critical importance to any action taken at the front of the crowd. These are points which could profitably be incorporated in Metropolitan Police Training.'*[84]

---

84 Red Lion Square Disorders of June 15, 1974: Report of Inquiry by the Rt. Hon. Lord Justice Scarman by Leslie Scarman. (HMSO)

From the mid-1970s until at least 2001, standard police public-order training for junior and senior personnel stressed the need to ensure that when policing crowds in confrontational situations, it was essential to allow an 'avenue of escape' for public safety reasons. Such practice was built into all major operations and continues to this day. An example of this is Notting Hill Carnival, the planning for which always incorporates sterile areas, which can be opened to accommodate crowds, if pressure becomes too great. None of this advice and training was taken into account at the G20 or during the 'kettling' of demonstrators during the student disorders of 2010. This was clearly against the spirit of the Scarman findings, and all police practice that has developed since 1974. Scarman also made a salient observation about the way police should manage crowds of demonstrators, something which HM Inspectorate, in their scathing review of the G20 debacle, referred to as the concept of 'no surprises'.

> *'...I think it would be a good general principle that where they propose to take action against a static crowd, the police should first give a warning; only exceptionally should no warning be given.'*[85]

It is intriguing to note, once again, how the failure to maintain an organisational memory can lead the police into difficulty time and time again. Scarman's warning was built into Met training and practice and was the approach adopted

---

85 Ibid

by all senior practitioners during the 1980s and 1990s but was apparently abandoned after 2001 as generations of experienced and able public order practitioners moved on or retired.

The College of Policing guidance and all police force directions make clear that compliance with ECHR guidelines,

> '...must be demonstrated during planning and debriefing in order to maintain a transparent decision making process... and that this is particularly relevant with regard to "...assessing feasible options..."'

In this connection there is a crucially important judicial decision which governs the use of 'kettling' as a tactical option. *Austin and Saxby v The Commissioner of Police for the Metropolis (2005)* arose from the May Day 2001 containment of protesters and non-protesters at Oxford Circus in London under circumstances remarkably similar to the containment of protesters during the G20 in 2009 and since. Following a series of legal challenges, the case was determined in March 2007 at the Court of Appeal before the Master of the Rolls, Sir Anthony Clarke. The extensive and detailed judgement has been cited by the Met as validation of their use of the tactic and it undoubtedly played a part in their decision to 'kettle' demonstrators in London in the years since, right up to 2022. However, close reading of the judgement casts its use in an entirely different light, indeed it is difficult to find the authority that Met senior officers claim. At paragraph 119, the Master of the Rolls finds,

> 'a) Where a breach of the peace is taking place, or is reasonably thought to be imminent, before the police can take any steps which interfere with or curtail in any way the lawful exercise of rights by innocent third parties they must ensure that they have taken all other possible steps to ensure that the breach, or imminent breach, is obviated and that the rights of innocent third parties are protected;
> b) The taking of all other possible steps includes (where practicable), but is not limited to, ensuring that proper and advance preparations have been made to deal with such a breach, since failure to take such steps will render interference with the rights of innocent third parties unjustified or unjustifiable; but
> c) Where (and only where) there is a reasonable belief that there are no other means whatsoever whereby a breach or imminent breach of the peace can be obviated, the lawful exercise by third parties of their rights may be curtailed by the police.
> d) This is a test of necessity which it is to be expected can only be justified in truly extreme and exceptional circumstances; and
> e) The action taken must be both reasonably necessary and proportionate.'

Effectively, the court placed a major obstacle in the way of legitimate use of containment. The police are put on notice that any interference with *'the lawful exercise of rights by innocent third parties'* may only be embarked upon following the most rigorous review of other options and confirmation *'that there are no other means whatsoever'* open to police. The final nail in the coffin of any claim that the 'kettling' of innocent protesters is legitimate is where the judgement directs that police must apply a *'test of necessity'* and requires that the circumstances must be, *'truly extreme and exceptional'*. Despite vigorous claims to the contrary by the Met, the court of public opinion has clearly shown that few people believe that any of these conditions were met then, or indeed since. The events that took place were a tipping point in terms of the way the police deal with legitimate public protest in this country. All sides looked over the precipice and did not like what they saw.

Until at least 2001, the Met's Public Order Branch (CO11) was regarded as a national and international centre of excellence. However, in light of their stewardship of policing in the last few years it is doubtful whether that is still the case. There are lessons that the Met and the wider police service must draw from their management of public order events in our capital city, the student protests, and the policing of lawful protest generally. Even if a tactical option teeters on the edge of being technically legal, that does not make it proportionate, nor does it confer respectability on its use. Strict legality must be weighed in the balance with the ethical and moral imperatives, the implications for civil liberties, and the damage to policing as a whole that results from the image of an over-mighty and thuggish police force.

There is a growing body of evidence that a significant minority of today's police officers are alienated from the public, see them as 'the enemy', and have little or no interest in preserving legitimate rights of protest. Such individuals inflict damage on civil society out of all proportion to their numbers. A healthy democracy cannot function without respect for the rule of law, the maintenance of civil liberties, and accountable policing. George Clemenceau's oft-quoted comment to Woodrow Wilson at the Paris Peace Conference in 1919 that 'War is too important to be left to Generals' (*La guerre est trop importante pour être laissée aux généraux)* could, with value, be re-cast to describe the law-and-order challenges facing twenty-first century Britain – 'Policing is too important to leave to Chief Constables'. Indeed it is probably too important to leave to politicians until something is done about the cavernous democratic deficit that currently exists.

CHAPTER 6
SEXUAL PREDATORS – A BETRAYAL OF TRUST

Police Constable Wayne Couzens, who was given a whole-life term of imprisonment at the Central Criminal Court in August 2021 for the kidnap, rape, and murder of Sarah Everard, is a predatory monster, a fantasist who believes that he is irresistible to women especially when he is wearing a uniform, and a gun fetishist who actively sought occupations which allowed him to carry and use firearms. Almost by definition he is precisely the sort of man who should never be recruited as a police officer, yet not once but on five occasions he was given the opportunity to place the public at risk.

In 2002 he was appointed as a Special Constable in the Kent Constabulary, where he worked part-time as a volunteer in police uniform around Deal, Dover and Folkestone. In 2011 he applied to join the Civil Nuclear Constabulary (CNC), a non-Home Office force which provides security for the nuclear power industry. After initial training he was posted to Sellafield in Cumbria where he served for eight months, before transferring to

Dungeness Power Station in Kent, to be nearer his home in Deal. The CNC are the only police force in the country in which officers are fully armed at all times when on duty – and as was to become clear, this was very much an attraction of the job for this appalling man, who saw the possession of firearms as a demonstration of his sexual potency. His nickname, used openly by CNC co-workers, was 'The Rapist', because he made female officers who worked with him feel uncomfortable. In June 2015, Couzens indecently exposed himself and masturbated in front of a woman in Dover. The allegation was promptly reported to the Kent Police who did absolutely nothing other than record the crime. There was no investigation worthy of the name, and the matter was 'swept under the carpet' without his employers, the CNC, even being informed. It is a matter of conjecture as to why no attempt was made to pursue this serious allegation more energetically, but the suspicion must be that his status as a serving CNC officer, and his previous time as a 'Special' with the Kent Constabulary for eight years, persuaded his former colleagues, out of misplaced loyalty, to close their eyes to what he had done. A shameful breach of their duty which is now (in 2023) the subject of a disciplinary inquiry.

In September 2018 Couzens transferred to the Metropolitan Police and was posted to Bromley in south London as a neighbourhood beat officer. In February 2020 came the fifth and final opportunity to divert this unsavoury individual from the path of perdition. He applied for a transfer to the Met's Parliamentary and Diplomatic Protection (PaDP) Command, the so-called 'elite' armed unit that protects foreign embassies in the capital, and the Parliamentary Estate in the Palace of Westminster. He was appointed without any sort of in-depth vetting and was soon providing armed coverage at the House of Commons, the House of Lords, and outside 10 Downing Street.

During his trial for the murder of Sarah Everard, evidence emerged that just six days prior to her kidnap, Couzens had exposed himself yet again at a fast-food restaurant in south London, and yet again police action had been conspicuous by its absence, despite the fact that his credit card details had been preserved, along with the registration number of his car. The investigating officers in that case are now (in 2023) facing disciplinary proceedings for 'gross misconduct', a classic example of closing the stable door after the horse has bolted.

Couzens belonged to a WhatsApp forum in which he and colleagues regularly exchanged views about policing. As with evidence of his earlier indecent exposure, these social media messages emerged at his trial. The content is outrageous and defies description, and yet again, in 2023, another stable door is being slammed shut as Couzens' colleagues on the forum become the subject of disciplinary action.

It would be tempting, indeed reassuring, to hope that the Couzens case stands alone as an example of perversity by a police officer, but nothing could be further from the truth, for in terms of criminality in the Met, the PaDP where he served with a group of like-minded colleagues, seems to be in a league of its own.

Three days after Couzens was jailed, PC David Carrick, a serving member of the PaDP and former colleague of Couzens, was charged with one count of rape following an attack on a woman on the night of 4 September 2021.

22 February 2019

Wayne Couzens
Messy one, lovely.
Remember Forster, it's
got to be consensual!

Matthew Forster
They've only got to say yes once

21 March 2019

After Jonathon Cobban describes responding, while on duty, to an unconscious woman who had been drinking.

Wayne Couzens
Did you [perform sex
act on] her to see if she
was ok?

Jonathon Cobban
I considered it. But she was a
right old lump. So I just raped
a bystander instead

21 June 2019

Wayne Couzens
Mate they aren't gonna ditch you with
your skill sets, unless you [perform a
sex act on] a DV [domestic violence]
victim! Oh, Jon in that case you're
probably f***ed

Jonathon Cobban
That's alright, DV victims love
it... that's why they are repeat
victims more often than not.

Joel Borders
No, they just don't listen!

29 June 2019

*During a discussion with other officers about racially diverse areas of London, described as 's***holes'.*

Joel Borders
You know when it's getting near to the
end of night shift in Hounslow because
you can hear the call to prayer

Wayne Couzens
You can add Peckham to that list. I
was on VCTF [Violent Crime Task
Force] the other shift in Peckham,
another Somalia village!!!!

On 24 November 2021 and 10 January 2022, he was further charged with an additional twelve counts of rape (and sixteen of related outrageous sexual offences) that occurred between 2009 and 2018 against seven other women. On 17 March 2022, Carrick was charged with a further twelve offences, some related to new complainants, that took place between 2003 and 2015. In April 2022, in his first appearance before the Parliamentary Home Affairs Committee (*his predecessor Dame Cressida Dick having been forced to resign by the media storm surrounding the rape and murder of Sarah Everard*), the Acting Met Commissioner Sir Stephen House ruefully confessed that an inquiry into PaDP's culture had found the unit suffered from 'a lack of supervision' – a description that re-defines the concept of management ineptitude.

Matters were to get even worse for the Met and the PaDP. In November 2022 Carrick was charged with an additional nine sexual offences added to the 44 he was already facing, bringing the total to 21 counts of rape, nine counts of sexual assault, five counts of assault by penetration, three counts of coercive and controlling behaviour, two counts of false imprisonment, two counts of attempted rape, one count of attempted sexual assault by penetration, and a further count of causing a person to engage in sexual activity without consent. On 16 January 2023, at Southwark Crown Court, Carrick pleaded guilty to 85 offences against 12 women, including 24 counts of rape, which were committed between 2003 and 2020. This represented the longest indictment of sexual offences against one offender placed before a UK court since 1958. He was sentenced to 36 life sentences with a recommended minimum term of thirty years.

However, no-one should breathe a sigh of relief and assume that the cancer of gross sexual misconduct has been cut from the body of policing by the arrest and conviction of these two creatures. The reality is that the abuse of women and girls and young children, by serving police officers, is a scandal that has been bubbling under the surface for decades, hidden from view whenever such cases arise by official sophistry, denial, and the wholly false claim that such offending is something that is perpetrated by the occasional 'bad apple', whilst policing as a whole is in good health. The truth is that sexual offending by police officers is at epidemic proportions in every force in the country, for reasons that will be discussed in due course.

In 2018 and 2019, detailed research for an ITV documentary entitled 'Exposure – Predator Police Uncovered', screened in October 2019, exposed the detail of individual cases dating back to 2015. Only those cases where officers were convicted before a court and subsequently dismissed for gross misconduct were included in the data, thus ignoring matters where no further action followed an arrest or allegation. In just four years, 2015 to 2018, a total of 251 cases involving 253 officers were discovered. Offenders were shown to have served in each of the 43 forces in England and Wales (plus the British Transport Police, and the States of Jersey Police). Whilst the vast majority were constables and a few PCSOs, a significant minority were officers of sergeant, inspector, chief inspector, superintendent, and chief superintendent rank. There was even a case involving a Chief Constable. It must be stressed that these were only those cases that had resulted in prosecution and internal police disciplinary proceedings. It is a 'rule of thumb' in all criminal investigation that those matters which are detected probably amount to no more than 25% of the total amount of offending. It is thus safe to assume that around a thousand such offenders were active during the review period and continue to be active to this day. Research showed that on average an officer was convicted or dismissed for sexual misconduct every five days, and that police officers were seven times more likely to be dismissed for sexual misconduct than teachers or doctors.

The egregious nature of the offending disclosed is both shocking and distressing. Much of it involves officers preying upon vulnerable women, often victims of domestic abuse and other crime, where the offenders have actively targeted and pursued them for their own sexual gratification. Shockingly, a large number of cases involve the making and distribution of extreme child pornography. Without exception all involve a power dynamic where men (it is almost exclusively men) have authority over women, and all involve the offenders relying upon their status as police officers to dominate their victims. The following are just a few of the cases, drawn at random from the datasets, which demonstrate the detail and extent of what is actually meant by the bland official term 'police sexual misconduct'.

March 2015
Police Sergeant 'A' *(Cambridgeshire Police)*
Appeared at Norwich Crown Court and convicted of 13 offences including 3 counts of rape, 3 counts of indecency with a child, various sexual assaults and taking an indecent

photograph of a child. Sentenced to 14 years imprisonment (subsequently increased to 20 years on appeal in March 2017). Placed on the sex offenders register for life. *In 2005 whilst on duty in uniform, 'A' had been arrested for taking 'up skirt' pictures of young girls using a 'spy pen' in a branch of Tesco's. He was given a police caution but was not charged with a criminal offence and was not placed on the sex offenders register. He appeared before the then Deputy Chief Constable, who allowed him to keep his rank and his job, after hearing that he had agreed to seek counselling. All his most serious offending took place after the initial 'incident'. The trial judge, when sentencing 'A', criticised Cambridgeshire Police in the strongest terms for their decision not to prosecute him for the 2005 offence.*

September 2015
Police Constable 'B' *(Metropolitan Police)*
Appeared at Southwark Crown Court charged with possessing and distributing extreme pornographic images. Sentenced to 4 months imprisonment. Placed on the sex offenders register and made the subject of a Sexual Harm Prevention Order. *Was found in possession of still and video images on his phone showing acts of bestiality with animals and sexual activity with children. Evidence was advanced that he had distributed the material to police colleagues at Bethnal Green Police Station.*

November 2015
Police Constable 'C' *(Hertfordshire Constabulary)*
Appeared at the Central Criminal Court, Old Bailey, charged with making, possessing, and distributing 110 grossly obscene still images and video footage, stored on his mobile phone, and 3 counts of misconduct in public office. Sentenced to 4 years imprisonment. *Targeted vulnerable young girls from broken homes or with a drug habit, whom he met in the course of his duty. Arranged to have sex with a 14-year-old girl who had run away from home, whose disappearance he had been ordered to investigate.*

March 2016
Police Community Support Officer 'D' *(West Mercia Police)*
Appeared at Shrewsbury Crown Court charged with rape of a girl under 13 years of age and bestiality. Sentenced to 11 years and 4 months imprisonment (with extended licence period of 4 years and 8 months). Placed on the sex offenders register for life. *Took still images and video footage on his phone which showed him committing the rape and having sexual intercourse with a dog. Was initially suspended from duty in April 2014 when arrested for the offences but remained a paid employee of West Mercia Police for almost 2 years until he was formally dismissed in March 2016 following his conviction.*

April 2016
Detective Constable 'E' *(Merseyside Police)*
Appeared at Liverpool Crown Court charged with Misconduct in Public Office and was sentenced to 4 years imprisonment. *Whilst working in the Merseyside Police 'Family Protection Unit' targeted vulnerable female victims of domestic abuse for sex viz.* **1.** *Bombarding them with hundreds of 'sex-texts' – sometimes more than 70-a-day – whilst on duty.* **2.** *Sending them lewd and obscene pictures and videos.* **3.** *Asked for nude pictures and videos of his victims in return.* **4.** *Convinced the victim of an attempted rape to retract her complaint against her wishes, then lied to her claiming that he had sought protection for her.* **5.** *Had sex with one victim of abuse after asking her to dress up for him.* **6.** *Recommended that no further action be taken against the ex-partner of a woman, because she would not send him nude pictures of herself.* **7.** *Received oral sex from a victim whilst a junior colleague waited outside the room, later returned and had sex with her three times.* **8.** *Received a sex act from a woman whilst completing a statement retracting her domestic violence complaint.*

July 2016
Police Constable 'F' *(South Wales Police)*
Appeared at Cardiff Crown Court charged with two counts of rape of vulnerable women. Sentenced to 18 years imprisonment. Placed on the Sex Offenders Register for life. *Drove one of the victims to the top of a remote Welsh mountain*

and attacked her and told the other she would not be believed if she reported him. (Was identified during the course of the inquiry as being responsible for other offences of indecency committed in 2014 against vulnerable victims of domestic abuse.)

November 2016
Detective Chief Superintendent 'G' *(Metropolitan Police)*
Appeared before a Metropolitan Police Disciplinary Tribunal charged with Gross Misconduct (4 cases) and was dismissed from the force. Subsequently appealed the finding and sought a Judicial Review against the decision; however, both applications were rejected. *As the Divisional Commander for a London Borough, acted in a grossly improper way by, 1. Asking female members of his staff inappropriate questions about their underclothing. 2. Putting his tongue in the ear of female members of staff. (2 counts) 3. Simulating oral sex with a banana in front of a senior member of the management team of the London Borough. 4. Taking the scarf from a female police officer and rubbing it in his groin area in a sexually suggestive way.*

December 2016
Woman Police Constable 'H' *(Metropolitan Police)*
Appeared at Southwark Crown Court and convicted of Misconduct in Public Office. Sentenced to 22 months imprisonment. *Became involved with a vulnerable woman, who was*

the victim of rape, when she was working for the Met's Sexual Offences, Exploitation and Child Abuse Command. Had sex with her on numerous occasions, including in the toilet of a McDonald's restaurant.

April 2017
Inspector 'J' *(Kent Constabulary)*
Appeared at Lewes Crown Court charged with three counts of making and distributing grossly obscene images of women and girls, two counts of voyeurism, two counts of taking indecent videos and two counts of distribution of indecent videos. Sentenced to 9 years imprisonment. Placed on the Sex Offenders Register for life. *Using the name 'Hubbabubba71' 'J' posted sexual images and videos he had made and used language which was graphic, obscene and sadistic on a messaging app. Distributed and shared material with other paedophiles in the UK, USA, and Thailand in which he described explicit sexual fantasies involving violently raping and murdering young girls.*

June 2017
Unnamed Police Constable 'K' *(Metropolitan Police)*
(Force refused to name the officer to protect the identity of the victim)
Appeared at Manchester Crown Court charged with a series of penetrative sexual assaults on a 14-year-old girl. Sentenced to 7 years

imprisonment. Placed on the Sex Offenders register for life. *The female victim, aged 14 years, had been repeatedly raped by her natural father, and was placed in the foster care of a Metropolitan Police officer and his wife in order that she could be in what was assumed to be a safe environment. However, the officer abducted the girl and took her to a hotel in Stockport, where he subjected her to sexual assault over a series of days. Her natural father, aged 60, appeared at the same court and was convicted of raping her, and another girl aged 17 years, and was sentenced to 21 years imprisonment.*

August 2017
Police Constable 'L' *(Kent Constabulary)*
Appeared at Canterbury Crown Court charged with rape and sexual assault. Pleaded not guilty but convicted and sentenced to 19 years imprisonment. Placed on the Sex Offenders Register for life. *Raped and sexually assaulted a young female victim, under the age of 16 years. Used police handcuffs to restrain her on a bed, then made a video of the abuse. Forced the victim to give oral evidence at the trial, during which she collapsed in the witness box.*

And finally, proof positive that the Metropolitan Police Parliamentary and Diplomatic Protection Command (PaDP) has had a continuing, and less than enviable, track record of employing and retaining prolific sex-offenders within its ranks alongside Couzens and Carrick, without any obvious management intervention to curb their excesses.

December 2017
Police Constable 'M' *(Metropolitan Police, PaDP Command)*
Appeared at the Central Criminal Court, Old Bailey, charged with 4 counts of possessing and distributing extreme pornographic images of children and bestiality. Was convicted with three co-defendants, one of whom was a school supply teacher. 'M' was sentenced to 20 months imprisonment suspended for 2 years, and 250 hours of unpaid work. *The officer stole social media photographs of a Canadian woman who had committed suicide at the age of 21 and used them to pose online as a 17-year-old girl called 'Emily', creating an alter ego named Emily Whitehouse in order to exchange explicit chat and obscene material with three other paedophiles online. Officers investigating the online chatroom searched 'M's home and uncovered a database of 1,691 indecent and extreme images, with one featuring an infant being abused and others showing children as young as seven. 'M' pleaded guilty to four counts of possession of indecent images – 645 of the most serious category A pictures, 201 category B, 449 category C, and 396 extreme pornographic images of bestiality.*

Any organisation, but particularly the police service, which harbours individuals who possess the capability to commit offences of the sort described has a real problem. These are not just examples of unacceptable behaviour, they are a litany of criminality which shames the officers involved but, more importantly, demonstrates a failure of professionalism by police leaders on an epic scale. In each and every case Chief Constables, Commissioners, and their media-advisers indulge in a masterclass of corporate hand-wringing, always stressing that offenders like Couzens and Carrick and the others are but a tiny minority, whilst all those who work with them are incorruptible heroes, free of any hint of blame or taint of responsibility. There are always 'lessons to be learned' from such cases, although what those lessons are is never defined and certainly never put into effect. The uncomfortable truth is that sexual misconduct by police officers is (to paraphrase Oscar Wilde) *'The crime that dare not speak its name'*. There are cases involving sexually incontinent police officers preying upon vulnerable women that go back fifty or even one hundred years. It is important to note that reliable statistics on police sexual misconduct in England and Wales between 1900 and 1930 are difficult to find. However, there were some well-documented cases from the 1930s, 1940s, and 1950s which confirm that the excesses of the twenty-first century are nothing new.

One high-profile case that occurred in the 1930s involved PC Harry Hammond of the Metropolitan Police, who was stationed at Cannon Row Police Station. He pursued a 15-year-old kitchen maid who worked in domestic service at a grand townhouse in Belgravia. His attentions were spurned however, and in 1935 he violently indecently assaulted her at her place of work whilst he was on duty in uniform. There was a 'hue and cry' as he made off after the assault and, unusually for the time, he was arrested by a colleague, Acting Sergeant Martin. Hammond was subsequently sentenced to 3 years imprisonment, and the case led to a scrutiny of police conduct.

In 1947 PC Arthur Davey of the Brighton Borough Police was convicted of sexually assaulting a woman who had sought his assistance whilst he was on duty in uniform. He was arrested and subsequently sentenced to 4 years imprisonment.

In the 1950s there were several cases in which police officers were accused of sexual misconduct. In 1951 a City of London Police officer, PC William Lambe, was convicted and imprisoned for raping a woman. In 1957, two Metropolitan Police officers, a sergeant and a constable at Golders Green police station in north London, were charged with indecently assaulting two women who were in custody in the police cells. Both officers were convicted and imprisoned.

It is worth noting that these cases probably represent only a small fraction of the actual incidents of police sexual misconduct that occurred in those early years, as many victims may not have reported the abuse they suffered. In addition, prevailing attitudes towards sexual assault and harassment were often dismissive and victims were seldom taken seriously. This, coupled with the fact that the police in those days were seen as beyond criticism, created an environment in which female victims were automatically deemed untrustworthy, and were assumed to have an ulterior motive in making any sort of allegation against a police officer.

During research for this book I interviewed a long-retired Metropolitan Police detective, now in his nineties. As he told me about his days as a Detective Sergeant in the 1950s, his powers of recall were impressive, supported by diaries and notebooks he had kept at the time. In relation to a question about how rape was investigated in those days, he made an inadvertent but very telling comment. Anxious to underline how fair he was, he remarked, 'I always made it a rule, when interviewing rape victims, to have a WPC in the room, and no matter what the victim's age, I'd make sure that she was accompanied by her husband, or brother, or father, you know, someone who was an adult, a man who could explain things to her'. Clearly, in his mind, 'woman' was synonymous with 'child'.

However, the problem of police sexual misconduct today is different in substance and severity, which in turn is a function of wider changes in society and in the way that the police service is managed and led. The advent of the internet and social media and, more significantly, the almost universal possession and use of sophisticated mobile phones, incorporating high-specification cameras and memory capability exceeding anything that would have been possible even a few years ago, has changed everything. Where once an individual who had perverse sexual desires might have kept a stack of pornographic photographs in his desk drawer, or a collection of hard-core magazines in his briefcase, nowadays the world is different. He can carry an iPhone in his jacket pocket on which he has uploaded 10,000 grossly obscene images of girls and children, and simultaneously store a hundred high-definition videos depicting sexual abuse. He can make and distribute such images himself without the need for any sophisticated equipment beyond the phone itself. In addition such individuals can, and do, download, and share such material with other offenders and with colleagues. Worse still is the misogynistic attitude towards female victims of crime (indeed women as a whole), adopted by many male officers as a barely concealed badge of their toxic masculinity. The WhatsApp messages shared between Couzens and his fellow officers are far from rare. The following are just three examples of comments made by Metropolitan Police officers during research for this book (under conditions of strict confidentiality), which display attitudes that run very deep amongst male officers, who may have joined the police with the best of intentions but are too often tainted by peer-group pressure and the need to be 'one of the lads.'

> *'Most DV [Domestic Violence] victims we come across are "slappers" [slang for sexually promiscuous women], who've got a right-hander from the bloke they're living with because they've been putting it about themselves. That's almost always the case when it's a white girl living with a black guy. It's hard to have any sympathy'.*
> *Male PC with 3 years' service working in a Borough Domestic Abuse Investigation Unit.*

> *'We've got a woman sergeant on our team, a woman inspector i/c response, and a woman Borough Commander. What's that all about? It's just the Job ticking boxes. Three Doris's [slang for female police*

officers] and not one of them is anywhere near as good as the guys who used to do their jobs'.
Male PC ('Police Now' graduate entrant) with 2 years' service.

'I dealt with a response call to a woman alleging she had been raped on her way back from a night out clubbing. I did what had to be done, but she had a skirt on that was so short you could see next week's washing, and she was dressed-up like a Russian prostitute. Sorry, but she was definitely asking for it, and only had herself to blame'.
Male PC with 6 years' service (selected for transfer to a provincial force outside London).

Such attitudes betoken a view of the world in which the needs and desires of men should be seen as paramount, and women are of second-order priority. There is also an enduring victim culture whereby male police officers interpret as unfair and discriminatory any support for female officers, as they see it as being at the expense of their own career progression and opportunities. Sadly, research shows that the comments expressed here are typical of the current generation of men entering the service, which raises a fundamental question. What is to be done to challenge this collapse in standards and morality in policing? Already, the legacy of Couzens and Carrick, not to mention the hundreds of others who are less well known, has destroyed the career of one Met Commissioner, and may well bury her successor unless Mark Rowley comes up with a remedy in the very near future.

The fashionable solution advanced by the media and various commentators is that the current problem is a function of unsatisfactory vetting of recruits when they apply for and enter the service. There is a certain amount of validity in this – vetting has a key role to play in ensuring that obviously unacceptable applicants are rejected, but deeper analysis raises a number of issues. Vetting to exclude those who might indulge in sexual misconduct in the future assumes that the risk factors can be identified in the new recruit years before offending becomes apparent. But can it really be the case that individuals have the propensity to offend imprinted in their DNA in some way? And can it really be recognised? This seems highly unlikely, and on that basis, it would be foolhardy to see vetting alone as the silver bullet. There is also the fact that any vetting procedure is effectively 'a photograph in time' so, logically, vetting should be a continuing process, repeated regularly throughout an officer's career. This is, after all, what happens in terms of security vetting for high-risk posts requiring security clearance. In the wake of the Couzens scandal, HM Inspectorate conducted a thematic inspection of vetting policy in England and Wales. The lead Inspector, Matt Parr, was scathing in his findings, saying that 'hundreds of applicants' who joined the police in the three years up to 2022 should never have passed their background checks. Many had failed to declare 'big red flags' such as 'prior convictions' with some having 'links with criminals that are too close and not explained' and many were 'not being entirely honest on their application'. One in 10 officers looked at by Matt Parr's team should never have made it through vetting and whilst it was a random sample, it still amounted to hundreds of officers who should never have been employed. Significantly, however, HM Inspectorate could offer no vetting solution that would meet the challenge of police sexual misconduct.

As with so many aspects of policing, the key to 'making a difference' rests upon the twin pillars of inspirational and effective leadership. Police leaders are not confined to those sporting silver braid on their uniforms, or crowns on their shoulders; leaders exist at every level of the organisation. Indeed it is those leaders on the shop floor, senior and experienced constables and sergeants, who matter the most because they are closest to the action. It is beyond doubt that those officers who worked with Couzens had a shrewd idea what he was like. When women referred to him as 'The Rapist', what did they do? When Detective Constable 'E' (see above) was having oral sex with a victim in a locked room, what did his colleague waiting outside think he was doing? When Sergeant 'A' (see above) escaped sanction after taking 'up skirt' photographs of schoolgirls, what on Earth was going through the mind of the Deputy Chief Constable when the decision was made not to prosecute him? It all comes back to the quality of leadership. On each and every occasion when an officer of any rank, senior or junior, has the slightest suspicion that another officer is committing offences, or even suspects him of being on the path to committing offences, his responsibility is clear and unambiguous. Report what he knows, throw caution to the wind, and pursue the allegation to the bitter end.

By reporting such allegations he or she starts a process that requires the management hierarchy and 'top team' to support them and take assertive action against the alleged offender. Too often in recent decades misconduct and downright corruption has been swept under the carpet because of misguided group loyalty, 'canteen culture', or fear of reputational damage. Those attitudes must be consigned to the dustbin of history because everyone, from top to bottom in the force, has an immutable obligation to maintain ethical standards at every level of interaction, anything less is unacceptable. This in turn presents senior leaders with the challenge of how to enforce standards. Until the 1990s there was a specific disciplinary offence within the then Discipline Code of 'lack of supervision', which placed an obligation on all officers with supervisory responsibility to actively intervene to prevent or report misconduct. To knowingly fail to do so rendered that supervisor liable to disciplinary sanction, up to and including dismissal. The Police Code of Ethics, issued by the College of Policing in 2014, is likewise unambiguous when it refers to 'Challenging and reporting improper conduct', i.e. *'I will report, challenge or take action against the conduct of colleagues which has fallen below the standards of professional behaviour'*. This covers all officers, including constables who are the colleagues of offenders, and carries a disciplinary sanction in the breach. In essence, this is the overarching solution to the problem of police sexual misconduct – unflinching and rigorous supervision by managers, and ethical intervention by working colleagues, with responsibility placed fairly and squarely on the shoulders of those in charge. As soon as it becomes known that a few constables, sergeants, inspectors, superintendents and even Chief Constables have been shown the door marked 'Exit' for failing to do what they are paid to do, and sacked without pension, the example of the execution of Admiral Byng in 1757 for neglect of duty, will concentrate the minds of many and will act *'pour encourager les autres' (to encourage the others).*

The challenge confronting senior management in policing their own personnel is daunting, even to experienced investigators who have been involved in this area of criminality for many years. Figures obtained by the *Observer* in 2023[86] show roughly one in 100 police officers in England and Wales faced criminal charges, including for sexual offences, in 2022 alone. Investigative journalists discovered that the Police Federation, the staff association for 140,000 serving and former police officers from constable to chief inspector, received 1,387 claims for legal support from members facing criminal charges in the year ending December 2022. This showed that the number of officers facing criminal charges has skyrocketed by 590% since 2012 *(in that year, just 235 claims were made for legal support by its members).* The organisation is a statutory staff association, meaning all police officers become members by default when they join any force in England and Wales, which angers critics of the system who claim that the federation is always ready to 'defend the indefensible' and is a 'major obstacle' to dealing with racism and misogyny in the police. The *Observer* investigation also found a sharp rise in the number of misconduct and gross misconduct claims recorded by the Police Federation. The net total related to the two shot up from 418 in 2018 to 598 in 2022, a 43% rise. Misconduct charges are less serious and relate

---

86 Andrew Kersley and Mark Townsend, 'The Observer' 25th February 2023

to the breaking of workplace rules, whilst gross misconduct relates to more serious acts, including criminal actions, that could warrant immediate dismissal.

For example, two officers (PCs Deniz Jaffer and Jamie Lewis), who shared photos of the dead bodies of murdered sisters Bibaa Henry and Nicole Smallman and described the pair as 'dead birds', both faced gross misconduct charges, before eventually being jailed in December 2021 for 2 years and 9 months each for misconduct in a public in public office. As with Couzens and Carrick the officers were part of WhatsApp groups, and during their trial at the Old Bailey it was disclosed that one – a group called 'the A team' – contained 41 police officers and the other contained friends of Jaffer and was proudly and publicly named 'Covid Cunts'.[87]

And so, we arrive at a position in 2023 where a public attitude survey in London[88], commissioned by Global UK Media and compiled in conjunction with the polling company JL Partners, found that just 39% of respondents said they could either strongly (7%), or somewhat (32%) trust the Met while 35% said they strongly or somewhat distrust it. Breaking the data down further, among women just 37% could trust the force while 36% could not. But the trust amongst young women is of greatest concern. Of those under 35, only 4% could say they strongly trust the Met, while 26% said they could somewhat trust it. That leaves seven out of 10 women under the age of 35 unable to say they trust their city's police, a truly appalling state of

---

87 Vikram Dodd, 'The Observer', 6th December 2021
88 Will Taylor and Connor Hand, LBC, 9th March 2023

affairs. There is also a broader issue, not so well reported, that has a direct impact on public confidence in the police. In a recent book by the novelist Holly Bourne, published in 2022, she describes how the isolation of lockdown focussed the minds of many young women and forced them to confront deeply buried fears and anxieties linked to sexual assault and misogyny. The outrageous conduct of Couzens and Carrick acted as confirmation that many powerful men, and particularly police officers, are, in the final analysis, predatory. The damage that this has done cannot be overstated. It may well be that the Metropolitan Police has lost the confidence of an entire generation of women in London, and elsewhere, for decades to come. Someone in the top tier of policing needs to face up to this new reality, say a 'mea culpa', and commit themselves to a change of strategy that is something more than empty rhetoric.

CHAPTER 7
FROM THE SUBLIME TO THE RIDICULOUS...

The police have never been held in lower esteem than they are today. Little more than a decade and a half ago, police officers were regarded by the majority of the population as hard-working, committed public servants doing a necessary and valuable job. They had always had their detractors, and there were always the so-called 'bad apples' who let the side down, but overall, the relationship between the police and the general public was reasonably healthy. In just ten years, fifteen at the most, everything has changed. Middle-England, where once the police might have expected to see their most committed constituency has abandoned them, along with the vast majority of people from all walks of life who have the misfortune to come into contact with the police up and down the country on a daily basis. Speak to the average man or woman in the street, or at a dinner party, and you will hear the same stories over and over again, many at first-hand, some re-told as anecdotes, but all confirming that our twenty-first century policemen and women are universally viewed as something between a joke and an intellectually challenged army of bullies.

Supine and uninspiring leadership, thuggish brutality overlooked on a daily basis, arrogance and rudeness by junior officers, all have brought a once proud service to the position it now finds itself. Most worrying of all is the fact that an entire generation of police leaders has no organisational memory of what the service has lost – to paraphrase Donald Rumsfeld, 'they don't know what they don't know'. Officers who were recruited in the late 1990s and early 2000s are now moving into positions of influence, firm in the belief that the confrontational and pseudo-militaristic model of policing that we see today is the only option to be offered. They are firm in that belief because they know no other.

In February 2011 the Independent Police Complaints Commission (IPCC) published complaint statistics for 2009/10[89], and for senior officers – indeed for the public at large – they made uncomfortable reading. For the second successive year the number of complaints increased by eight per cent, to record levels of almost 58,400 *(by 2020/21 the total had soared to 109,151)*, but within that headline figure there were trends that should give us all pause for thought. Almost 50 per cent of all allegations related to rudeness, incivility and neglect of duty. Even the interim Chair of the IPCC at the time, Len Jackson, felt compelled to comment that *'the number of rudeness and attitude complaints… will require forces to develop an open dialogue with the public'*[90] – Whitehall mandarin dialect for *'This has got to change!'* No-one who cares about the maintenance of law and order

---

89 IPCC Complaint Statistics 2009/10 (Press Release 24.2.2011)
90 Ibid

in this country could view these figures with anything but concern – they expose worrying issues that we ignore at our peril. It is not a trivial point of manners but a reflection of the extent to which policing has changed for the worse in this country over the past few decades. As has already been discussed, until comparatively recently the general public could confidently expect efficiency and courtesy from their local constabulary. This contract with the public lasted until the early nineteen-nineties when, under the dual pressure of economic and social change, a new generation of chief constables and commissioners, who saw policing as a 'business' rather than a vocation based upon service, decided that things had to change.

The new policing, enthusiastically supported by successive Home Secretaries, was about targets, response times and 'measurable performance', lifted straight from the MBA syllabuses of the best universities. Beat patrols on foot in uniform were not part of this brave new world. Unless effectiveness could be measured and converted into a 'bottom line' cost it was of no use and had to be scrapped. Police discretion was submerged under a tsunami of directions, guidelines, and data-gathering.

Then along came 9/11 and the police service enthusiastically decided that everywhere, and all the time, they were on the frontline in the 'war on terror'. Almost overnight, we all changed from citizens to suspects. Terrorism legislation and spurious 'officer safety' policies led to the militarisation of policing, the abandonment of the concept of service, and the greatest change in attitude towards civil liberties that had taken place for a century. Police officers, the majority quite young – the average age of an operational PC is under 24 – have been trained to believe that they are continually under physical threat and must therefore be continually on their guard. Indeed, it is clear that a significant minority of officers see the public as their enemy and as a potential hazard to their well-being which must be dealt with aggressively.

There is no doubt that standards of behaviour and civility, across the whole of Britain, have changed for the worse over the past quarter century. Courtesy and good behaviour have been abandoned by many in our modern, celebrity-besotted, 'me' society. The police are products of that society; they attend the same schools, live in the same communities, and have the same attitudes and prejudices as the best and the worst of us. But police officers should be held to a different standard of behaviour. This change in attitude must be set alongside the simultaneous withdrawal from day-to-day street patrolling that has taken place. Once, all young officers would spend their first few years getting to know local communities and local people by patrolling designated beats, tightly supervised with disciplinary sanctions by their sergeants and inspectors. That has all been abandoned. Now new recruits, fresh from training which emphasises the primacy of their own safety over that of the public, learn from those senior to them, who also know no better.

A concerned officer from a rural force in the south of England recently gave me, in strictest confidence, a copy of the 'Instructors Briefing Notes' from a training programme being run in his force for constables and sergeants – the tone is chilling. Under the heading 'Conflict Resolution' officers are told the following:

'What the public consider rude is [sic] usually just no-nonsense commands and attitude. Unfortunately, when you try to reason with people, they take advantage. Therefore, when you need immediate compliance, you must use stern, unambiguous commands that require no interpretation on the part of the person being talked to. Through experience you must learn to COMMAND AND DOMINATE ALL INTERACTIONS.'

The emphatic block capitals appear in the original training notes. There is no mystery about why police officers are so rude and discourteous today – they are actively trained to be.

It is therefore hardly surprising that of the 58,399 allegations of misconduct recorded by the IPCC 11,576 were of rudeness and incivility. It is also deeply worrying, and one would expect that the senior leadership of the police would be as concerned as you or I. The official response from the then spokesman on Complaints and Discipline, Deputy Chief Constable John Feavyour, of the Association of Chief Police Officers (ACPO), to his credit, acknowledged that a problem exists, and he encouraged the public to complain if they considered that an officer's conduct had been unsatisfactory so that 'appropriate action' could be taken. But sadly there is little evidence to show 'appropriate action', which should mean disciplinary sanction by middle managers, is ever effective. I know from bitter personal experience as an investigator that the default position for too many junior officers is to 'close ranks', refuse to co-operate, and deny that anything improper has occurred.

Every time one is confident that the police service has finally plumbed the depths and can sink no further in terms of its public reputation, details of yet another act of crass stupidity or organisational arrogance emerge, which confirm the urgency of the need for change. The following four examples, selected at random, are offered as a masterclass in how to destroy a once proud institution – each demonstrates breath-taking lack of imagination, slavish adherence to procedure, and an almost total absence of leadership.

(1) ASSAULT BY MARSHMALLOW

On a spring morning in March 2011, groups of children were making their way to school in the small town of Torpoint in Cornwall, just across the Tamar estuary from Plymouth. Like most kids, they were in high spirits, joking and laughing about the day ahead. Nathan Watch, just 13 years old, was walking with a group of two or three of his classmates to Torpoint Community College in the town when one of them – it has never been established who – took a small, soft, pink marshmallow sweet from a paper bag. In jest, the sweet was thrown at another boy who was walking past; nothing more than a childish prank – certainly not a crime. By all accounts no-one gave any further thought to the matter, although the lad on the receiving end of the marshmallow mentioned the incident during a mobile phone conversation with his parents shortly after.

The boy's parents, for reasons best known to themselves however, interpreted the incident as something that required police intervention and made an emergency call to the Devon and Cornwall Police. One might have assumed that the force would have had more important matters to concern itself with. The bustling city of Plymouth, with its population of a quarter of a million, stands on the other side of the Tamar Bridge from Torpoint, requiring all the policing effort that the force can muster. Anyone with a modicum of common sense receiving such a call, certainly in former times, would have politely pointed out that children throwing sweets at each other is not a matter for police, offered suitable advice and rung off.

However, common sense is clearly in short supply amongst the emergency-call handlers of the Devon and Cornwall Police, who immediately logged the 'incident' as an 'alleged assault' and promptly dispatched an officer to the school even though the cash-strapped force is struggling to maintain an acceptable service across two busy counties, and at 8%, has the lowest percentage coverage by uniform police officers of any police force in England and Wales. The officer, a sergeant, raced to the scene accompanied by a constable (because, as we have seen, all modern police officers prefer to patrol in pairs, irrespective of the need to do so). Upon arrival, the officers spoke to staff, told them they were investigating what was now grandly described by them as an 'attack' and had Nathan and his friends plucked from their classrooms 'for interview'.

The school telephoned Nathan's father at home and told him that his son had been accused of 'common assault' and that he would be interviewed as it was a 'police matter'. The concerned father asked if anyone had been injured and was promptly told, 'No, the assault [was] carried out with a pink marshmallow'. Somewhat bemused, he refused to attend the school to be present when Nathan was interviewed, instead demanding that any interview take place at his home, at a time suitable to all concerned. This was interpreted by the officers as a reason to detain Nathan, remove him from school, and convey him to his home by police car, in full view of staff and pupils. His friends were then interviewed and had formal statements taken. The whole sorry saga swallowed around four hours of police time for both officers and became a standing joke across the south-west of England as the TV news and media picked up the story. Yet no-one at the helm of policing in Devon and Cornwall seemed to see anything wrong with such a ridiculously disproportionate response to a non-existent problem. In a bland statement issued by the force headquarters, hinting at deep mystery, the only comment was that an 'incident' had taken place near the school and that 'further enquiries are being made'.[91]

The force has subsequently declined to disclose whether or not a case file was prepared for the Crown Prosecution Service, and whether any charges were preferred or recommended. In the weeks following the 'attack' a blanket of silence fell upon Torpoint and its clearly under-employed police and one is left with the distinct impression that all concerned are acutely embarrassed by the whole business.

(2) KUNG FU FIGHTING!

In 1974, Carl Douglas took his disco hit 'Kung Fu Fighting' to number one in the charts in Britain and the US. Produced

---

91 'Police quiz boy 13, over assault with marshmallow' The Sun (1.4.2011)

on the back of the craze at the time for Chinese martial arts movies starring Bruce Lee, the record sold over nine million copies worldwide, won a Grammy, and made Douglas a very rich man. The lyrics are pure hokum, written, as Douglas has confessed, whilst he was under the influence of painkillers after injuring his foot playing football and watching two kids doing 'kung-fu' moves in the street in the early 1970s.[92] To the vast majority of people the song is little more than aural wallpaper, or so one would have thought until the Hampshire Constabulary became involved.

On 24th April 2011 at Sandown on the Isle of Wight, Carl Ledger, a local entertainer and singer, was appearing at the Driftwood Beach Bar where he had been booked to entertain the customers. One of his regular numbers, always a favourite with the audience, is 'Kung Fu Fighting' and he was halfway through the song playing to a packed house. It was Easter Sunday, and the bar was busy with holidaymakers, when he was approached by a Chinese man who had been walking by the premises in the street outside. This individual, accompanied by his mother, then stormed into the bar and began to shout and swear at Ledger. The man was asked to leave but he continued to shout and allegedly made lewd gestures at the singers on the stage, before storming off. Once the commotion was over, Ledger and his band thought nothing more of the incident, finished their set and left the Driftwood in the early evening.

A few hours later Ledger was enjoying a meal in a local Chinese restaurant (it would be difficult to make this up!), when two uniformed constables from the Hampshire

---

92 'Kung Fu Fighting' Songfacts.com

Constabulary entered and said that they wanted to speak to him. They told him that the Chinese man had made an allegation of 'racial abuse', to which one of the officers added somewhat pompously, 'the law is the law, and this is [our] duty'. Ledger was then arrested and bailed to appear at Newport Police Station for further enquiries. He duly appeared and was questioned at length about a matter that neither he nor anyone else (other than the police on the Isle of Wight) could see was an offence. Even Carl Douglas, the composer of the song, thought that the whole incident was ridiculous. Contacted at his home in the US he confessed that he failed to see any hint of racism in the lyrics; it was just a 'bit of fun'.

In a po-faced statement, the Hampshire Constabulary went to great lengths to justify their actions. A police press spokesman confirmed that a 32-year-old man of Chinese origin had claimed he was subjected to racial abuse because of the lyrics of the song sung by the hapless Mr Ledger. He added, 'If a victim believes that an alleged crime is racially aggravated, the police will treat it seriously. Investigations into this incident are continuing.' The spokesman then went on to say that a 34-year-old man had been arrested on suspicion of causing harassment, alarm or distress under section 4a of the Public Order Act 1986, aggravated by racial abuse, adding portentously, 'He has been bailed for further enquiries'.[93] Subsequently, to the surprise of no-one, the police decided not to bring any charges in respect of the incident and Mr Ledger was released from his bail. Yet again, in what is a pattern in instances of this sort, there

---

93 'Pub singer arrested for racism . . .' Daily Mail (27.4.2011)

was not the slightest hint of an apology from the force for their overbearing and disproportionate behaviour, merely confirmation that 'no charges will be brought', and the self-justifying comment, 'Anyone who perceives they are a victim of a racially aggravated crime is entitled to make a report to the police and we will treat a report seriously.'[94] Putting aside the fact that their conduct is barely justified by their cavalier re-definition of what justifies a 'crime', there is absolutely no admission that they threw discretion and common sense to the winds, merely the hollow excuse favoured by all those who blindly follow orders – 'the law is the law, we were only doing our duty'.

(3) HITLER IN SOMERSET

Pitcombe, near Wincanton in Somerset, is everyone's idea of a picture postcard English village. Indeed to call it a village is something of an exaggeration – it is little more than a hamlet with just twenty houses dotted along the A359, surrounded by lush farmland. The parish church, St Leonards, dates from the 12th century. It is the sort of place where nothing happens for decades at a time and where crime is practically non-existent.

In early April 2011, however, the villagers of Pitcombe were visited 'en masse' by the forces of law and order in the shape of 'half a dozen' officers from the Avon and Somerset Constabulary who over the course of three days made

---

94 'Kung Fu singer faces no charges'. Southern Daily Echo (downloaded 7.5.2011)

door to door enquiries, closely questioned residents, and searched for witnesses to a heinous crime[95]. Local people, who had become used to a level of policing that often left much to be desired ('...'If my shed was broken into would I have received such a tenacious response?' said one), marvelled at the new-found diligence of their local police and wondered what major offence was under investigation; murder perhaps, or high-value burglary? No, the reason for this unaccustomed activity was much more mundane.

It was election time in the county and Councillor Mike Beech, a well-known former chairman of Pitcombe Parish Council, was standing as the Conservative candidate for the vacant local seat as District Councillor on South Somerset District Council. Election posters for all candidates were on display around the village, including one showing the smiling face of Mr Beech, which had been pinned to the notice board near the village hall. In the dead of night, it was assumed, someone armed with a fibre-tip black pen had crept towards the notice board and drawn a 'toothbrush' moustache beneath Mr Beech's nose on the election poster in an effort to make him look like Adolf Hitler. Everyone regarded it as a comic piece of democratic satire. Mr Beech was not greatly offended – as a veteran local politician he has experienced greater criticism than the odd piece of comic graffiti – but having mentioned the incident to the Tory 'political hierarchy' he was advised to report the matter, which he duly did on the basis that he wanted the matter noted.

---

95 'Comedy Hitler moustache drawn on election poster,' Daily Mail (25.4.2011)

Immediately, the Somerset (East) Division of the Avon and Somerset Police, under the command of Chief Superintendent Nikki Watson, swung into action with what was subsequently described as 'Operation Overkill'. Over a three-day period officers descended upon Pitcombe, usually in the evenings, to conduct house-to-house enquiries into what they grandiosely referred to as '...an investigation under the Public Order Act.'[96] Bemoaning the fact that there was no CCTV in the village they appealed for witnesses to help them track down the individual who had drawn the offending moustache on Mr Beech's poster. They stressed the seriousness of the matter by announcing that the very act of defacing the poster was something that, '...could be deemed to cause harassment, alarm or distress to an individual.' Local residents however were slack-jawed with amazement, referring to the exercise as 'an outrageous waste of taxpayer's money.'[97]

The miscreant was never tracked down; the whole exercise was a monumental waste of time and police resources, but in common with so many other similar instances, there has never been the hint of an apology from those who lead the force. What of Mr Beech? Clearly the 'Hitler moustache' debacle did his electoral prospects no harm at all – he was duly elected and now serves as a Conservative Councillor for Somerset South District Council. Indeed perhaps the last word should go to him, obviously deeply embarrassed his only comment to the press was, 'This is something I'm trying to forget.'

96　Ibid
97　Ibid

And, as an aside, it is worth noting that Chief Superintendent Nikki Watson, who presided over this farrago of nonsense, obviously suffered no lasting career damage. In 2022 she was appointed the Deputy Chief Constable of the entire Avon and Somerset Police.

(4) THEFT IN A CHURCH? NOT A JOB FOR THE POLICE

St Andrew's Church, Timsbury, Hampshire, has stood in the village from 1400, when King Henry IV was on the throne. Built of stone with exquisite mediaeval images painted on the fifteenth century plasterwork, and the original oak pews still in place, it is a popular location for visitors interested in church history, and passers-by, all of whom are welcome. The parish churchwarden, John Glasspool, a retired GP and Timsbury resident, takes his duties very seriously. He has done much over the years to raise the profile of the church as a place of worship, whilst safeguarding it against vandalism and theft, including by the installation of CCTV. During 2022 Mr Glasspool and other members of the church council noticed that a series of thefts had taken place from the donation box in the nave of the church, and they decided to do something about it. The CCTV coverage of the slit in the wall-safe donation box was improved and the box was 'baited' it with a £5 note inside. A few weeks later, in September 2022, the churchwarden was astonished to play back the footage to reveal a man, in his sixties, wearing a distinctive padded jacket and a flat cap, accompanied by a woman who appeared to be his spouse. After a quick check for any witnesses, the thief got to work, first using a torch to look inside the slit, revealing the £5 note. Then, using a length of wire, with the torch gripped between his teeth, the elderly villain managed to gently edge the money out through the opening, whilst his companion quietly looked around the Grade II listed building. As soon as he'd managed to make his illicit withdrawal, he handed the money to his female accomplice and the pair left. On camera footage from outside the church Mr Glasspool identified the couple as they entered their car which was parked near the lychgate of the churchyard, and then drove off.

Armed with the camera footage and the registration number of the vehicle, he contacted the Romsey (North) Neighbourhood Policing Team of the Hampshire and Isle of Wight Constabulary, only to be told that they were 'too busy' to do anything about the theft. When Mr Glasspool persisted, pointing out the registration number of the 'getaway car', he was told it was only 'circumstantial evidence' and not a matter for police.

A couple of days before Christmas, the same pair returned, hoping perhaps for a bumper yuletide haul, but this time the box was empty. Again, armed with more CCTV footage the churchwarden contacted the local police, only to be told that they would note it but he 'shouldn't get his hopes up' because the police were far too busy to deal with the theft of small sums of money. When it was suggested that the pair might be stealing from other churches, the officer said, 'That's a thought. If you hear anything let us know', clearly unaware that it was the job of the police to look for links between offences. No amount of argument elicited any worthwhile response from the local police, in essence the churchwarden and the parishioners of St Andrew's were told that they were on their own. Eventually, the church council regretfully took the decision that the church would have to remain locked except during services.

A complaint to the Police and Crime Commissioner for Hampshire, Donna Jones, generated a letter in response which advised Mr Glasspool to 'dial 999' if he saw the couple again, which was less than useless as a strategy because attendance by officers at Grade 1 calls in Hampshire takes an average of 18 to 20 minutes (even after the 60 seconds it takes to answer the call in the first place)[98]. The Hampshire and Isle of Wight Constabulary refer to the fact that attendance at such calls takes more than the target of 15 minutes in more than 30% of cases as 'a quality standard'.[99]

---

[98] Hampshire Chronicle, 30 May 2022

[99] Hampshire Constabulary, Force Performance Profile, March 2022

CHAPTER 8
WHERE TO NOW?

Something has to change. From the leafy suburbs of the Thames Valley to Manchester council estates, and from madrassas in Bradford to chapel villages in Snowdonia, policing has become something that is done *to* you, rather than something that is done *for* you. In a decade we have allowed ourselves to become a nation of 'suspects'; to be photographed, checked, stopped, searched, DNA data-based, required to identify ourselves, and told that we must account for our actions whenever we are ordered to do so. We have swallowed the line that every additional obligation placed upon us, every fresh infringement of our liberty, is necessary because of 'the terrorist threat', or to 'deter pædophiles', or just 'to defeat crime'. If you seek to argue against the prevailing trend, you are promptly categorised as someone who is clearly 'anti-police' and therefore not to be trusted. You are obviously an apologist for criminals, and for extremists who would kill our families with bombs on the Underground. A large proportion of the population, probably the majority, gives every impression of being content to submit to each new rubric on the spurious grounds that 'I've got nothing to hide, so where's the problem?' Like generations of ordinary people before them, they would rather live quiet lives and trust that the ubiquitous 'powers that be' have their best interests at heart.

Hardly anyone beyond the 'Comment' column in the 'Guardian' is prepared to challenge the fundamental change that has taken place, or to marshal a cogent argument dealing with how we might respond constructively to it. There is nothing to be gained from ranting about the Government, or the Opposition. Both in their different ways have supinely allowed events to wash over them, not fully understanding the issues involved, and both are equally guilty of 'short-termism' dressed up as action, with every initiative and review that they launch. At the heart of the problem is a failure to properly define what we want and what we need from the army of police officers who are increasingly absent from our streets. No reasonable person would claim that we do not need effective policing in these crowded islands, indeed the most committed anarchist would no doubt run straight to his nearest police station if he was robbed in the street, demanding attention, and the immediate dispatch of half a dozen detectives. The issue is not about policing *per se*, it is about the way it is delivered, and increasingly it is about the attitude, character and abilities of the officers who deliver it. In these straightened economic times, there is also a real debate to be had about how to pay for a bloated public service which undoubtedly ranks below health, education, and the armed services in importance to the average taxpayer.

There is value, for want of a better phrase, in getting back to basics.

The adjectives that describe the sort of policing that a liberal democracy should aspire to are all words that define aspects of service, a concept which is fast disappearing from the relationship between the police and the public in Britain. Too often, senior officers argue that their personnel are accountable, visible, efficient, and courteous, when the experience of the man or woman in the street tells an entirely different story. One has to hack through the verbiage, much of it self-serving, and expose the enduring realities, a process that is painful for any big hierarchical organisation. This is particularly so for the police because despite constantly claiming a willingness to accept criticism, in truth they do not believe that they ever do anything wrong.

There is a famous photograph that was taken at the Sovereign's Trooping the Colour ceremony some years ago. It shows a young subaltern from one of the Guards regiments leading a detachment of men past the Queen, sword held before him in salute to the Sovereign, marching with his left foot forward. Behind him the serried ranks of guardsman are all marching with their right foot forward. The caption beneath the picture when it appeared in a newspaper was 'Shock! Entire Regiment Out of Step!' So often this is the view of the police establishment and increasingly of junior officers. It is not they who need to change, it is the rest of us who are out of step with them. By degrees, over the last two or three decades we have arrived at a position where too much effort is focussed upon what the police service 'likes' to do, rather than what it 'must' or 'should' do. Absence of effective leadership has ensured that much of this activity is driven by the attitudes and prejudices of junior officers on the shop floor who do not have a 'service ethos' and who, being young, enjoy the rough-and-tumble of physical policing, rather than the staid but necessary business of quiet preventive patrol.

The following comment, from a 23-year-old constable serving in a rural force in Wales, sums up the attitude of many of his peers:

> *'When I finished training, I was posted to M-------- [a small market town]. God, it was boring! Nothing to do, no-one to nick, just driving round and round the same streets on the same shitty council estates, listening to the same people whining about their lives. Market day, when the hill-farmers came to town, was the only time the place livened up – and then not much! I couldn't wait to get away, and last year I was selected for the Divisional Support Unit. We do "real" policing. No-one fucks with us, and if they try, their feet don't touch the ground till they reach the custody sergeant. I'm a door-opener, I'm trained to use the big ram we carry to smash down doors on raids or when we're looking for someone. I suppose we don't really need to use it as much as we do, but it's a real buzz going into some of these places mob-handed, and it scares the scum that we are dealing with shitless! I reckon I'm responsible for more broken front doors in council houses than anyone else in [a Welsh county]. I want to stay on the DSU for another couple of years and then go for promotion, or CID, anything other than so-called Neighbourhood Policing. I've had a belly-full of that.'*[100]

---

100 Confidential interview (2009) – Author's research

This young man sees nothing wrong with what he is doing, indeed he is proud of himself because by his assessment, he is a 'good cop'. His definition of policing, and that of his colleagues and managers, is narrow, aggressive, and inwardly focussed. Culturally it dismisses the concept of community, which is supposed to be the cornerstone of today's approach, but he and those like him are nonetheless the face of operational activity in his rural fastness and in many other places up and down the country. Policing at the cutting edge is defined by the attitudes and norms of those delivering it and if senior officers really want to offer a different model (which is debatable because many have the same mindset and are a product of the same system as their junior personnel), they have to be assertive in the way in which they supervise those in their charge.

In essence, the problem is that everyone involved in policing believes that they have got it right. Chief Constables sit in their headquarters and receive reports that, for example, Neighbourhood Policing Teams have been set up around their force and as far as they are concerned, they have built the New Jerusalem. Whether or not the officers on those teams have any degree of commitment, or have the right attitude to the public, or are even delivering anything of value, is of precious little concern. A system has been put in place, a box has been ticked, an order has been given that henceforth there will be Neighbourhood policing and *ergo* there is Neighbourhood policing – job done! No experiment ever fails in the police service. Simultaneously, junior officers such as the young Welsh constable quoted above believe that they know intuitively how to police an area, and irrespective of any broad strategy handed down from above, continue doing what they have always done. Since 1981 there have been no less than eighteen major structural reorganisations of the Met alone, each paid lip-service by middle management and comprehensively dismissed by the majority of rank-and-file officers as irrelevant to them. The fact that none of these much-vaunted changes have ever really met the needs of the public, speaks volumes about the extent to which those at the top delude themselves that they are making a difference, and those at the bottom believe that they know best.

Frankly, the needs of the public are comparatively few and relatively straightforward. Most people do not have an atom of interest in the intricacies of police delivery; have absolutely no idea who their local Chief Constable is (and could not care less), and are supremely disinterested in the police as an organisation. All they want is for police officers to be there when they need them. They want to feel secure when they go to bed at night, confident that their property, their person, and their family will not be violated. They want their immediate neighbourhood (as opposed to their 'community' which can and does mean something different) to be peaceful and well-ordered. On the rare occasions when they need the assistance of a police officer, they want him or her to come to their aid promptly and upon arrival to act professionally. They quite rightly expect the officer to have the training, knowledge and power to deal with their problem, hence the general antipathy towards PCSOs who provide none of these things. Above all, the public expect the police to be the guardians of where they live and work. The most effective way for this guardianship to operate is by prompt and assertive intervention, coupled with enforcement, when comparatively minor breaches of order take place. Prompt intervention means literally that; it does not mean having the facility to telephone some faceless 'beat manager' in order to make an appointment to see him or her within 24 or 48 hours. Prompt resolution, almost by definition, requires the very thing that the police service has chosen to abandon – officers on the ground in uniform. The public do not need to know the officer's name; they have no particular desire to be his friend. Basically, all they want is the provision of a service that they pay handsomely for through the tax system.

All of this is what is sometimes referred to as 'first tier' policing. It is the most manpower-intensive of three tiers and generates virtually all the activity that other, better qualified, officers must subsequently deal with. It is the bedrock of the way in which the police operate in almost all western democracies and used to operate in the UK. It is essentially local in nature, operating on the scale of individual streets rather than towns or boroughs but requires significant investment of visible personnel on a 24-hour basis. That is why the Met's 'Safer Neighbourhoods' scheme and the Neighbourhood Policing model rolled out across the rest of England and Wales are simultaneously right and completely wrong. Policing at the neighbourhood level is precisely what Mr and Mrs Public want; the old-style 'beats' were of course based upon identifiable neighbourhoods, so there is nothing new there. The new neighbourhood model is patently not based on 'neighbourhoods' however, it is based upon Wards, which are local authority electoral areas containing anything up to a dozen or more discrete neighbourhoods. Thus, whilst the overarching aim of trying to base policing on localism should be applauded, the Met's model and the Home Office driven scheme which mimics it were fundamentally flawed from the outset. To achieve any of the intended strategic aims would require allocation of uniform police officers to each neighbourhood in numbers that all forces, as currently structured, would refuse to countenance. Back-filling with PCSOs adds nothing to the mix and in the long run is counter-productive, for reasons discussed elsewhere. In addition, the closure of police stations and the wholesale withdrawal of police officers to unified 'hubs' in cities and counties, far from the areas that they are charged with policing, is a strategic error of such magnitude that it will take years, and the investment of millions of pounds, to remedy.

THE CHALLENGE OF 'LOCALISM'

Localism needs to be precisely defined, as it can mean different things to different people. The Chief Constable of Bedfordshire might assume that he or she is the local police chief and can speak for the county and all the towns therein, but suggest this to either of the BCU commanders, in Luton and the force HQ respectively, and you will find that they claim to be more closely aligned with 'their' local people. Drill down further, however, and you will discover that people in both places see themselves as being residents of much smaller units than these larger towns or indeed the county as a whole. The need to have a shared understanding of what 'localism' means has assumed importance because both major political parties have adopted the concept as the cornerstone of their approach to law and order, offering different versions of 'power to the people' in an effort to more closely align the wishes of the public with the quality of policing that they receive.

David Blunkett was Labour Home Secretary from 2001 to 2004. During early 2009, some years after leaving office, he was invited to conduct a review of police accountability for the Prime Minister, Gordon Brown, which reported in July of that year. His report[101] rehearsed all the difficulties linked to the gap between public expectation and on-the-ground delivery and waxed lyrically about 'partnership working at CDRP level', whilst railing against 'politicisation', but his report, whilst acknowledging the need to truly reflect local needs, made no worthwhile recommendations. In truth, the purpose of his intervention was nothing more than an obvious attempt to steal a march on the Tory police reform spokesman Nick Herbert (who subsequently became a Home Office minister in the coalition government after 2010). In 2007 he had produced a 243-page analysis entitled, *'Policing for the People'*. The Conservative solution, promised as a manifesto and policy commitment, was to replace statutory police authorities with locally elected police and crime commissioners, supported by elected Local Policing Bodies (LPD's)[102] *(which never saw the light of day, and were ignored as the subsequent enabling legislation passed through parliament).* It is worth examining these proposals in more detail

---

101 'A People's Police Force – Police Accountability in the Modern Era' Rt Hon David Blunkett MP (2009)(published by the Home Office)

102 Police Reform and Social Responsibility Bill – First Reading 30.11.2010

because in many respects the concept of an all-powerful Commissioner poses more questions than it answers. Herbert's review argued that,

> *'The police should be locally accountable to the public, through the direct election of police commissioners to replace police authorities and through a "right to policing" for local communities. Elected commissioners would work with partners to deliver local, joined-up justice. At the national level standards should be ensured by a strong independent inspectorate and a streamlined set of national indicators to measure what matters.'*

Putting aside the ever-present danger of politicisation of the elected commissioner's post and the threat that that would undoubtedly pose for the operational independence of policing, the principal flaw in the proposal was that it did nothing to meet the need for localism. The 'right to policing' was little more than aspirational management-speak and was not enforceable. The intention of the proposed legislation was that the Commissioner would mirror the role of the Chief Constable; but quite who would have primacy, beyond what existed at the time in terms of police authorities, was never explained, nor was it defined in the years since the introduction of PCCs.

Police and Crime Commissioners, almost by definition, need to have a very specialist skillset if they are to add value to the policing effort and properly exercise their intended powers of holding Chief Constables to account. People with such abilities are rare. The vast majority of individuals serving on the former police authorities had already disqualified themselves by virtue of the fact that they were garlanded with failure in their role. They were the last people to entrust with such an important job. Likewise, retired former senior police officers could not and should not be considered for the post as they would be perceived, rightly or wrongly, as being 'too close' to force hierarchies. Who then are left? – Only political activists with a party-political machine to support them, and single-issue zealots who believe that they understand the complexities of policing having observed it from the outside. Undoubtedly, there is a compelling argument for overview, but without radical re-working of the concept, elected commissioners in the form proposed have shown that they are not equal to the task and are not the answer.

The Herbert report provided an analysis of why police authorities, which had always been an anachronism, had outlived their usefulness. In the late nineteenth century local 'watch committees' met weekly to run police forces. At that time there were of course many more forces than the 43 we have today in England and Wales. Most small boroughs and county towns had their own constabularies, often with personnel numbering no more than a few score officers. To that extent the problem of ensuring localism was met, although petty corruption, nepotism and what was known as 'aldermanic interference' were common. The watch committees had the power to hire and fire individual officers of all ranks and often used it. In 1964, following a series of scandals, watch committees were abolished and were replaced by police authorities which were meant to hold individual police forces and their Chief Constables to account on behalf of local communities under what was known as the 'tripartite system'.

In 2012 the Home Office website described the relationship as:

"A three-way system of responsibility ensures forces run smoothly:

- *We [i.e. the Home Office] fund the police and have overall responsibility as overseer and coordinator.*
- *Chief police officers have responsibility for the direction and control of regional forces.*
- *Police authorities make sure local forces operate efficiently and effectively.*

This system prevents political interference in policing and avoids giving any single organisation power over the entire police service.'

However, the tripartite system was never a contract between equals, and particularly after the Labour landslide in 1997 the balance of power shifted inexorably, year by year, towards central control by government and Home-Office senior officials. Very little has changed in the years since, notwithstanding the appearance on the scene of Police and Crime Commissioners in 2012/13. Home Office departmental officials work in an almost symbiotic relationship with the cabinet members of the National Police Chiefs' Council (NPCC) in devising and implementing policing policy, effectively side-lining any local input. Describing why police authorities were no longer 'fit for purpose', Herbert quoted the lobby group 'Direct Democracy'[103],

> *'The police and the public have never been more remote from each other. Police Authorities – appointed bodies comprising local councillors, Home Office-appointed "independent" members, and local magistrates – are supposed to represent the community in the supervision of the police. They are one of the three pillars in the "tripartite" structure implemented in 1964, the others being the Home Secretary and the chief constable. Over the years, and especially since 1997, the police authority has become by far the weakest of the pillars. Chief constables are accountable in practice not to the representatives of the community but to the Home Office in Whitehall, which works to ensure – through targets, central funding streams, and bureaucratic audit and inspections. The Home Office has imposed "de facto" national control of police forces."*

Police authorities were deliberately reconstituted in the 1990s to include members appointed by the Home Secretary, ostensibly with the aim of insulating the police from what was seen as local political interference. The actual effect was to almost completely emasculate them. Police Authorities became comfortable fee-paid quangos who seemingly interpreted their role as being something between a rubber

---

[103] 'Policing for the People – Interim Report of the Police Reform Taskforce (2007)' Conservative Party

stamp for the force budget, and a cheerleader for any force initiative that the Chief Constable told them to support. As the then government minister, Lord Rooker, said during a debate on Police Reform in 2002,

> *'No-one is going to kid me or anyone else that [police authorities] actually represent anyone. Let us not beat about the bush. The fact is that if one person in three knows the name of his Member of Parliament, I doubt whether more than one person in a thousand knows the name of any member of the police authority in his area.'*[104]

Thus, as one examines this first tier of policing it becomes clear that whilst there seems to be common agreement across the political spectrum about the need for localism, the application of the philosophy has eluded government over many years. Failure by the Home Office to meet the needs of local people has ensured that the core requirement of such a system – fully trained, fully warranted police officers committed to visible uniform reassurance and preventive patrol – has been almost wholly absent from policing for a decade.

Above first tier activity the problem has not been so acute, largely because policing at the second and third tiers is mainly delivered by specialists, and seldom involves visible uniform patrol. Second tier policing relates to those areas of criminal activity which are clearly beyond the competence

---

[104] Debate on the Police Reform Bill 2002, Hansard, 16 April 2002

and expertise of officers working at the BCU or borough level. Thus murder, all serious and series crimes, drug-trafficking, and crimes committed by criminals who are crossing force and regional boundaries would fall into this category. The officers deployed to deal with such matters need special skills, experience, and the ability to work creatively with the minimum of supervision. HM Inspectorate published a path-breaking report in 2005 entitled *'Closing the Gap'* which identified the fact that most of the smaller forces in England and Wales lack the resources and capability to deal with second tier criminality and that the only feasible solution was a programme of strategic amalgamations to release latent capacity. This was all the more important as the need for the police to have a coherent approach to the delivery of all protective services, such as MAPPA (Multi-Agency Public Protection Arrangements), became apparent. At the last minute, however, the Home Secretary, John Reid, gave in to lobbying from the police staff associations and a number of shire authorities, and the plan for phased amalgamations was dropped because New Labour perceived it to be electorally damaging to them. Notwithstanding, cross-border joint operational units have developed in various places, the success of which has raised further questions about the relevance of having full Chief Officer teams in small forces managing a mere two or three BCUs.

Just as there is always a degree of overlap between first and second tier activity, so it is that the boundary between second tier policing and the third tier is relatively porous. Third tier operational activity is confined to top level organised and international crime, counter-terrorism, and anti-terrorism – effectively all offences and threats that might hazard the social, economic and security well-being of the nation. The lead in such activity, other than terrorism, currently rests with the National Crime Agency (NCA) which formally came into being on 1st October 2013, following a merger of the Serious and Organised Crime Agency (SOCA), National Crime Squad, the National Criminal Intelligence Service, the National Hi-Tech Crime Unit (NHTCU), the investigative and intelligence sections of HM Revenue & Customs on serious drug trafficking, and the Immigration Service's organised immigration crime wing. Currently around 40% of the NCA's efforts are devoted to combating drug trafficking, 25% to tackling organised immigration crime, around 10% to fraud, 15% on other organised crime and the remaining 10% on supporting other law enforcement agencies. Whilst, under the present system, the vast majority of second and third tier personnel are drawn from the ranks of first tier officers who have 'cut their teeth' on low-level activity, it need not necessarily be so. Indeed, many of NCA's best investigators are customs officers and immigration officers with skills that are every bit as developed as those of career police officers.[105]

PAYING FOR POLICING IN A TIME OF AUSTERITY

In the years prior to 2008, those senior officers and Home Office officials responsible for leading the police service

---

105 Following the formation of the coalition government in 2010, the Home Office had already begun consultation on proposals to merge all third tier operations within a larger National Crime Agency

could disguise their failure to deliver by writing cheques which the Treasury always cashed. A £7 billion radio system, PCSOs, IT projects that over-ran and seldom worked, and overtime payments larger than the gross national product of some sub-Saharan African countries, were all paid for as if money was no object. Indeed, money was no object, because it was a brave Home Secretary or Prime Minister who would have risked the opprobrium of tabloid journalists had either not given 'our brave boys and girls in blue' what they claimed they needed to fight crime.

And then the sky fell on the City of London.

Without any meaningful debate, the Conservative/Liberal Democrat coalition government grasped the nettle and introduced challenging and robust cuts to bloated police budgets. An upper range of twenty-five per cent cuts over a four-year cycle (2011 to 2015) was phased in. The 2009 Home Office budget for 2010/2011 was originally £10.3 billion, with policing forming by far the most significant element. Therefore, each ten per cent reduction was equivalent to at least £1 billion per annum. The consensus view was that reductions on this scale could only be achieved by structural change. Salami-slicing various allocations would not address the problem, because between 85% and 92% of spending is locked into the cost of personnel. Thus, two 'big hit' areas immediately presented themselves and were identified by policymakers at the Treasury, and special advisers to senior politicians. They were, in order of importance, reducing the headcount of police personnel, and removal of the right to paid overtime for constables and sergeants.[106]

---

106 These two issues, together with a programme of equally contentious

In England and Wales, police headcount decreased precipitately after the global recession in 2008. Home Office data shows that the number of fully warranted police officers fell from a peak of 144,353 in March 2009 to 114,700 in March 2019, a reduction of around 20%. The reduction in police officer numbers was almost exclusively due to austerity measures introduced by the government in response to the economic downturn. The impact on levels of crime is less easy to discern. Between 2008 and 2018 overall levels of recorded crime actually fell, against a background of a reduced police headcount, which intuitively should not have been the case. One study claims that the reduction might possibly have been due to the fact that fewer police officers on the street meant fewer opportunities for victims to report offences[107], although closer analysis of Home Office figures shows that the reduction, across all crime categories with the exception of violent crime, was statistically real, and ran in parallel with the reduction of police officers.

The second 'big hit' area, paid overtime for constables and sergeants, and the way in which it was managed, had long been regarded as an unreformed abuse. The 2008/2009 overtime bill for forces in England and Wales was £412 million[108], which was the equivalent of £14 from each of the UK's 29 million taxpayers and represented about seven per

---

topics, were the subject of the 'Independent Review of Police Officer and Staff Remuneration and Condition' – the 'Winsor Review' – which reported in early 2012.

107 Bradford B. (2011). 'Police Numbers and Crime Rates – A Rapid Evidence Review'. London: Her Majesty's Inspectorate of Constabulary.

108 Home Office data 2008/2009

cent of the total cost of police pay. Senior officers sought to justify this enormous expenditure (over £870,000 in just one Met BOCU (Redbridge) alone in 2010), by claiming that paid overtime was a highly flexible way to get more officers where they were needed quickly. There may well be occasions when paid overtime lends flexibility to operational planning but unfortunately the Police Federation was not always 'on message', often claiming that many officers relied upon regular overtime payments to boost their ordinary earnings. This is no doubt true, but unfortunately for rank-and-file officers, the overtime budget was never intended to be an extra pot of money to help with their mortgages, or pay for foreign holidays.

At a time when the British public was howling for the heads of MPs and bankers to be placed on spikes on Westminster Bridge for their 'greed'; when legions of taxpayers were and are in daily fear of redundancy, police overtime arrangements have a vanishingly low priority. There is little doubt that the police service has very few friends when it comes to its stewardship of public money. The perception of the police service, held by the average man or woman in the street, is of a job that is secure (when theirs is not), with a 'gold-plated' final-salary pension, which they can only dream of. There are well-reported scandals such as Met's 2012–14 inquiry into misuse of its corporate credit card involving 1,183 officers and the loss of £3.7 million, which have further reduced the bargaining power of the entire police service. As a Met borough commander officer commented to me,

'It is highly unlikely that ordinary taxpayers will go

to the barricades to preserve overtime rights for their local bobby, even in the extremely unlikely event that they have any idea who he is!'[109]

It is also worth remembering that the world continued to spin on its axis when the right to paid overtime was removed from Inspectors some years ago, and there is every reason to believe that beyond some initial grumbling, the rank and file in the police service would get used to the change reasonably quickly. With the employment market as it is, and with a hundred applicants waiting in the wings for every police job, the danger of a mass exodus by experienced officers angered by the loss of overtime can be effectively disregarded.

Other ideas, which will no doubt make many officers quake in their boots, are also floating in the ether. Since April 1st, 2006, the cost of pensions in payment has been removed from police operating accounts. PCCs now hold a separate account for this purpose, into which are paid officers' contributions and a new employer's contribution. Deficits are topped up with a grant from central government, whilst any surplus is recouped. This arrangement was originally seen as lending clarity to the funding process, but another interpretation is that it has drawn pension policy ever closer to the Home Office, and by implication, the Treasury. People with detailed understanding of the arcane subject of pension accrual acknowledge that although it would not be easy to reduce benefits, 'something has to be done', because the burden of paying generous pensions to

---

109 Confidential interview – Author's research 2012

an ever-increasing number of retired officers is radically undermining the ability of the Home Office to fund present manpower needs. In fact, there is a disaster scenario emerging for the years ahead. At present (2023) there are at least four forces in England and Wales where the cost of paying pensions to retired personnel is already greater than the amount paid in salaries to serving officers, largely due to the well-known, and much quoted, actuarial fact that people are living longer. In the context of policing however this is exacerbated by the fact that final-salary pensions are paid at thirty years' service which means that the vast majority of officers start to draw their pension between the ages of 49 and 55 which increases the pension liability exponentially, as many of these pensioners will now live well into their seventies, and beyond, drawing pensions that are index-linked to inflation. Turning the final-salary pension into an 'average through service' scheme or even a 'money purchase' scheme are options that do not generate much opposition from junior and mid-service officers (because any changes would only affect new joiners). Such changes have been gradually introduced since the updated Police Pension Scheme was applied in 2015 and will deliver considerable savings in the future. Thus, in terms of the overall funding of the police service, there is no greater challenge than the obvious and pressing need to reduce the pensions burden. The Conservative administrations of Cameron, May, Johnson, and now Sunak, have signally failed to confront the power of the staff associations, and government must make some hard and painful decisions in the years to come. Compelling all serving officers to transfer to a newer, and far less generous, pension scheme is probably the way forward, but will be a management challenge of immense proportions.

Indeed, it may well be that when the history of policing in the twenty-first century is written, a lengthy chapter will focus upon the present economic downturn and the fact that for the first time in a quarter of a century, those at the helm are being forced to reappraise what constitutes 'core' policing, so that non-core activity can be radically pruned.

FINDING THE DETECTIVES

It would be difficult to advance any sort of cogent argument that second and third tier activity should be curtailed – both are undoubtedly core business, but that is not to say that sensible economies should be disregarded. As recruitment into the NCA has demonstrated, the ability to be a good detective is not a skill that is bestowed on police officers from birth, and once this is accepted it is a small step to directly recruiting a proportion of investigators from other bodies such as Customs, the Benefits Agency, UK Borders Agency, and the Special Investigation Branch (SIB) of the Military Police, etc. Indeed, once the principle is established it would not be beyond the wit of man to devise a competency and skills framework, coupled with a training programme, to allow for direct-entry detectives/investigative agents at the upper tiers in much the same way that the FBI operate in the United States.

In UK policing, 'detective' used to be a coveted role that only the best and brightest police officers achieved. This was in part helped by extensive media and drama coverage of the CID in real-life forces, and a large proportion of bright men and women offered themselves for detective duties early in their service. However, this is no longer the case, and a crisis now exists where the detective role is something that very few police officers are willing to step into. This has resulted in a shortage of detectives nationally, which was noted as early as 2008 and has become increasingly dire. In a 2019 report by Her Majesty's Inspectorate of Constabulary and Fire & Rescue Services' (HMICFRS), it was shown that 14 per cent of all detective posts in England and Wales were unfilled, despite valiant attempts to recruit suitable personnel from the existing workforce. The College of Policing, charged with the responsibility of making policy and developing training solutions in England and Wales, was faced with the dual problem of dealing with a shrinking police officer establishment coupled with an intractable shortage of detectives. The first issue was addressed by intensive lobbying of government to provide funding for a substantial 'uplift' in the police personnel headcount. The problem of insufficient detective capability is yet to be adequately faced.

To partially meet the manpower deficiency in forces, the government announced increased funding to recruit 20,000 new police officers by 2023 to combat the reduction after the austerity measures enacted in the early 2010s. Whilst this was a much-needed boost, it did not go far enough. Indeed, as the Police Federation pointed out, this increase merely reset workforce numbers at slightly over the 2010 level.

However, the UK population that forces will be responsible for at the end of the uplift programme in 2023 will have increased by 4 million, with the level of crime also increasing in proportion and becoming more complex. This suggests that the overall police force workload will continue to be under considerable strain. As detectives are primarily recruited internally, the staffing of their ranks is directly related to the increase in fully warranted officers. Yet, as shown by the reluctance of current internal candidates to strive to be detectives, this uplift funding increase is unlikely to resolve the shortage of detectives. Therefore, a different strategy is needed – the Direct Detective Entry Scheme.

The Metropolitan Police pioneered this approach in 2017. The scheme allows individuals to join the force and become designated detectives by the end of their two-year probation, without first having to perform ordinary uniform duty. Over this initial period, they must gain their core competencies as police officers and sit examinations to test the specialist investigative skills required for their intended role, leading to accreditation. In 2020, 354 applicants were accepted which made a reasonable contribution to the Met's 5,000-detective shortfall, even taking into account the number of officers who left before or after the initial two years. Other forces have since adopted this approach under the 'Police Now' banner, but the jury is out as to whether or not this is a solution to the problem overall. Clearly direct entry for detectives must be part of the mix, and this will require a profound attitudinal change within the police service where such innovation is not welcome, particularly amongst junior personnel.

There will be little need to test the market. With the right incentives and an attractive career structure, good quality applicants would be queuing for miles for such a job.

Other advantages would flow from such an arrangement, such as the opportunity to set up a workforce who, whilst paid well (as they would have to be to attract the best qualified applicants), would not have such extravagantly generous allowances and pension rights as currently serving police officers. Conditions of service and pay could be matched more closely with comparable employment and responsibility in the private sector. Disciplinary arrangements could be severed from the ridiculously unwieldy police misconduct system and linked directly to employment law. Most importantly, the investigation of cross-border serious crime and top-tier international crime could be put on a truly professional footing with the opportunity to match personnel skills acquired elsewhere to the needs of the organisation, which is not currently possible when the pool of talent from which to take applicants only contains police officers, who have seldom done anything other than policing.

Direct recruitment of a proportion of investigators – perhaps the majority – would allow the workforce to be enhanced and truly skills-based. For example, there are currently only a handful of investigators who have any sort of language skills and perhaps only one or two with an even cursory knowledge of Arabic, Farsi, Mandarin Chinese, or Russian. High level skills in accounting, finance, corporate law, and computer science are virtually non-existent. The opportunities for change, if applied imaginatively, could create a sea-change in the way that we approach policing and the investigation of crime in the UK. It would be necessary to get governance and accountability right, but the chance to establish a new, more efficient, and probably cheaper investigative framework is an opportunity not to be missed.

'Governance and accountability' is merely management-speak for having the right organisation in place to allow any job to be done well. In this context the size and capability of police forces comes into play, as does the role and composition of the NPCC teams who run them.

There is an optimum size for a police force which will allow it to have sufficient capacity to deal with core activity and unplanned challenges simultaneously. As Her Majesty's Inspectorate have pointed out[110], at least fifteen to twenty of the forty-three forces in England and Wales are incapable of dealing with more than one major enquiry or one major incident at a time without a serious impact on their mainstream activity and capability. Tiny forces such as Bedfordshire, Wiltshire, Warwickshire, Dyfed-Powys, Cumbria, Dorset and Suffolk are essentially 'one-trick ponies'. For example, when the Ipswich prostitute-murderer Steve Wright struck in December 2006, Suffolk Police were placed in the position that they had to scale back all other activity in the county, overspend on their operational budgets, and go cap-in-hand to the Home Office and other forces for money and assistance. If the force had then been confronted by another major crime or an operational challenge such as widespread flooding, they would have been unable to cope.

Thus, the logic of HMIC's recommendations of 2005

---

110 'Closing the Gap – A Review of the Fitness for Purpose of the Current Structure of Policing In England and Wales.' HMIC (Published 13.9.2005)

shines through. Notwithstanding the somewhat parochial objections of county police authorities and one or two Chief Constables of the dinosaur variety, the need for a programme of amalgamations is indisputable. With regional forces covering three or four counties and having a strength of between 3,000 and 5,000 officers, the number of police forces in England would reduce to around a dozen, whilst Wales would probably have a single force for the entire Principality. The Scottish Parliament have already had their say north of the border, when in 2013, the eight pre-existing forces in Scotland were amalgamated to form 'Police Scotland', a single unitary force for Scotland, with headquarters at Tulliallan Castle, Kincardine in Fife.

FINDING THE NEXT GENERATION OF CHIEF CONSTABLES AND COMMISSIONERS

All of which raises real questions about the role of Chief Constables under any new arrangement. With fewer than twenty in the entire country, any claim that they might make to be champions of their local communities would, of course, be nonsense. The Chief Constable of a new force for the whole of southern England, or Wales from Wrexham to Pembrokeshire, would have regional strategic responsibilities that have little to do with local accountability. The real powerbrokers of significance to local people, as today, would be the BCU and Borough Chief Superintendents, and those officers at neighbourhood level who work under their command. NPCC officers would, to an even greater extent than is the case today, become little more than facilitators and providers of support services for those below them.

This in turn raises the question – why do Chief Constables need to be police officers at all?

At the proposed level of intervention there is a greater need for sophisticated and highly developed management skills, the ability to negotiate, and strategic sensibility of a high order. Policing skills *per se* would have very low importance in the grand scheme of things, certainly at the level at which these individuals would operate. In many respects the role of these new 'super' Chief Constables would be comparable to that of *Préfets* and *Sous-Préfets* of Police in France. Prefects operate under the Minister of the Interior, which in a British model would be the Home Office. They effectively act as an interface between the government and the police, managing the senior officers and co-ordinating the high-level strategic activity of all the emergency and security services. Their main duties include representing the state to local government administrators and elected officials; the co-ordination of the security and public safety role of the police and gendarmerie forces; taking charge of and handling major crises; emergency defence procedures, and a whole raft of administrative functions relating to licensing, immigration, data-collection etc. They also have a wide remit in terms of audit and inspection of the police and emergency services with powers, unheard of in this country, to refer doubtful cases to administrative and financial review courts. Almost all Prefects are trained for their role in the École Nationale d'Administration (ÉNA) (hence the reason why graduates are referred to as énarques), and can best be described as a cross between senior civil servants and chief executives. They have been an integral part of French policing for decades and have always worked successfully 'hand in glove' with the police professionals under their charge.

Essentially, the gradual replacement of Chief Constables by such a highly qualified cadre in the UK would allow for the removal of Police and Crime Commissioners, who add absolutely no value to policing, have no genuine local mandate, and are a majestic waste of public money. They would provide a strategic link between government and the new larger forces; could form the core of a strengthened and independent inspectorate and would clarify the position of BCU and BOCU commanders who, as the most senior police professionals, provide the focussed localism that policing requires. One or two of the new breed of British *préfets* and *sous-préfets* would no doubt be recruited from the ranks of the best serving Chief Constables, but it need not necessarily be so. Individuals of outstanding quality and potential from the upper echelons of the civil service, the private sector, or even the military, might well be excellent candidates for the posts. The appointment of key leadership roles, at the helm of the largest and most complex urban forces such as the Metropolitan Police, West Midlands Police, Greater Manchester Police etc., must not and should not be left to 'Buggins' turn', or the vagaries of which Deputy Chief Constable might be available when a vacancy falls due. Such individuals have profound regional and national responsibilities and should be selected from the widest and deepest available pool of candidates. Almost by definition this should include talented men and women from beyond the insular world of senior policing, where broad experience is rare, and seldom valued to the extent that it should.

REDEFINING THE ROLE OF CONSTABLE

The professionalisation of the upper tiers of the police and removal or redefinition of the current Chief Officer structure. (i.e. Assistant Chief Constable/Commander and above) would allow for the long-awaited realignment of community level policing with the needs and wishes of the public. Shorn of the responsibility to investigate anything more than lower-tier crime and disorder (everything else being undertaken by directly recruited professionals at the second and third tier), the majority of police officers could then be deployed on patrol in uniform in increasing numbers. The ready acceptance of PCSOs by the police service was a tacit acknowledgement that preventive patrol is a low-skill, low-status, activity that can be done by anyone – that view must be reversed. Fully trained fully warranted police officers must be returned to 'neighbourhoods' in large numbers; their performance not measured by arrests or apprehensions (which increasingly would cease to be their primary responsibility, being devolved to trained professionals). The key indicator of their efficiency would be the proportion of their time spent on patrol, in uniform, in designated neighbourhoods.

Despite the protestations of the Police Federation and other vested interests, it would not be difficult to find the personnel to achieve this, so long as there was a focussed and radical pruning of non-core activity. Legions of officers are currently employed on duties that do not require the special powers of a police officer (i.e. the power to detain someone and place them under arrest), indeed it has been estimated that between 3,000 and 4,000 officers fall into this category in England and Wales alone. This is a scandalous diversion of resources, and any such functions could and should be privatised so that the officers can be returned to core patrol duties. A far from exhaustive list of functions from which to harvest these individuals is set out below:

i) All police training officers, involved in initial recruit training or development training within forces, including Dog-Handler, Mounted Branch, and Firearms training, and all specialist and management training. Such skills are easily found in the private sector, at a considerably reduced cost.
ii) All officers attached to Policy Departments, Diversity Units, Community Engagement Teams, Quality Assurance Teams, and any form of liaison activity with outside bodies. These are quintessentially jobs for paid non-police professionals. Likewise, all the many officers engaged on intelligence analysis (as opposed to intelligence-gathering).
iii) All officers engaged on operational activity that does not require a power of arrest, such as Specialist Search Teams, Underwater Search Units, Helicopter Observers, Specialist (Body Search) Dog Handlers. All such functions could be 'bought-in' from the private sector.
iv) All officers involved in peripheral activity such as Wildlife Liaison, Schools Liaison, Recruiting, etc.

PCSOs would not fit into such a redefined model and would need to be ruthlessly removed from the mix. They do not have the skills, or the training, to provide the sort of real neighbourhood policing that is wanted. In truth, they were never intended to be anything more than a poor imitation of policing designed to fool the public into thinking that there was a visible presence on the streets. Now that the personal reputations of senior officers and politicians no longer depend upon the success of the concept, its failure could be quietly acknowledged with the saving of £282 million per annum in salary costs alone. This sum would buy a considerable number of real police officers to add to those liberated from non-jobs up and down the country, even after redundancy payments for PCSOs are taken into account.

Trying to understand the welter of statistics describing police deployment is akin to deciphering the Dead Sea scrolls. Hedged around with ill-defined role categories such as 'front line', 'middle office', 'back office', 'visible' and 'available', the overall figures lump together real police officers with PCSOs. Even with this artificial inflation of the totals, the most recent pre-pandemic research[111] paints an alarming picture of the Met, a force that cost the taxpayer £5 billion per annum. Despite adopting the widest possible definition, figures show that barely more than 11% of the total police strength of the force is visible and available at any given time. Of the 43 police forces in England and Wales the Met is placed at a disgraceful 24th position, whilst Merseyside, where Bernard Hogan-Howe, who would eventually become Commissioner of the Met, was the Chief Constable until 2009, was ranked 'best' with a much more creditable 17%.

---

111 'Demanding Times – The front line and police visibility', HMIC (June 2011)

How, apart from winkling unproductive 'non-combatants' from their offices, can the number of visible patrolling officers on the street be increased? The answer presents yet another management challenge for the police service which will require those at the top to do what they have been studiously avoiding for years – to confront their workforce.

The London Borough of Camden is one of thirty-two police borough commands in the Met, and fairly typical of police command units in London and elsewhere[112]. Camden is a busy area, comprising Hampstead in the north, Holborn in the south and Kentish Town at its heart, and has a total strength of 790 police officers, which might seem more than sufficient. Drill down however and it becomes clear that mere totals are misleading. Discounting officers attached to squads dealing with single-issue problems such as 'hate crime' and domestic violence, and factoring in sickness absence rates of around 8% to 10% and 'training abstractions' of up to 12%, the pool of available personnel is quickly reduced. Annual leave, two days off per week, and the requirements of a 24-hour shift system, all mean that

---

112 In 2017, two London boroughs were amalgamated with Camden for policing purposes. These were:
- Islington Borough: Islington was merged with Camden to form the Central North Basic Command Unit (BCU). This means that the policing services of both boroughs are now managed under a single command unit.
- Westminster City: Westminster was merged with Camden to form the Central West Basic Command Unit (BCU). This means that the policing services of both boroughs are now managed under a single command unit.

officers may spend as few as 161 days at work each year. It is thus hardly surprising that on most Saturday nights Kentish Town Police Station struggles to parade more than six or seven officers to police the heaving pubs and clubs around Camden Lock. All of this is disturbing enough but is compounded by what amount to unsupervised and unrestrained 'Spanish Practices' by junior officers, reminiscent of the worst days of trade union militancy.

Not only in London, but across the country, junior officers regard patrolling in uniform on their own as something that they will not tolerate. On spurious 'officer safety' grounds and the alleged need for 'dynamic risk assessments' under the Police (Health and Safety) Act 1997, Constables demand that they patrol in pairs and regularly confront their Sergeants and Inspectors on the issue. This is compounded by the fact that the Met now regard 'response policing' as a specialism which requires officers to operate in pairs in vehicles – foot patrols have been wholly abandoned. It is a classic example of the tail wagging the dog, amply demonstrated recently on a widely read police 'blog' which has attracted over 7 million hits in two years. An ill-tempered campaign against single patrols attracted hundreds of responses, almost all of which ridiculed their senior managers and challenged their right to interfere with paired patrolling.

However, it is blindingly obvious that robustly enforcing single patrols would double coverage on the streets within a few hours. Couple that with some radical pruning of unnecessary squads and teams and the Met would start to provide what the people of London so earnestly need and deserve. Whether the new Commissioner has the organisational support of his top team to achieve this is the unknown factor. If he is to challenge the existing culture and 'take on' his workforce, it will require a level of management intervention and granite-faced leadership that his four most recent predecessors were not equal to when they faced the same problem. Sir Mark Rowley has inherited a force in which an entire generation of young constables have no experience of patrolling a beat alone, in which their Sergeants and Inspectors have lost the skills of supervision and robust management, overseen by a cadre of senior officers, many of whom are good managers but poor leaders.

Such a major programme of redeployment, privatisation, and civilianisation, coupled with a re-evaluation of what should be a 'fair rate for the job' for first-tier officers could generate significant savings over time. In essence, our expectation of such officers would not be that they should be multi-skilled – able to deal with anything and everything from the simplest incident to the implementation of a counter-terrorism strategy. We could and should expect that they be no more than they used to be – a constantly visible presence on our streets, able to respond promptly and professionally to most incidents, with the common sense and knowledge to 'hold the fort' until trained professionals could attend and take over in more complex situations.

In fact, markedly similar to the sort of policing provided by the eponymous George Dixon.

This would be a lesser role than today's generation of policemen and women aspire to, but would more properly represent their real function and would undoubtedly meet the needs of the long-suffering taxpayers. Salary levels would have to come down (or at least not increase), in order to reflect the reality of their new role, but in essence this need be no more than a long overdue re-balancing of police pay, which has received much more generous increases than other comparable areas of the public sector in the last two decades, albeit less so since 2012. At present, the overwhelming view of the public is that policing at a neighbourhood level is virtually non-existent anywhere in the UK, and that the few police officers that are deployed to such duties are scruffy, rude, aggressive, disinterested, and completely lacking in any understanding of the 'service ethos'. What follows is the verbatim description of one person's encounter with street level policing in London recently. She is middle-aged and middle-class, and has no particular animosity to the police, but the service (or lack of service) she received is depressingly familiar and by no means exclusive to the capital. Police officers act in this way in all of our big cities and in rural communities every day of the week, and then wonder why public confidence in them has plumbed new depths in recent years.

> 'We live in a riverside house on a private estate near Tower Bridge. My husband and I were just about to go to bed when we heard a commotion outside our house. A man, who was obviously very angry about something, was standing in the road shouting. He then launched himself at our car, which was parked at the kerb, and began furiously kicking the doors, leaving enormous dents. He then stomped off along the road. My husband, who is 62, decided to go after him but I was worried that he would get assaulted or

even stabbed, so I dialled 999 for the police. When I eventually got through, they told me that they were "far too busy" to send anyone and refused to help. A crime had been committed, my husband was pursuing the offender who might be dangerous, and the police refused to come! I dashed along the street to find my husband and discovered that the man, who had caused £600 damage to our car, had got into a black cab and had got away, but my husband had written down the registration number and cab plate number, so it would be easy to trace the driver and find out where he had taken the man. We immediately called the police again and told them, but they were not in the least interested, didn't want any of the details we had recorded and told us to contact our insurance company – then they hung up! You've really got to ask why we even have a police force in this country if they can't even help with simple things like our problem.'[113]

The last sentence says it all. If the police do not see it as their job to come to the aid of the average law-abiding member of the public on the rare occasion when they need help, one really does have to ask whether we need them at all. It would be simpler, easier, and much, much, cheaper to employ Group 4, or Sure-Guard security officers. Then, at least we would be able to get rid of them and employ someone else if they failed to deliver.

Life imitates art. For too long we have been seduced

---

113 Confidential interview – Author's research 2009

by the notion that every police officer is a hero who risks his life for you and me every time he puts on a uniform, that every detective is an Ian Rankin super-sleuth, that every policewoman will one day be the DCI in 'Prime Suspect'. Wrong, wrong, and wrong again. As has become depressingly clear over the last few years, the police are a reflection of the society they serve, and it was ever thus, even in the days when the fictional George Dixon patrolled our streets. The difference then was that they were led and supervised; now they are 'managed' and 'developed'. Where once we had police forces that saw themselves as public services, we now have semi-accountable organs of government whose public face is presented by highly paid media professionals, whose core function is seemingly the protection of their powers and privileges.

Whilst conducting research interviews for this book, I spoke to an American colleague who has served at a senior level in a number of large forces on the east coast of the USA. Now retired and working in academe, he is a seasoned observer of public policy on both sides of the Atlantic and is no apologist for policing in his home country, but his comments about the situation that we find ourselves in at the end of the second decade of a new century were succinct and deeply depressing. Looking across a landscape strewn with the wreckage of mishandled terrorist operations, oppressive legislation, and strategic inadequacy; occupied by police officers who are trained to see their fellow citizens as an enemy race, he shook his head and commented sadly,

> *'How did you get it so wrong? You used to have a police system that was the envy of the world. People*

used to beat a path to your door to find out how you did it. No guns, no night-sticks, just honest cops who cared about the people on their beat rather than what the mayor at City Hall wanted. Now look at you, you've turned into an army of occupation. What a waste!'[114]

How true, what a waste.

---

114 Ibid

AFTERWORD

Policing is necessary, policing is important. It is no exaggeration to say that it impinges upon virtually everything that we do or need to do in a modern liberal democracy. Good and effective policing holds the ring between responsible civil society and those who would wish to disrupt our lives, damage our property, or threaten our well-being. It ensures that communities are safe and well-ordered so that commerce and employment can prosper, and it should protect and preserve civil liberties and democratic values of accountability. All senior officers and the vast majority of politicians, of whatever hue, take refuge within a blizzard of statistics and performance indicators and claim that everything they do is garlanded with success. They say that policing, in their hands, delivers exactly what the public wants. However, to paraphrase Mandy Rice-Davies, 'Well they would say that, wouldn't they!' Such individuals have a vested interest in preserving careers, constituencies, and pensions.

The truth is rather bleaker. In researching this book I have conducted scores of interviews with serving and retired officers of every rank from constable to Chief

Constable. I have spoken to victims of crime, 'players' in the criminal justice system, and the ordinary man and woman in the street. I have canvassed the views of 'special advisers' and listened to the indiscreet and unattributable comments of Home Office officials. No-one believes that we have got it right. Indeed a significant majority of police professionals take the view that something radical needs to be done if we are to preserve anything of value from a police system which, despite protestations to the contrary from various apologists, shows every sign that it will soon no longer be fit for purpose.

As with all aspects of public policy the key issues that need to be confronted are money, leadership, and the 'art of the possible'. Each is linked to the others to a greater or lesser extent but in terms of the form and function of British policing, the current state of the economy will almost certainly be the main driver for change. Put simply, the police are living beyond their means and blithely assume that the days of wine and roses, which they had known until the economic downturn of a decade ago, would go on forever. Police forces waste eye-watering sums of money each year on poorly supervised personnel, unnecessary and unaudited projects and initiatives, and the pointless duplication of functions within and between forces. The scandalous annual waste of a quarter of a billion pounds of public money on PCSOs has already been discussed in detail, as has the failure of police managers to do anything about profligate waste of resources on unsupervised paid overtime for constables and sergeants. To an extent however, enormous as these sums are, they represent just part of the problem. Of greater significance is the structural change that reduced funding will force on those responsible for shaping the police system of the 2020s, 2030s and 2040s.

Today's Chief Constables may want to whistle in the dark and assume that the economy will be back on its feet again in a year or two, and that everything will be back to normal soon, but most economic commentators take a much starker view. It could be twenty or thirty years before the UK's fiscal position returns to true stability, and it is unlikely that we will ever have the tax revenues that were available for the public sector from 1996 to 2012, because they were largely generated by an over-inflated housing market and unsustainable levels of personal and corporate credit. Such has been the shock to the banking sector and the political establishment, that it is inconceivable that we will go that way again. Even without factoring in the damage done by Brexit, the public sector is going to have to plan to operate in an environment where funding will reduce year-by-year for decades, with all that entails for resources and personnel. Steering organisations through such waters will require leaders of exceptional quality and bravery, and most people that I have spoken to do not feel that the police service is currently over-burdened with such individuals. There are, of course, one or two 'stars', but the vast majority of senior men and women in the police *(and too many of those waiting in the wings)* give the impression of being unimaginative functionaries, ever willing to toe whatever is the current 'party line' in an effort to ensure patronage and promotion.

For this, if for no other reason, the police service needs to look outside the tent for the next generation of top people. As already discussed, the election or, more probably the appointment, of suitably qualified individuals on the *prefet* model may be the way to force change, together with a radical programme of direct recruitment of specialists and generic investigators.

Bravery and effective leadership will also be necessary as Superintendents at borough and BCU level dragoon more and more uniform constables out onto the streets and force them to stay there, patrolling beats on their own. Since the 1960s the bean-counters in forces and at the Home Office have tried to convince senior police officers and the public at large that preventive patrol by uniform police officers is a waste of resources, for the spurious reason that such activity does not always, or easily, produce measurable outcomes. Because you cannot count (and therefore cost) the crimes that were prevented by a PC walking along the High Street at 3am, the assumption has been made that his patrol has no value. The fact that this is precisely the sort of policing that most people in this country want has been comprehensively ignored for decades. Such a change in philosophy will come hard to young, and not so young, constables as they are forced back onto 'beats' and are measured by how long they spend there. They will need to be led and inspired, and they will need to be supervised by Sergeants and Inspectors who have lost the skill of supervision, even if they had it in the first place.

Time is running out, and this is where 'the art of the possible' comes in. Nothing can happen without impetus from politicians. Officials will not generate change unless they are firmly directed to, and will produce all manner of reasons why this or that change process should not be embarked upon. If Home Office (or indeed Treasury, or

Cabinet Office, or No 10 Policy Unit) officials are allowed to manage the process, nothing will change and nothing worthwhile will happen, because most senior civil servants are wed to inertia. What is needed is a strong political lead, and recognition that British policing, so long the envy of the world, is in very real danger of becoming an expensive and ineffective basket case.

ACKNOWLEDGEMENTS

Thanks are due to the many serving and retired police officers, and members of police staff, who gave their time willingly during what must have seemed interminable interviews. To the Librarian at the London School of Economics, and particularly to the Chief Librarian at the NPIA Library at the Police Staff College, Bramshill, for her unstinting assistance and help with finding research material. Lastly to the family of Peter Woodhams and his partner Jane, for allowing me to reproduce the photographs of Peter's injuries taken after the first attack on him, when he was so cruelly let down by the Metropolitan Police.

GLOSSARY OF TERMS

ACPO	Association of Chief Police Officers
APSG	Accelerated Promotion Scheme for Graduates
BAWP	British Association for Women in Policing
BCS	British Crime Survey
BCU	Basic Command Unit (*a provincial police 'Division'*)
BOCU	Borough Operational Command Unit (*Metropolitan Police*)
BPA	Black Police Association
BTP	British Transport Police
CID	Criminal Investigation Department
CNC	Civil Nuclear Constabulary
CO.11	Metropolitan Police Public Order Branch
CPS	Crown Prosecution Service
CT	Counter-terrorism
GES	Graduate Entry Scheme
HMIC	Her Majesty's Inspectorate of Constabulary
NBPA	National Black Police Association
NCA	National Crime Agency
NHTCU	National Hi-Tech Crime Unit
NPCC	National Police Chiefs' Council

NPIA	National Policing Improvement Agency
PCSO	Police Community Support Officer
PSNI	Police Service of Northern Ireland
SOCA	Serious and Organised Crime Agency
SNT	Safer Neighbourhood Team (*Metropolitan Police*)
TSG	Territorial Support Group (*Metropolitan Police*)

ABOUT THE AUTHOR

Born in London and educated in the Home Counties and at the London School of Economics *(BSc (Econ) in International History and Philosophy),* David now lives in Cambridge with his wife and family, having retired from the Metropolitan Police in the early 2000s where he was a Deputy Assistant Commissioner at Scotland Yard and one of HM Assistant Inspectors of Constabulary at the Home Office, reviewing the performance of police forces across England and Wales.

In a long and varied career, he served in the UK and abroad *(attached to the New York City Police Department in 1988 and seconded to South Africa in 1994 organising the Peace Monitors in Johannesburg, Pretoria, and the Transvaal, for the first post-Apartheid elections).* In the late 1980s he was the Bramshill Visiting Lecturer in Social Policy and Comparative Policing at the City University of New York (CUNY). He was the head of policing for Notting Hill and at Tottenham in the early and mid-1990s and went on to be responsible for all public order and counter-terrorism operations in north and west London in the late 1990s as a Scotland Yard Commander. In the 2001 New Year Honours he was awarded the Queen's Police Medal for 'Distinguished Service'

ABOUT THE AUTHOR

He writes on history, policing, and public policy subjects and has been published widely in the print and on-line media. He is a regular contributor to programmes broadcast on relevant subjects on television and radio. In addition, he holds various public appointments related to the regulation of the legal profession.

He is also an avid student of the role of the Confederate States Navy during the American Civil War.